AF413088

Observed, Lived, Experienced

Observed, Lived, Experienced

A Year of Everyday Life in China

Translated from the Original German
by Herb Parker

Helen Wolf

VANTAGE PRESS
New York

For H.K.
in
gratitude

whilst being there
I knew nothing of
here

then living here
I was yearning for
there

was I then there
I was longing for
here

being again here
I would like to be
there

H. W.

Contents

Preface to the English Translation

The account of my one-year stay in Y. was written in German and published in 1987. I never expected the positive and wide resonance that followed and was sorry not to have published more books for my interested readers.

As word of mouth spread, I had several enquiries from abroad as to whether the book was available in English. In order to comply with their wish, I started to translate my work from German into English myself but was surprised by the peculiar experience of writing a new work on one and the same theme. So I decided not to do it and was, of course, very happy to unexpectedly receive help from Sydney, Australia. An old childhood friend, Herb Parker, was so kind as to spontaneously offer his help in undertaking this strenuous and long-term task of translating the book into English. I owe not only to him my heartiest thanks but also to his wife, Margret, for her compliance in spending much of her free time alone.

Then again, time went by after I received the translation. Not only many hours were spent revising it; moreover, it had to be retyped into the computer and then printed.

Despite the years between 1987, when I first published my book, and 1990, when the translation arrived, the facts of Chinese everyday life I have described still exist today, maybe with some alterations. Fundamentally little has changed; therefore, the value of the information in this book is not outdated.

H.W.

Hamburg, March 1993

xi

Translator's Preface

The authoress of this fascinating account and I grew up together as children in China before and during the early stages after "liberation" (1949). As classmates through primary school and the early years of high school, we lived through the Japanese occupation of China, the defeat of Germany and Japan, the brief American involvement that followed, a few years of civil war between the Kuomintang (KMT) and the Communists, and finally the early years after the People's Republic of China was established.

As children of German parents, the authoress of multinational descent, living in the former German Concession of the old "treaty port" of Tianjin (in former writing Tientsin), we were largely sheltered from the tumultuous events of those years and lived as members of a foreign culture in an "alien" land. And yet the influence of growing up in China was profound and lasting. I can recall some of the unrest, such as Japanese tanks rolling through the streets, three bandits being beheaded in a square near our home, American LSTs discharging GIs, then civil war with distant gunfire, preparations for street fighting, and the eventual fall of Tianjin, with Communist troops rushing past our house. There was uncertainty; there was fear.

My family left China in 1951 headed for Germany, but whilst in Hong Kong awaiting a ship my parents received the news that we would be able to go Australia, where I have lived ever since, except for a three-year stint in Europe in the sixties. The authoress went to Germany at the beginning of 1953, and for many years we lost touch, until we met again in Hamburg in

1979 through another classmate of ours from the good old China days. Unlike me, the authoress has kept up with the Chinese language and sinology in general, of which she has made a real study; this has, in turn, enabled her to travel to China as almost "one of them."

It has been a real pleasure to read the account of her travels, particularly as my wife and I, with our children, were also in Beijing (Peking) during the same year, although my attempts to contact Helen by telephone in Y. were fruitless. I share her views about the changes in China, and reading her account brought back many old memories.

I have enjoyed translating this book and hope that my doing so will enable many more readers to enjoy it, not the least my wife and children.

Herb Parker
Sydney, Australia, 1990

Introduction

It was the encouragement and stimulation on the part of friends
and acquaintances to write down and record my eventful year
in China from February 1985 to January 1986 that caused this
book to be written as a collection of facts, a record of my experiences, and reminiscences.

It is not a conventional account such as one might expect
from the typewriter of a journalist or an enthused China
tourist. Rather, it is an attempt to give the reader a picture of
the real everyday life of the Chinese, with all its large and small
joys, the many problems and inconveniences, inadequacies and
banalities, as I found them in a small Chinese community. It is
also an account of my difficulties with the Chinese bureaucracy
and a description of life in China today, as seen by a "foreigner
returned home."

I have tried my best to be as objective as possible in giving
this account of my experiences and adventures. In this I have
probably not always succeeded, because it is seldom possible to
relate with total objectivity events and experiences that touch
one deeply.

In the interest of protecting those who told me this and
that, most names have been changed and given only as initials,
also the city in which I lived. Cities and life in all of China do
not differ much, so Y. may stand for any of them.

China is a large country, many-sided, multicultural, and
rich in history. It is the country of my heritage, my childhood
and adolescence. I was born there and lived for eighteen years
in the Chinese world, including some years after the Commu-

nist takeover in 1949. I had grown to be a part of China, thoroughly familiar with her mentality and her culture, when I arrived in what was to me a totally alien and foreign land, Germany. The homesickness of the early years and a silent longing never entirely left me; they became the driving force behind a growing desire to revisit China as soon as I could. When after the "decade of unrest," as the period of the Cultural Revolution between 1965 and 1976 is known today, the great bamboo gate opened just a little, later even allowing single travellers into the country. I took the advantage of the first opportunity. I visited China in 1980 and again three years later. During these two visits, I was able to make some good contacts, and many friendships resulted, which survive and prosper to this very day. As I am able to speak Chinese like a native, and as I also inherited a little of my Chinese grandmother's appearance, most Chinese looked upon me as one of theirs. And thus it came as no great surprise one day when I received an enquiry as to whether I might be interested in teaching German at a technical college in a coastal province.

The longing to find that part of my roots again that had been suddenly severed by political events many years before had never quite left me and led me to yield to the temptation to accept this most appealing offer. I resolved to leave behind my family, my friends, and many customs that had become dear to me for a whole year so that I could experience once more the everyday life in China in what, by Chinese standards, was a relatively small city of a mere 700,000 inhabitants.

I had plenty of time to consider the step I was taking. After I had lived in the Federal Republic of Germany for over thirty years and become accustomed to conditions there, the German part of my roots, inherited from my grandfather, had taken hold also. And still I ventured the step backwards!

And so I started my preparations for the great adventure. Packages with books and warm clothing were sent off, and a great many farewells were said. The day of my departure moved ever closer, and suddenly I found myself at the airport in Frankfurt, and events all started happening at once.

H.W.
Hamburg, April 1987

Observed, Lived, Experienced

Flight: Frankfurt–Beijing

Frankfurt Airport, 6 February 1985

I had checked in at the counter for foreign airlines and been processed into the departure lounge. As far as I was concerned, the flight, Frankfurt–Cairo–Karachi–Beijing, was free to leave, the sooner the better. But nothing happened. There was no sign of an aircraft anywhere. At last a call came to board a 747 coming from New York, which was continuing to Paris.

After forty-five minutes' flying time, we landed at Orly, where ongoing passengers were requested to disembark and change to another aircraft. However, there were no signs whatever of any means whereby we could continue our journey. Then followed hours of nerve-wracking uncertainty and nothing but conflicting replies to our various questions. There were no refreshments, nothing.

After nearly three hours of waiting, we finally boarded another jumbo, also coming from New York and packed full. Service was poor and unfriendly. Children were left to play with the levers and controls on the doors, and the cabin crew squatted on the floor in full view of the passengers, quite immersed in a game of cards. But four flying hours later, we had at least managed to progress a little closer to the East. Cairo came into view, followed by a one-and-a-half-hour stopover, but we were not allowed to leave our seats. During this time, various rumors started to circulate that another transit stop was scheduled for Dubai. And there was additional uncertainty as to whether our connecting flight to Beijing would be waiting in Karachi. Children ran about, noise, tom-tom, not a drop of booze to lull one to sleep, which would have made conditions and the endless waiting slightly more bearable.

At last a small group of travellers with Beijing as their common destination crystallised from this commotion. There were about sixteen of us, Chinese, British, Japanese, and Germans, all sharing the same concern about being able to make the connection to Beijing at 6:00 the following morning. We were scheduled to arrive in Karachi at 4:15 local time, but our actual arrival time turned out to be 8:00.

There we were! No sign of any ground personnel. When anyone did happen to appear behind the counter, it was not the right person to advise us about our ongoing flight; and as for anything like a "missed connection," nobody was responsible. We had no idea what was to happen to us next. "Why don't you spend a few pleasant days in Karachi [at our own expense, of course] and take the next plane to Beijing in two or three days' time?" we were told. But evidently no one was tempted to accept this proposal. We besieged the counter and by so doing only succeeded in making the ground staff surly and uncooperative. In the end, they simply closed the counter and left us to our fate, or so it seemed to us.

The clock in the transit lounge moved to 9:00, 10:00, 10:30. Suddenly it was announced that a CAAC aircraft (China), coming from Zurich, would depart for Beijing at around 11:30 and had some empty seats. But which of us would make it on board? A somewhat more competent-looking airline employee arrived with a bundle of forms, sat down behind the counter, and started filling them out. In no time at all, we raced over with our passports, and he wrote out new tickets for the flight to Beijing. There were fourteen available seats.

And so the great lottery began as to which of us would be lucky enough to be chosen. The man seemed to derive some enjoyment out of our nervous and tense situation, and his cheerful manner was quite infectious. With the words, "Have a good flight," he hustled us onto the ongoing flight, which was scheduled to take off at 11:35.

Five minutes before departure time, we were indeed seated in the somewhat decrepit-looking Boeing 707. I was one of the first to board; and as I entered the cabin, I said to a uniformed attendant in Chinese, "I am so tired; I'm ready to drop!" Well, in that case there was no need for me to walk all the way to the rear of the plane; why not make myself comfortable right here in first class? This kind offer I accepted with gratitude. But next problem: where to put my hand luggage and my heavy coat? Every vacant nook and cranny was stuffed full of boxes, cartons, bags, and cushions. The backrests of all the seats were strictly vertical, and behind them there were long objects wrapped in foam rubber and other things.

The process of clearing the seats took some time. The stewardess did not seem to be particularly pleased at having to rearrange the purchases the crew had made abroad, but at long last a place was found for everything. I placed my hand luggage half under my seat, which gave me a support for my feet. As for my overcoat, I did not even take it off, after seeing that the Chinese passengers were all sitting there bundled up in their padded coats and jackets. It was certainly not too warm.

Be that as it may, takeoff took place at 11:35 without any further difficulty, and we set course for Karachi to Beijing non-stop, approximately six hours' flying time. After I had succeeded in making myself a little more comfortable and was about to take a nap, the stewardess came around again, distributing to each passenger sweets, a kind of sweet lemonade, a small key ring with CAAC insignia, and a pair of sleeping socks, pink for the ladies and sky blue for the men. A little while later, the cook, resplendent in a white apron, came by and asked me whether I was a "first-class or other-class passenger." I told him I was "other class." Quite satisfied, he strolled off, and I had the distinct impression that he had only been wanting to test my Chinese. I feel certain someone had told him that there was a foreigner sitting in the window seat, third row, who spoke Chinese.

I took a look outside and downwards. The landscape under us looked a light grey-green colour in the haze. There were rivers, some mountains in the distance, and the sky above us was clear and blue, nothing special at all; I was probably too tired for any real impressions. The monotonous and rather loud droning of the jet engines did have a soporific effect, but I did not find it particularly pleasant. We were given something to eat. The Chinese passenger in front of me received a square cloth, grey rather than white, which was placed on his lap by the stewardess. She then served him various pieces of meat and assorted vegetables out of a variety of bowls and dishes on a tray and handed him a fork, a spoon, and chopsticks, all made of plastic. He must have been an important official deserving such special service. I, not being a member of the hierarchy or a bona-fide member of the first-class section, was given a plastic tray, different food, more modest eating utensils, no serviette, and no special smiles. The passenger in front of me was later served green string beans as an extra dish, together with a mug of hot tea. After the meal a hot, damp face towel served to refresh him. Indeed, differentiation between the classes must be!

Suddenly I noticed the mountains, and what a gigantic spectacle they were! Coming from Karachi we flew over two of the Himalayas' ancillary mountain chains, Hindu Kush and Karakorum. We were moving in a northerly direction towards Urumchi. Somewhere beneath us there must have been the Pakistani cities Rawalpindi and Peshawar, with the Indus River snaking its way between them. The mountains seemed close enough to touch, and I started feeling a little uneasy. My imagining what might happen if we were to run into heavy turbulence and if any sizable air pockets would have resulted in our being impaled on the sharp peaks kept me distracted from enjoying this impressive and grandiose spectacle. But no, these were not appropriate thoughts! Snow-covered peaks glistened in the bright sunlight, above them a brilliantly blue sky and clear air. I could see as far as the eye could reach, and there seemed to be endless mountains running forever, all crystal clear! The sheer extent of these mountains is impressive in itself, and it took an hour before we left this particular region.

The world of mountains ended as abruptly as it began, and suddenly we could see nothing but desert. The Tarim Basin was clearly recognizable, but there were no signs of human habitation anywhere. The landscape seemed to be dipped in ochre brown paint, with nothing but an occasional watercourse meandering through the brown earth to break the monotony. This unchanging picture, hour after hour, gave me a feeling of hovering still in the air, as if I were a predatory bird up in the heights observing its prey below. Had it not been for the noise of the motors I might have taken this deceptive feeling to be real. Right in the midst of this seemingly endless and unchanging sea of sand there were a number of terrace-shaped raised plateaus, giving a bizarre effect. For a few hours we followed high, scraggy conical outcrops of brownish coloured rock, which eventually gave way to more ochre-coloured desert. Soon dusk started to fall, and there was a bluish sheen over the mountains. Farther down in the valleys it was already dark. Very soon it was pitch-black outside, and of the six hours' flying time we flew some three hours in total darkness. Underneath us nothing at all could be seen. There were no lights, however few or small, nothing at all to indicate that there were human beings living underneath us, and there were no clouds that might obstruct the view. Eventually we approached Beijing; here, too, was a total absence of lights, and still we suddenly found ourselves making our approach for landing. Everything around us was black, which creates a rather strange feeling when one has become disoriented. During the landing manoeuvres a certain amount of tension became apparent, and it seemed as if the NO SMOKING and FASTEN YOUR SEAT BELT signs were only intended for conscientious foreigners. The Chinese passenger in the seat in front of me merrily went on smoking, as did a number of others around me. A few started to collect their possessions, and some passengers even stood up and scrambled for a place near the exit, as if we were travelling on a train. The stewardess, seeming bored rather than energetic, urged a few passengers back to their seats. The approach was a little shaky, and there was still nothing to be seen outside, but we landed, albeit a little bumpily, in a thick fog. The plane touched ground, and I took a deep breath of relief.

Flying with a Chinese aircraft and crew is something that has never yet given me a feeling of confidence. Whilst the crews are certainly given the necessary training, it has always seemed to me as if rules of conduct, safety precautions, etc., were not taken too seriously.

Once we had come to a stop and the doors had been opened, customs officials came on board. I thought that the necessary formalities would now be completed on the plane before disembarkation, but it was not so. They had come on board merely to check on their own countrymen and on the purchases they had made abroad. The rest of us were allowed to get off the plane straightaway. In the hall we found the usual turmoil characteristic of all airports. The customs and other formalities were completed quickly and smoothly, with the officials being friendly and helpful. I next went to the bank counter, where I exchanged money at an exchange rate of 1 deutschmark to 0.85 yuan. My suitcase was already moving on the conveyor, and the luggage trolly I had been able to secure stood ready. Everything went beautifully. Another German woman and I were heading in the same direction towards the university, and we decided to share a taxi. Our acquaintances who were to have met us had of course gone home on account of the arrival delayed by some four hours, but in their place there were countless taxi drivers at the exit of the hall, holding large signs with the word *taxi*. We were barely inside the large hall, which impressed us as being bare and cold, when the numerous drivers crowded in on us. There were people everywhere, cries, shouts, chattering, loud negotiations about fares and destinations. It was chaotic! I had to be careful to make sure that a taxi driver did not simply grab my bags and place them in his vehicle, thereby making me a captive passenger. The commotion taxi drivers caused soliciting passengers added further stress to my mind, already overtaxed from the long flight. I was really taken aback by the masses of people all talking to me at the same time, and in addition I was not familiar with Chinese prices, although I remembered from earlier visits that most taxis did not have meters, so that fares were calculated on an ad hoc basis. But my instinct told me: *Careful! Don't be taken advantage of; don't accept too quickly.* One driver quoted one figure, another a different one for the drive of some forty kilometres to the university by driving right through the city. At last we were sitting in a car, the driver having asked thirty yuan, which seemed to me to be a fair price.

The drive took a good hour. Compared to my visits in 1980 and 1983, the main streets were now better lit, although not as brightly as we were used to at home. But at least there was now enough light to be able to distinguish pedestrians and cyclists. Neither Chinese drivers, pedestrians, nor cyclists, it seems, had any problems in this regard, not in the past or today, and I admire their skill and their "feel" for these conditions.

We were driving along at moderate speed, and with an occasional flash of the headlights I thought that surely nothing much could happen. Nevertheless, I saw two accidents during the drive, with one of them involving casualties, as we saw an ambulance racing past with siren blaring. It was evidently a collision between a car and cyclist. I had gradually become accustomed to the diffused yellowish lighting on the streets, just as I would later have to get used to the darkness in smaller streets.

At last I arrived at my destination. As I had phoned my contact from the airport despite the late hour, there he was, standing by the university gate, and he greeted me most heartily. The driver was instructed to take us to the guest house inside the grounds, and my friend then paid the fare. I was taken to the gatekeeper, introduced to him, and given my room keys.

I had been travelling for more than twenty-five hours and longed for a bed and a drink of water.

Eventful Days in Beijing

On the evening of my arrival I was too exhausted to absorb any-thing my attendant, the man who was to be my "guide" during my stay in Beijing, tried to tell me about matters such as room, board, and reimbursement of expenses through future employ-ers. All I wanted was to sleep and be left in peace.

The way Chinese friends fuss over and care for their guests is quite touching. Another friend rode over on his bicycle, despite the long ride, the dark and cold, just to say "hello" to me and ask how I was. He not only told me about plans for the following days, which I was to spend with and as part of his fam-ily, but also made arrangements on behalf of a mutual friend, who had been unable to come himself. For more than an hour I forced myself to stay awake and alert, listening to and acknowl-edging their various suggestions politely. But in the end my attention started to lapse, and I asked the gentlemen to excuse me because I was terribly tired. Some more time passed before they finally left, but not without offering advice as to how a rest-ful and undisturbed night's sleep might be accomplished. I was not to open the window, because draughts were harmful. I should keep the door locked, because one never knows. Should I be cold during the night, then an additional blanket taken from the other bed would ensure comfortable warmth. It was just before midnight when they finally left.

I was thirsty, and after almost two days without a proper wash I felt grubby. However, because of the late hour water had been turned off. The thermos contained only remnants of water, which I drank despite the stale taste. I decided I would do without a wash, and dead tired, I fell into bed.

The time for breakfast was from 7:00 to 7:30, but I slept through it. I woke around ten o'clock to loud hammering on my door. The girl responsible for the floor stood there with two full thermoses, which she wanted to exchange for the empty ones. She commented on how late it was and asked why I was still asleep. My explanation that I had only arrived from Germany around midnight and was still not adjusted to the time difference seemed to still her curiosity.

In the communal bathroom there was only cold water left. If I wanted to take a shower or have a warm wash, I was politely requested to keep to the proper times, 6:00 to 8:00 A.M. and 4:00 to 8:00 P.M. The bathroom was partly tiled, and above the tiles the walls were the usual painted bare concrete. Here as in the shower the paint was peeling. A number of clotheslines crisscrossed through the room for small items of laundry. During my stay nothing whatsoever was stolen. Adjacent to this room there was a small niche for the hot water boiler, which delivered "boiling" (eighty degrees Celsius) water at certain times for the various thermoses. It was usual to replace the contents of the flasks each morning and evening, even if the water had not been used.

One morning, as I was returning from breakfast, I was greeted in the corridor by such dense steam that I could barely see my way. Evidently the girl in charge of the floor either had not closed the tap or had failed to open the outlet valve, and the water was boiling over. Instead of one of the guests opening a window, all ran to their rooms in a crouch, under the cloud of steam. I opened the windows in the corridor, only to find the girl running from the other end of the floor to close them again, with a comment that it was too cold outside and the steam would dissipate in time. Then I understood why nobody had opened a window.

As I already mentioned, I overslept on my first morning in

China. I then had a wash, but not as thorough as I would have liked. Not only was it too cold, but I did not want to undress completely before unwelcome male eyes. Finally I fled back to my room. It was not unusual for a woman to be housed on the men's floor, but there was a problem in that none of the communal rooms, such as shower, toilet, or bathroom, could be locked. I was glad to be back in my relatively warm room, even though it could not have been more than sixteen degrees Celsius.

Having missed breakfast, I searched through my luggage, where I found a piece of cheese, a little butter, and two stale rolls, all carefully saved from the flight. I also found a tea bag and had my breakfast sitting at the desk in this cold environment, with a feeling of homesickness and lack of sleep. But this did not last long, because I had to hurry if I was to meet my guide, the contact, at eleven o'clock as arranged, not keeping him waiting.

During the night a light snow had fallen. The landscape looked quite lovely in its white covering of what seemed like powdered sugar. Even the ugly spots, such as broken brick walls, blocks of stone lying about, rubbish, and dirt, all looked clean. And the frozen pond, which during summer held foul-smelling greyish black water, gave a silvery sparkle. The whole surroundings gave one an impression of peace and tranquillity. There were very few people about. I met with a few cyclists on the snow-covered paths, wearing thick padded jackets, and on their heads fur caps with lowered earflaps, plus the mouth protection that is tradition in wintertime. The walk to the house of my guide took about ten minutes. I had been invited to a meal of *jiaozi* (a type of ravioli), and when I arrived I was very warmly greeted by my host at the door. Immediately I was offered a cup of hot tea and invited to sit on the *sha fa* (sofa), but I was discouraged from taking off my overcoat just yet, because the temperature in the room would be quite a bit colder than I was used to in Germany. And indeed it was not especially pleasant to sit in a room with the temperature around sixteen degrees for a lengthy time. The bare stone floor did little to combat cold and the draughty windows even less.

For this reason it is customary in many houses to glue virtually all window frames shut with strips of paper at the start of the cold season, in order to keep out the cold wind from Siberia. This custom was still familiar to me from my childhood, and on looking at the thus-sealed windows I reminisced about the times when I had performed this task with our "boy," I for my part for fun, but he because that was part of his job. And so, after many, many years, there I was sitting in a room in North China able to experience this familiar spectacle once more.

After I had also been greeted by my guide's daughter, I was introduced to his old mother. We were all sitting in the living room, which also served as bedroom for the parents, and conversed with one another perfectly and pleasantly. A small anteroom, a kitchen, a Chinese toilet, and an additional room for the daughter plus two balconies completed this apartment of some forty square metres for a family of three in a better-than-average situation. The mother was in Germany at that time, and the grandmother was keeping house for her son. For this small family this apartment represented considerable comfort compared to the single room of some fifteen square metres in a commune to which they had invited me a few years earlier.

It was time to think about lunch, and I was quite surprised when the son sent his old mother out to buy *jiaozi* from a street pedlar. I had been used to the old custom of everyone, including the guest, taking part in the preparation of the small dumplings. It was a happy and sociable task, helping to roll out the dough and then form and fill the *jiaozi*, and by comparison the purchase of ready-made dumplings seemed like a breach of custom. I also felt most uncomfortable at the thought that the seventy-year-old mother had to go out into the cold on my account. My offer to accompany her was firmly rejected by both mother and son. Meanwhile the granddaughter fetched the folding table from a corner, set it up, put some chairs around it, and brought the bowls and chopsticks.

While the grandmother was cooking the *jiaozi* her son kept me busy with a German text. My host was a lecturer in German at a university in Beijing. His grasp of German was quite outstanding, but he did have a few problems with idiomatic figures of speech and certain phrases not in common use. He was in the process of translating from German into Chinese a children's book about the family life of Karl Marx.

The first bowl of steaming *jiaozi* was brought in. I was confronted with dark dumplings with thick pastry, but little flavour of meat or vegetables. Instead there was a lot of fat. It is quite common to use unbleached flour, and use of the latter is particularly common with street pedlars. These pedlars also sell homemade but uncooked noodles, baked Chinese flat bread (known as *da bing*), and *jiaozi* or *baozi* (steamed yeast dumplings with various fillings according to season, in winter usually including Chinese white cabbage).

During the meal I asked the grandmother how she liked Beijing, as she had told me earlier that she originally came from Hunan Province. She stated quite bluntly that the North was not to her liking at all, the climate being too dry and too cold in winter. The northerners did not understand her dialect (true, I had some difficulties understanding what she wanted to say). She would be very happy as soon as she could return to her familiar surroundings and to her old friends and neighbours. She complained in particular about the poor choice and quality of vegetables in winter. The only available varieties were cabbage, whitish mushrooms, onions, and sweet potatoes, and in addition the prices were much too high compared to those in her home village. No, she did not enjoy living in this meagre part of the country, particularly as it was always covered in dust and yellowish earth. "The people here eat too much flour; we in the South are rice eaters. But I can't even buy such good and tasty rice here." On a return visit in the summer I learnt that she had returned home soon after this conversation.

Indeed, the difference between North and South is considerable. I had often experienced the way in which southern Chinese, mostly people from Shanghai, spoke in a derogatory manner about the northerners: "these peasant people with their rough and ready manners, with almost no business sense." Often the opinions expressed were so belittling that I, as a northern Chinese by birth, went strongly on the defensive in favour of my fellow northerners.

These verbal duels, which usually took place in an atmosphere of jolly togetherness, always served to enliven the general conversation. It is also not uncommon for northern Chinese to be critical of the southerners, particularly the eating habits and cuisine of the other provinces. Sichuan food was too hot, Shaanxi too sour, Shandong too unimaginative, and Guangdong too sweet; such was their opinion of the famed Chinese gastronomy. Nevertheless, in the end they invariably agree that theirs is a culture of refined cooking going back thousands of years, and all feel part of the great Han family.

Not long after the meal I took my leave, as it was not customary to stay on after eating for any length of time. The Chinese do not practise the transition from eating to our customary relaxed phase of chatting and cosy togetherness. In China that happens during the meal. During official functions the invitation ends once the last course, usually soup or fruit, has been eaten. Lately it has come to be regarded as especially Western and progressive to offer the guest a cup of coffee at the end of the meal, with milk and sugar already added. For my part I clung to the old tradition of drinking a cup of hot *jiaozi* soup, which is the stock in which the dumplings had been boiled, said to aid the digestion and contribute to one's general well-being.

On the following day my companion and I travelled downtown to the city and to the security bureau, the *gong'an ju*. In the meantime I had learned that my companion had been instructed by my employers, the Technical Institute, to make all necessary arrangements for my journey to Y. and to meet the resulting costs. The money that had been made available to him was intended to be sufficient for fares, accommodation, and meals for three days, after which I was to meet my own expenses. Having agreed on the conditions, we set out for the *wai bin gong'an ju*, the security bureau for foreign visitors. Although I had already had my passport appropriately stamped by the Chinese consulate general and was thus able to travel without the need for any additional visa to cities such as Y., which were not yet "opened to foreigners," my companion was determined to play it safe. The officials were all very friendly and amused at the earnest efforts of this very correct man. My visa was for an unlimited stay in China, and the only additional thing I had to do was obtain an exit visa from the *gong'an ju* in Y. on leaving there. Otherwise it was "Have a pleasant voyage" and "We are pleased that foreign experts are here to help us with our development into the year 2000." Our next stop was the railway station in Beijing. The university-owned car took us there quickly and waited there for us, ready to take us back to the campus.

Tickets for foreigners, overseas Chinese, and citizens of Hong Kong and Macao were sold in a special room within the large station hall and not available anywhere else. Only native Chinese travellers were served at all the other windows. The latter must always be prepared for the possibility that tickets are not available for the particular day they wish to travel.

Rail tickets are scarce in China; rail networks and passenger trains are inadequately developed. Freight trains have priority everywhere in the entire country, where all rail lines are single-track. I often experienced a long wait in a passenger train on a siding whilst a very long freight train had to be allowed to pass before the passenger train could eventually resume its journey at a leisurely pace, usually sixty kilometres per hour.

But back to the special ticket room. A long queue of people was lined up at each of the three windows. Window number 1 was for preordered tickets, number 2 for tickets to be used immediately (if available), and number 3 for sleeping cars.

It is advisable to be armed with a great deal of patience and goodly number of alternative days for travelling, because the constant *mei you* (not available) and other negative indicators almost seem to be deliberate after a while. The long waiting and time wasting has brought many foreign travellers to despair while trying to travel China independently.

The fault lies not with the lack of willingness on the part of the personnel behind the windows, but with the lacking infrastructure already mentioned. This applies in particular to rail travel on routes other than the principal north–south routes, Beijing to Guangzhou and Beijing to Shanghai, or the north to northeast routes, Beijing–Shenyang or Beijing–Dalian.

There I stood, in the special room, near the end of a queue of some twenty people. Patience! That word is law in China, above all else, and without it one does not get far in this large country. During the coming months I would have to relearn the art of patience, which was to be a most beneficial experience.

When my turn finally came, Dame Fortune smiled on me! Without difficulty I obtained my ticket for the desired day, or rather not exactly a ticket, but a slip of paper pressed into my hand on which the number of the train, date of travel, compartment, and sleeping berth number were written. This piece of paper had to be taken to another female official (I found that train personnel were almost always women; men were usually employed in the technical professions), who had set up her worktable in a far corner of the special room. Her task was to collect the slip of paper and the money and issue the appropriate tickets.

When it came to payment, my companion, much to my surprise, lost his composure for the first time. Until now we had not had any bad experiences with officialdom. From earlier travels I knew that there were considerable differences in the applicable train fares depending on whether the traveller was a foreigner, a Chinese from Hong Kong or Macao, an overseas Chinese, or a native Chinese. But I also knew that foreigners in the employ of a Chinese organisation paid the same fares as native Chinese, and this meant in my case 75 percent less than the tourist price of some ninety yuan. And this was where I received the big surprise. My companion, who was responsible for all expenses in connection with my employment, refused to pay the ninety yuan being demanded. He based his refusal on the fact that I would be working at an institute and could present all necessary documented proof. Therefore, according to rules the tariff for foreigners did not apply in my case. (Much later, after I had already arrived in Y., I learned that my ticket was only 50 percent dearer than the Chinese rate; it seems, therefore, that an intermediate fare also exists.) Be that as it may, for the time being I had to prove my credentials.

I took out of my bag all the various documents and the official letter and presented them to the ticket lady. She looked through everything carefully and, having read my preliminary contract, offered the comment that we foreign experts were not badly paid at some four hundred yuan per month. She thought I did not look as old as my date of birth indicated and asked how I came to speak Chinese, together with other questions in the same vein. She was quite friendly, and I began to think that the game was about won. Considering the way in which my companion had spoken to her, she might well have reacted angrily, but no, she remained polite. But that did not help. Indeed, she conceded, a contract of employment was certainly quite useful, but where, if I pleased, was the proof of employment from my work unit? I explained that I did not have it as yet, as I would only be given it on arrival at the institute. But that explanation was not acceptable because, she argued, anybody could turn up on that basis and demand a ticket at the standard fare. In the end my companion had no choice but to dig deep into his pockets. On leaving he made the comment: "This high expenditure may lead to difficulties with the manageress of the bureau for foreigners." He then handed me all receipts for money expended so far and said in passing that I might as well take care of the remaining formalities and justification myself personally on arrival, rather than have him take the trouble to record it all in writing. All I had to do was tell the manageress truthfully everything that had happened. In hindsight this was quite a clever move on his part. He had nothing to do with the affair, did not have to justify himself, and had no more documents on which to base his justification. But for the time being it was all the same to me.

I was glad that all had been settled so quickly, and also at not having to travel into the city again. It would all have meant time and expenses, and as yet I had neither the training nor the mental attitude to stand by and see precious time being wasted without becoming impatient. Quite apart from the time, it was an expensive business having to order a car every time. Use of public transport would have taken an infinitely greater amount of time. In any case, we would probably only have been able to attend to one matter at a time, and this would have meant a number of trips to the inner city. It was certainly more comfortable this way, because it would have been no pleasure to stand waiting at the bus stops in this cold or to be jammed like a sardine into one of the draughty, overcrowded buses. But travelling by car was not cheap, quite apart from the difficulties and problems of obtaining the use of one. If I wanted to use a car owned by the university, then it had to be ordered at least two days in advance; if, on the other hand, one happened to have a friend sitting in the car park, then it could occur that a car was available immediately. The difference in pricing between public taxis and cars from the university car park was so great that I resolved to get to the bottom of the matter. If I had paid thirty yuan to travel by university car to a particular destination, then the taxi would charge only ten yuan for the return journey. This puzzled me.

One day, when I was about to use one of the university cars again, I asked about the reason for the price variation. I was told that the problem lay in the fact that the university car had to travel back empty. And who should pay for the petrol and driver, if not the passenger? It makes sense, doesn't it?

The university campus is situated a long way out of the city proper. One rarely sees vacant taxis in the streets. When I happened to get myself lost, I was most surprised to notice that the driver took no notice of my attempts to hail him, even though the VACANT sign was showing green. When the first taxi passed me thus, I thought that the driver probably had not seen me. But when it happened several times I started to wonder, and again resolved to find out why.

I found the answer on my next trip by taxi. The taxis belonged to a number of different taxi control stations, which at that time were appearing everywhere like mushrooms. Also, it was once more permissible to earn private income from taxi driving. Each control centre directed its drivers to particular waiting spots, which were only found as a rule outside hotels for foreigners or outside "Friendship Stores." It was not possible to order a taxi via one of the control stations. If a visitor happened to know the telephone number of a "hotel-owned" (i.e., organised by the control centre) communication station he could try his luck there, always assuming he could find a telephone and was willing to pay for the return journey as well.

As of yet, China does not have public telephone booths as

we know them; however, anyone who knows the language and can read Chinese will notice signs in many of the shops indicating that their telephone is available for use by the public. Local calls from private connections cost nothing; however, a fee is charged for these so-called public telephones.

Taxis travel from their allocated stand to the desired destination, where they will wait as long as the passenger wishes it and is willing to pay. However, if the latter is not the case and there is no customer seeking a taxi at the destination, the taxi will travel back to its stand empty. On the way back, though the cab is empty, the driver will not stop to pick up a passenger.

During a conversation with a taxi driver I was able to learn something about the reason for the apparently wide variations in taxi fares. There were price categories of 0.50, 0.60, 0.70, and 0.80 yuan per kilometre and basic hiring fees ("flag fall") of 2.40, 2.60, and 2.80 yuan. Where the tariff was only 0.50 yuan there was no flag fall and the taxi had no meter, being a locally made vehicle of the Shanghai make. These cars were somewhat rattly and shaky, mostly with sagging upholstery, and compared to 1980 one saw very few of them outside the many tourist hotels for foreigners. Generally the Shanghai taxis these days saw service with various institutes, factories, and universities, in their own car park with their own fares, usually 0.70 yuan for foreigners. For a "Japanese" of the more basic type the client would pay 0.60 yuan (60 fen) per kilometre plus a flag fall of 2.40. Larger and more comfortable cars "made in Japan" with airconditioning generally cost 70 fen. For 80 fen per kilometre the driver would not only drive; besides playing with the automatic windows, he would also operate the built-in cassette recorder: "Wyyyyy Emmmm Siiii Ehhh" (YMCA) and other disco sounds at full volume. The flag fall in such cases is usually 2.60 or 2.80. The fare is no less if the passenger does not want music or complains about the volume. "But you foreigners listen to such music; in fact, we got it from you! Peculiar, these foreigners. If you play disco, they don't appreciate it. In fact, some don't want to hear anything at all during their journey, or else very old folk tunes, which are so unfashionable." The drivers making such comments were usually rather young drivers who tried to give a modern impression and probably thought themselves very "Western": "We are not really that backward, you know!" During one of the drives I learned something new about the fare structure. The highest fare is charged for a Mercedes, with 1.20 per kilometre and a flag fall of at least 3.00 yuan. But I never did see a taxi with that "Lucky Star" in the city traffic. Apparently, there are only very few, and these are so sought after by wealthy Chinese that it seemed to me that a Mercedes could only be obtained by the dark labyrinths of "connections." It is probably the dream of every Chinese of substance to sit in such a luxury car just once and perhaps even drive it.

My driver simply could not understand my needing only "a basic set, four wheels." My simple wish for "four wheels and to get there without of having to wait at bus stops, what more would I want?" seemed to me to be something totally new to him, and I am sure that it shook severely his mental picture of a "typical foreigner."

My naive idea that money was only money was also in need of some correction. At least in those places where there were a lot of foreigners there seemed to be various means of payment. I did not notice this so much during my eight-day stay in Beijing, because I always received so-called FEC (Foreign Exchange Certificates/Currency) for my deutschmarks and spent only these green and blue notes. It was much rarer for foreigners to receive the country's currency notes of higher value, for example ten-yuan notes. In fact, legally foreigners are not supposed to have them at all.

Having FEC meant that one could shop in special shops, to which the local population could only gain admittance in the company of a foreigner, and buy goods destined for export or at least of better quality.

My salary was paid to me in local currency, the *renminbi* (people's money, RMB). FEC could only be obtained in exchange for hard currency. As a result of this dual money system I had a number of disputes during the coming months, because I did not want to be forced to exchange marks for FEC all the time. Particularly taxi drivers were reluctant to accept their RMB, which led to various quite heated arguments with them. Asking them why they thought so little of their currency and even despised it, I usually got the answer that they would like to shop in those Friendship Stores for a better selection. My impression was, above all, they wanted to hoard the FEC to exchange for hard currency, in order to get abroad.

Foreigners in Chinese employ receive an entitlement card, which allows them to shop with RMB in those special shops already mentioned, in sections or departments open to foreign tourists or businesspeople working in China. As this card is white, it is known simply as a "white card": *bai ka*. This *bai ka* is something akin to an "Open Sesame" for obtaining the unattainable in everyday Chinese life. The quality of the merchandise not always matched the sometimes quite steep prices on display. But from time to time one could find some very attractive special offers of items that were simply unobtainable elsewhere.

Such "specially reserved" offers could be found in all parts of this large country, particularly at "sightseeing" locations. Even bookshops had a special section, usually on the upper floor, where particularly interesting books could be bought. Not everything that was printed was intended for use by the average consumer. It was my impression that a lot of goods, whether they be books or quality merchandise, were intended primarily for export. Whatever was left over then found its way to a normal counter.

From friends I learnt something regarding Chinese translations of books by foreign authors. Mouth-to-mouth advertising worked extremely well. One of my acquaintances heard that on a particular day a certain bookshop would have for sale several thousand volumes of translated foreign literature. The shop was full to bursting with interested buyers. They forced their way through to the counter, had two or three books pressed into their hands, were told the price and where to pay, and by that time had already been pushed forward by the crowd. My acquaintance really had no idea what was happening to her. Once back on the street she looked at her buy and discovered that for several yuan she had bought books that were of absolutely no use to her. The books were dissertations by foreign authors on scientific subjects. Patiently she waited to come across someone who had suffered a similar fate and with whom she might be able to make a swap. She did have the good luck to exchange one of her books for a novel, but the English author held little interest for her, as she wanted to read German literature in Chinese translation. She took the book anyway, as for her a novel was preferable to a scientific work. Later she was able to exchange the other two books for some obscure works by Russian authors quite unknown to her. It seems that one buys when goods happen to be on offer; one then swaps those goods if they are of no use.

The days in Beijing passed very quickly, with almost every day bringing an invitation to dine, sometimes even twice a day. I was spoilt rotten, almost force-fed, in fact. The families I visited treated me as an honoured guest, and neither effort nor expenses were spared in preparing and serving delicious dishes.

Again and again I experienced this very warm and friendly hospitality, which was taken for granted by my hosts. On a number of occasions the host simply sat there and derived his pleasure from the appetite and enjoyment of the food being shown by his guest, to the point where the host sometimes forgot to eat. However, there were times when the hospitality was overdone, when there were new servings heaped on my plate again and again and my glass was instantly replenished even though only a few sips had been drunk from it. It was not regarded as impolite to leave something on your plate. On the other hand, if one ate up everything, the host was likely to take this as meaning that the guest had not had enough and pile more food on the plate.

In this way I was able to enjoy many cheerful and relaxed invitations in pleasant company. The better host and guests knew one another, the more openhearted were the conversations. Jokes, double entendres, flirtations, and gossip served to enliven the assembled guests during a feast of *jiaozi* or a hot pot (a type of fondue), Sichuan style (hot and spicy with three kinds of meat) or Mongolian (mutton).

In Beijing such occasions tended to be more stiff and formal, probably because the hosts were of more mature years and of the old school. I had to sit fixed to my chair, permitted or indeed almost forced to just eat and enjoy my food. I was not allowed to fetch a bowl or a chair or do any other form of work. The housewife usually spent her time standing in the kitchen, only coming into the room briefly to bring another dish to the table and quite delighted if one asked about the origins or method of preparation of the particular recipe.

By comparison such sociable dinners in Y. tended to be much more relaxed affairs, and by being crammed together into the one room of some fifteen square metres we all became very close to one another.

Apart from the many eating sessions, we also undertook a visit to an open-air museum of some very old bells, situated on the grounds of what was once a monastery. My friend took the trouble to have his wife's bicycle repaired specially to lend it to me. The ride from the university to the open-air museum took about thirty minutes. The idea was to make it a picnic in the open, which at minus five degrees Celsius was not a particularly inviting prospect.

On that very morning I was greeted by a pale blue sky, and even though the cold northerly wind was not as strong as usual, my face ached as I rode into the wind, as if I were being stung by a myriad of tiny needles. The street dust, mixed with fine sand, had the same effect as sandpaper. My companions with their mouth protection did not even notice the sand, which I was forced to inhale with every deep breath. My mouth was dry, and the sand grated between my teeth. Still, we calmly cycled along the streets.

The buses and other vehicles, which tended to come very close, took some getting used to, and I felt rather unsure of myself. Even the other cyclists did not seem to me to be at all that courteous or considerate in the traffic. Not only did the ceaseless ringing of the bicycle bells and being continually cut off make me angry, but I felt challenged to stand my ground in the traffic. Once I got used to it I no longer took any notice of the bell ringing. Cool, calm, and collected, I just pedalled on, taking no notice at all.

Unless a young cyclist happened to be trying to force his way through with ceaseless ringing of his bell, the masses of cyclists just moved along in a steady procession at a comfortable speed. There were few accidents and little unpleasantness. I only rarely encountered any kind of stubborn determination in the behavioural pattern of Chinese people. Differences of opinion were explained and discussed but seldom led to heated arguments, unless it was something really severe. Everyone seemed to try in his own manner to resolve his differences with others.

For example, the young cyclist mentioned above would have simply been allowed to pass after what the other cyclists would have thought an appropriate time. Pairs of young lovers, young men and young women, often rode side by side, chatting happily and holding hands, thereby taking up a significant portion of the roadway. Everyone went his own way, many deep in thought. It seemed to me not unlike a lazy, slow-flowing river, where one avoided the occasional rapids only to join the main flow again a little farther downstream. Every movement was calm, and it was with implacable calm that everyone rode along.

The gradual change in myself was quite remarkable. If during the first months I was apt to be uncertain, irritable, afraid, or overcautious, in time I developed a more stoic attitude to challenges and irritations not only in the traffic, but in all kinds of other situations where previously I had reacted instantly if I had to take some sort of stand. The learning process was making itself felt.

My only real concern, even towards the end of my stay, was with the car drivers, although this was less of a problem in Beijing than in the country. I just could not see that the common reckless driving style was in any way necessary or even rational. If I saw one of the large dark green, solidly built, and massive-looking trucks driving towards me in the distance with a huge cloud of dust behind it, I would move as far to the right of the roadway as I could, making myself as "little" as possible. I behaved similarly if I heard the continual horn honking of a truck some distance behind me. By contrast the Chinese cyclists allowed nothing to interrupt their calm or cause them to alter direction in the slightest. Only at the last moment, when they could practically feel the truck, did they finally deign to make way for the bigger and stronger vehicle. I envied their calm and their unshakable confidence in fate and in themselves.

As already mentioned, there were very few accidents on the special bikeways in Beijing. However, in the country such special bikeways did not exist, and there had been in recent times an increasing incidence of accidents involving pedestrians and bicycles. The import boom of foreign cars, mainly from Japan, led to chaotic traffic conditions, especially during the rush hours. I was told that in Beijing alone during the year 1985 some thirty thousand additional motor vehicles were registered for road use. Whether such claims are fact or idle boast is difficult to find out in China.

Traffic rules were still in their infancy throughout China, although Beijing in this respect was more progressive than smaller towns or country areas. However, although the rules might be few and basic, drastic measures were in force to ensure that they were followed and that the traffic remained under control. The rules were almost literally hammered into the population, and that on the spot and almost immediately. I saw this myself in Beijing. On the long Changan Jie, an eight-lane road that crosses Beijing from east to west, I observed on a number of occasions at different times of the day that police officers were posted on the centre strip at intervals of about ten metres, from where they controlled vehicular as well as pedestrian traffic. I guess it is true to say that policemen behave in much the same way everywhere. Arguments and backtalk are not really tolerated. I experienced the same thing now in Beijing. The result was, I was told, either the bicycle being confiscated or in the case of pedestrians an immediate and hefty fine. Any misdemeanour on the part of a car driver is punished by instant loss of his driver's license. A taxi driver told me once that very energetic measures were being taken in order to ensure adequate traffic control. Taxi drivers tend to be very careful and cautious in the traffic, because their very existence depends on their license.

Compared with my previous visits in 1980 and 1983 I found that the average person's traffic sense and behaviour on the road had improved significantly. No longer would pedestrians stroll along the street in thought or daydreaming, blissfully ignoring the traffic. Whilst I noticed an increased attentiveness in many of the people, there was also an increase in nervous movements and expressions, particularly with younger people. Some of that old calm had gone, too, and perhaps that is the price of progress in China.

Our excursion to see the bells from various epochs of Chinese history took place without incident. Unless you know your way about, the small, winding side lane was quite difficult to find. Only an almost illegible sign on a weathered wooden board affixed to the crumbling wall of a house showed us that we were on the right track. The sign had probably been there for decades. After a few minutes' ride in this lane we reached the right spot. At one time there used to be a monastery here. Some of the remaining buildings seemed to be in bad disrepair, although some attempts at restoration had been made.

A number of large and small bells stood in a gardenlike arrangement, exposed to the elements. In front of a number of the exhibits there were small tablets stuck in the earth, giving some basic information about the epoch and the history of the particular bell, as well as the material used in its manufacture, predominantly bronze. On average the bells were more than a thousand years old. As far as I can remember, no fee was charged to those who wanted to look at the bells out in the open. We walked around, admiring the handiwork of the ancestors with respect, and we finally came to the conclusion that today's craftsmen probably could not produce articles with such a high degree of artistry and polish. One of my acquaintances commented that such skills were being lost not only in cultures outside the Chinese, but that these traditional skills and artistic trades had been shamefully neglected in their own country. Efforts at restoring significant cultural items worthy of preservation were set in motion some time ago, but progress is slow and spasmodic. Traditional skills, such as the preparation of paints (made from pigs' blood) for painting walls or wooden structures in the traditional red, have been passed on only in a very limited sense. At one time there was very little interest in such activities.

On one occasion, in a park belonging to the Summer Palace I saw a very old man standing on a scaffold, busily trying to restore a section of an old palace wall with great effort. Somewhat astonished, I asked my companion at the time why a younger workman could not be found for this task, which could surely not be easy for an old man. In reply I was told that as yet there were no younger workmen sufficiently skilled in the use of the various powders typical of that particular period. Those older skilled craftsmen who are still alive are much sought after today, so that they can pass on their skill, their knowledge, and their experience to the younger generation. Fortunately, the Chinese authorities today have reached a stage where the cultural heritage of their country is once again regarded as worthy of preservation.

As I heard later, the Cultural Revolution was much less successful in country areas, in that much less was destroyed or ruined by the peasant population than was destroyed or ruined in the cities. The peasants had buried many articles, to dig them up later when the situation turned for the better, and thus preserved their treasured things with utmost care; likewise they have kept in mind their traditional beliefs. This is probably true, as it is difficult to explain otherwise how old customs and traditions could be preserved or why I came across many old and traditional objects of daily use, such as clay or ceramic pots or special stoneware vessels used for the preparation of healing herbal medicines. Superstition, too, has never been entirely eliminated in China. Whilst there have been very great changes in rural areas and much new technology introduced, it is the traditional peasant heritage that helped the rural population to weather all the storms of the Cultural Revolution. In the country I still found much tradition and knowledge handed down through the generations. In these areas the people do remember the old customs and try to preserve them. For example, efforts are now being made to restore remains of old temples that, once in good shape, become a source of tourist dollars. Though in Beijing, the temple we visited on this particular day was typical.

The sun was shining and even gave a little warmth if one stood out of the wind. As the outing was intended to be a picnic, with all the trappings, my friends had brought with them everything needed to hold body and soul together. We found a protected spot in the sun beside one of the paths belonging to a temple and sat down on a protruding ledge. The bag of tasty items started to empty rapidly. We ate smoked chicken, nibbled nuts, quenched our thirst with dried apricot and plum pieces, sweet/sour and slightly salty in taste, and chewed on beef jerky in order to stimulate the flow of saliva. For dessert each of us had a freshly peeled apple.

Despite the biting cold we concluded our most enjoyable meal in the open air, with much laughter and telling of anecdotes. If we had not been sitting in a sunny spot out of the wind, I doubt if I could have endured it.

So far we were the only visitors. After lunch, by which time it was two o'clock, and more by accident than by design, we had a look at an exhibition in one of the recently restored temple buildings, now opened to the public. An engraver showed his tools, pig-bristle brushes with various engraved Chinese characters. They were so small, only a magnifying glass made them visible. The engraver worked in classical calligraphy, from right to left and from top to bottom. In some cases he had engraved entire verses by Confucius or other Chinese philosophers. There were also works carved in ivory, bone, wood, and animal horn. The artist, a man of about eighty years from Sichuan, greeted me personally and immediately offered to do an engraving for me on an item of my own jewellery. Unfortunately, I was not wearing any jewellery at all and could only offer him my metal spectacle frames on which to practise his art. He took them into the light, put on a watchmaker's eyeglass, and in a matter of minutes my spectacles bore engravings in Chinese characters giving my Chinese name, the date, place, and best wishes for a long life, all on one part of my glasses. The engraving was decipherable only through a magnifying glass. The entire engraving was no more than seven millimetres long and contained fifteen characters.

Whilst all this was happening, one of my friends took care of the entrance fee for the exhibition. When entering the temple hall we had not seen any signs of admission fees, but by some way or other my friends must have been requested to pay, and my entry ticket was considerably more expensive than it would have been for a Chinese visitor. The price for the engraving was also quite a lot dearer. I paid ten yuan, which was supposed to be a "special friendship price," but his own countrymen paid only 2.50 yuan for the same work.

A family of foreigners joined us. They were Swiss, and the man was a manager of one of the numerous hotels for foreign tourists. These hotels usually belong to one of the well-known foreign hotel chains, which invest in a joint-venture enterprise in China and sell their know-how. In any case, this manager was promptly offered an engraving, at the "friendship price" of only ten yuan. He had already been in China for some time and was familiar with the prices, especially the "friendship prices," because his spontaneous reply, promptly translated into Chinese by an English-speaking Chinese onlooker, was: "Friendship in China is always a little more expensive," and he declined the offer with thanks.

Around four o'clock, having been outdoors in the cold since 10:30 that morning, we set out in our return journey. I was so frozen through that even vigorous pedalling into the wind barely served to warm me up a little. Back in my room at the guest house I made a beeline for the thermos and poured myself a mug of hot water, which filled me with a pleasant warmth and started to revive me. I held the hot mug with both hands, and gradually I felt some sensation returning into my frozen fingertips.

The weather during my eight days in Beijing was variable. Once or twice the sun shone from a pale blue sky, but most of the time the sky was bluish grey. The fabled deep blue sky of Beijing is a thing of the past. The environmental pollution is indescribable. For two days a biting "fog," as smog is called here, hung over the city, reducing visibility to less than ten metres. My eyes burned and watered, but the cause for this was merely my excessive sensitivity to fog, as a young man explained to me. It had nothing to do with pollution. I was told that some quite effective eyedrops in small plastic ampoules could be bought in the traditional pharmacies. Except "eyedrops," there was no indicated composition on the small bottle; nevertheless, they certainly eased my discomfort.

On another day there was a very strong northerly wind blowing. What little snow had remained was soon gone, and instead one seemed to be chewing sand. Small children and women protected their faces with a kind of veil made of muslin or tulle, whereas others wore mouth protection. Not similarly protected, I had to dismount from my bike a number of times to clear my eyes or remove fine grains from their corners. The storm tended to dry everything. I was told that the relative humidity during the winter months was never higher than 40 percent.

The evening before my departure for Y., I had another invitation for a major feast. I was to be ready at 5:00 P.M. As I had a prior luncheon invitation, I rushed back to the guest house at three o'clock so that I would have some time to relax and change. The president of my institute was giving a dinner in my honour. He and a number of other professors, including the brother-in-law of my helper during my stay in Beijing, were on their way to West Germany. They were in Beijing waiting for authorisation from the appropriate ministry for their departure as well as visas and flight tickets. "This is an important visit," my helper told me gravely and in some awe. I understood. This meant I had to be punctual, dress appropriately, and give some thought to what I might say in an after-dinner speech. At five o'clock I was ready in coat and hat and awaited what was to happen. But nothing happened. At last, just before six o'clock, the helper and his brother-in-law knocked on my door. Now there were the three of us waiting, but just what we were waiting for I still did not know; not to seem inquisitive, I did not ask. Several times the professor, the brother-in-law, went to the main entrance of the guest house as if he was on the lookout for something particular. After a while he came running up the stairs quite excited. "Quickly now, we can't let the president wait so long. Come on, hurry, hurry!" We literally ran down the stairs, but I did not know for what reason. In front of the main entrance stood a blue car of the Shanghai brand.

Quickly, quickly to the restaurant. Calmly the driver started, and after what seemed to me like a long drive we arrived at a newly opened restaurant situated in the old city of Beijing. The street was narrow and sparsely lit, but the restaurant was all the more brightly and colourfully lit. It was an establishment specialising in Hangzhou cuisine (from Zhejiang Province, south of Shanghai). In front of the entrance stood three gentlemen to welcome us. After brief introductions they led us inside and up many steps to the third floor. I supposed that the lower floors were intended for the "rabble." There was a lot of activity. All tables were set, and there was an almost indescribable noise made up of hundreds of voices, interspersed with the shrill shouts of the serving girls. It sometimes sounded as if there were open conflict, but the raised voices were merely intended as a signal to clear a way through the throng.

On the third floor, where we were headed, a quieter form of conversation with appropriate decorum was taking place, and I found the atmosphere relaxed and cheerful. On the lower floors the diners sat around smaller round tables, but in the upper rooms there were larger round tables set for eight to ten people each, located in separate niches with inlaid bamboo partitions. The serving staff consisted of young girls in traditional jackets of burgundy cloth, buttoned on the right side with the knotted traditional "buttons," and all attractively made up and with stylish hairdos. Long black trousers and shoes with moderately high heels completed their livery. A somewhat older but just as carefully made up girl acted as receptionist; she greeted us at the door and led us to the niche where the president and other gentlemen were waiting. I was welcomed very warmly and introduced to the gentlemen. There were the current president, the previous president, the local president, the incumbent chief of the foreign bureau, here a professor for this, and there another professor for that. This gentleman was in Germany for eight months; that one speaks good English; these gentlemen are with the group travelling to Germany; that gentleman is from the research branch of our institute in Beijing. Before long my head was swimming. Who did what? What was that one's name? Yet I had to form a clear picture in my mind quickly as to which of the gentlemen had an important role for the evening and which role that was. I then had to behave according to whom I should listen, of whom I could ask a question, to whom must I give my attention first, and to whom last. I had to orientate myself very quickly indeed. From the way in which the various men behaved towards one another I was able to deduce the hierarchy fairly well. Apart from the position held by one particular gentleman, I had been acquainted with the functions of the others present. I assume that he was the party secretary of the research institute in Beijing. In any case, here I was among illustrious and all male company; these people knew what behaviour was due to a lady and how she should be treated. According to the Chinese view that women do not drink strong alcoholic beverages, at least when in public, the usual additional small glasses were missing from the table setting. My host drew my attention to this and remarked that they would all limit themselves to a little light wine or beer. I thanked him for his caring concern, and from then on I either avoided or partook very sparingly even of these beverages, as I did not want to appear an unpolished barbarian devoid of all manners.

The meal itself was a once-in-a-lifetime experience. There were carefully selected delicacies such as eel, as thin as shoelaces, from the Western Lake in Hangzhou, freshwater cress from the same waters, and a type of carp from that region, and other specialties tempted the palate. Various opinions were offered by the guests, absorbed in eating, munching, and slurping, as to the various recipes and methods of cooking.

Once the obligatory speeches and toasts were over—one had to rise after each one and touch glasses with everyone round the table in turn and mumble something about friendship—the more casual and relaxed phase began. Increasing consumption of alcohol had the effect of making the gentlemen more talkative. Anecdotes, jokes, and the like went the rounds. After about two hours the host, in this case "my" president, gave the signal that the dinner and with it the invitation were concluded.

An arrangement was made with one of the many gentlemen present that I was to be picked up punctually at 4:30 P.M. the next day outside the guest house at the university. A car belonging to the Research Institute would then take me to the railway station. One or two companions were instructed to make sure that I got to my train safely and in time. With many good wishes and "peace on your journey" I was ushered into the Shanghai and driven back to the guest house. It was a somewhat odd feeling to be looked after and fussed over in such a caring way. For the time being it was very pleasant, I did not have to take responsibility for anything, and all I had to do was follow the instructions given to me obediently and pleasantly; no questions, suggestions, or any other contribution was expected from me.

I whiled away most of the following day with writing of letters and postcards, a stroll through the university campus, making a few small purchases, and reading. In the dining hall for foreign students and teachers I had my lunch.

This hall was large and could seat hundreds of diners. On one side was a section for foreigners, and opposite was the area for Chinese visitors and guests of the university. The university's own students and teaching staff either ate their meals at home or used one of the dining rooms intended for them. In the "foreigner" dining hall Western meals as well as Chinese cuisine were available. The food was not particularly tasty, and the price varied with the category of the menu. A Western meal with soup, a piece of meat in the form of a small steak or a slice of roast, accompanied by vegetables or potatoes, and possibly followed by a puddinglike dessert, cost around 4 yuan, which was simply unaffordable for students. Even teaching staff had to content themselves with more economical meals. As a general rule the monthly salary of experts, with or without academic degrees, was in the range of 300 to 700 yuan (0.85 yuan to 1 deutschmark) paid by Chinese organisations, institutes, or universities.

It was evidently due to these economical considerations that there was always a long queue at the counter where the Chinese dishes were distributed. One had to count oneself lucky if, on arriving at the window where the food was served at long last, there was still some choice among the various large pots and bowls. There was rice, different types of noodles and dumplings, combination dishes of stir-fried vegetables with slivers of meat, and pieces of fish or stew with noodles; dishes such as these, which varied from day to day, were typical of what the kitchen had to offer. So it was much cheaper to eat here. For example, a *mantou* (steamed yeast bun) or a bowl of rice, with combination, could be had for 1.50 yuan. Canteen food was rarely flavoursome and as often as not was not very nourishing either. Nevertheless, the cooks tried very hard to keep their foreign clients satisfied. The choice of drinks was not too bad, ranging from beer, all kinds of undefinable rather sweet juices and milk, to tea and hot water.

Before setting out at 4:00 P.M. to meet the gentlemen who were to take me to the station, I took care to pay for the additional five nights' accommodation. It came as a considerable surprise to me that I had to pay seventy yuan for this, despite the earlier arrangement made with the responsible clerk earlier that I would pay only seven yuan per night, which happened to be the same amount paid by my helper on behalf of my future employers when I first arrived. The employee who was on duty at that time had assured me that this was the arrangement, written it all on a piece of paper, and then stowed it somewhere in a drawer. It was then explained to me that there was only one disadvantage to the cheap room rate, namely, in the event of the guest house being heavily booked, the other bed in my room would also be let. If I was willing to pay the full price I would have more comfort as the sole occupant of my room. I decided on the cheap rate, and the question of full booking did not arise while I was occupying the room. This is why I was so surprised when I received the bill. The employee on duty this time knew nothing of the earlier arrangement and even doubted that there was any regulation such as I described. I insisted that she search through her records and through the drawer where the earlier clerk on duty had deposited the piece of paper with the details. Very reluctantly she did as asked, and lo and behold, the slip of paper was located. She then calmly wrote out a new bill for thirty-five yuan as well as a receipt for the same sum and in a friendly manner handed me both with a beaming smile. We parted the best of friends, and she even wished me a pleasant journey and expressed the wish that we might meet again at the same price.

I left my luggage with the gatekeeper and went to the home

of my helper, who was also to accompany me safely to the station. He was just in the process of conducting an important telephone discussion with some ministry. It seemed it was a real odyssey through the labyrinth of the telephone system and the bureaucratic hierarchy. At long last he seemed to have the right person on the other end of the line. I was becoming a little apprehensive, because we were supposed to be waiting outside the guest house at 4:30 P.M. sharp for the car and for my official companion, who had been charged with the task of getting me to the train safely and on time by the president on the previous evening. But my helper gave no sign of cutting the telephone call short. Once a telephone subscriber in China actually succeeds in getting the other party on the line, he will not let go easily. Since there is no charge for telephone calls within the city limits, it does not matter how long the call takes. At last, a few minutes after four-thirty we got on our way, but when we got to the guest house there was no car and no "official escort." The gatekeeper told us that the car and the man with the driver had left again a few minutes ago, because they did not know where they should start looking for us. So there we stood—now what? My helper looked rather helpless and became more and more nervous, asking, "What do we do now? Where can I get a car? How much time do we have?"

My train was due to depart at 6:30 P.M., and during the rush hour the streets of Beijing became hopelessly congested. It was not without reason that the gentlemen allowed two full hours for the ride to the station. My helper ran off, came back, then ran off again: "Mei you." In the end he tried to phone the car park of the Research Institute, and this time he was in luck. Another driver undertook the task and turned up at five o'clock. It was a real race against time, and in the end I managed to get aboard my train six minutes before departure time, with my tongue literally hanging out, with two totally unnerved and exhausted companions, namely, my helper and the chauffeur, struggling with my twenty-kilogram suitcase. But at last I was on the train from Beijing to Hefei, capital of Anhui Province. The stewardess did not miss the opportunity to give me a mild reprimand: "Why do you come so late? Don't you know that the train will leave in a few minutes?"

I stood inside. The two men had quickly jumped off the train again, after kindly stowing my baggage for me. With "See you in the summer," and, "Many thanks for your trouble and for helping with the baggage," I rolled into the night and towards my ultimate goal in China. I was feeling quite exhausted.

Train Journey to and Arrival at Y.

To the accompaniment of shrill whistling, jerking, and groaning the train pulled out of the weakly lit Central Station of Beijing. In my compartment, which was not much brighter, there were two men and a woman in a green uniform, complete with a peaked cap and insignias of rank, and the woman's barely two-year-old son. The huge astonishment at my appearance in the compartment was mirrored not only in the faces of the adults. The little boy immediately snuggled up close to his mother and buried his face in her thickly padded green overcoat, which bore narrow red epaulettes with two golden stars. He perhaps feared the *wai guo ren*, or foreigner.

It would be most unusual for Chinese travellers to come across foreigners travelling alone, especially in the winter or on this particular stretch. They expect to see foreign tourists in groups and in carriages especially arranged for them. Most foreigners these days fly the longer distances from city to city.

I certainly gained the impression that it was a most unexpected experience my cotravellers encountered in someone like me, quite alone and right in their midst, and speaking their tongue. Once the usual polite formalities had been dispensed with, such as where I was from, where I was going and why, and the perennially recurring interest in how I came to speak Chinese, it was time to start thinking about dinner.

I had had not a bite since my lunch at 11:30 at the dining hall at the university and was starting to feel quite hungry, with my stomach growling in protest. By chance a waiter from the dining car came walking past, whom one of the male passengers asked what was available in the way of something to eat. There was only noodle soup left, which was fine with me. When, after some minutes I was handed a steaming bowl with a lot of liquid, lots of noodles, and not much else and I wanted to pay, the waiter told me not to worry—it was already paid for.

One of my fellow travellers had paid the fifty fen (0.50 yuan) on my behalf. Time and again I experienced this very sincere hospitality and friendliness, which was apparently taken for granted, from people whom I did not even know. The foreigner, the guest, was always shown respect and courtesy, even if he/she did not know the language. I have very rarely experienced any kind of animosity or unfriendly treatment in China, either in the past during my youth or more recently. Here, too, in the compartment, everybody was very friendly and willing to help. The problem was how to deal with the undisguised inquisitiveness that always surfaced as soon as I started any kind of conversation, without hurting their feelings or offending anyone. My fellow travellers asked about my age, profession, family, income, etc.; they were particularly interested to know what people abroad thought about China today and about Deng Xiaoping, also, how the West judged the Cultural Revolution and similar questions. If I in my turn asked them, for example, what they knew about the Federal Republic of Germany, I was quite often surprised to find that they had considerable knowledge about the division of Germany, the strong currency *ma ke* (deutschmark), Chancellor Ke-er (Kohl), the Berlin Wall, and condemnation of that unworthy structure.

It seems that Chinese people do not feel abashed to ask or think it impolite to put so many personal questions to a stranger. I then in return asked them about their families, professions, and so on. And so I found out that the woman in uniform was a medical practitioner with the police in Beijing and that she and her son were on their way in order to spend the Spring Festival (Chinese New Year) with his grandparents near Hefei, Anhui

Province. She did not refer to them as "in-laws," but as "my son's paternal grandparents." If a father or mother has a child with him or her and one asked after the other parent, meaning wife or husband, the reply almost always refers to the "father" or "mother of my child"; rarely does one hear "my wife" or "my husband." The woman doctor told me that she had decided to travel by "soft sleeping car" (first class) because she wanted her little son, whom she affectionately called Dudu, to be comfortable during the twenty-hour journey. She said that the trains always tended to be overfull at festival time and that the "hard *chouchettes*" were always noisy and draughty, also that with so many travellers the carriages were not very clean. As a doctor she took great care with hygiene and wanted her little boy to learn the importance of it right from the start.

Little Dudu slowly seemed to thaw towards me, and after a while he even smiled and offered me a mandarin orange, which his mother had given him for me, holding it out with a tentative little hand. The two men, who were not related to mother or child, cared for and fussed over the little one in such a loving way that they easily could have been taken for his grandfathers. It is wonderful to be a child in China, particularly a son! We all took part in the usual game of questions and answers, and we all learnt a good deal from one another before we reached our destination.

Around nine o'clock an announcement came over the train radio, a kind of a public address system, that it was time to settle down for the night, and there was an additional appeal to smokers not to smoke in bed due to the risk of fire concluding the announcement. After a few bars of Chinese opera the loudspeaker above us became silent. Little Dudu was already nearly asleep in his mother's arms. Once the two men had climbed up into the upper bunks and mother and child had snuggled into their blankets, I dug out a small towel from my baggage, especially bought for this purpose, and spread it out on the somewhat grubby pillow. I felt little desire to get into the previously used padded blankets and therefore decided to keep my overcoat on. It was quite cold in the compartment, the heating did not function properly, and draughts sneaked through all sorts of gaps and cracks. And so, fully dressed with overcoat, woolen cap, shawl, and boots, I slept soundly through the night rolling towards Y.

Having thus slept soundly, I faced my arrival in the city of Y. the following morning. I decided to skip breakfast, but not a trip to the toilet and the "washroom." I would have preferred it the other way round, but when there is need one does not ask too long about hygienic custom or privacy. I brushed my teeth under the gaze of a young man and similarly washed my face and hands in the tiny washing cubicle. Fortunately, the train toilet could be locked from the inside, but the bidetlike basin, set into the floor with footrests cemented into it on either side, did not tempt one to linger. It was too dirty, and there was a very strong, cold draught from the train movement up the open drain. If there was no water in the cistern for flushing, usually it was empty; then whatever was left in the pan stayed there unchanged to await the next user. It required great self-restraint to use these primitive and quite revolting facilities, but there was no other choice. Having got it over with, I went back to the compartment, where the stewardess was already waiting for me in order to give me back my tickets, which she had taken into possession when I boarded the train in Beijing.

Another stewardess refilled the two large thermoses sitting in holders under the window with freshly boiled water. At the end of the sleeping car there was a tiny room, in which a kettle steamed away constantly all day on a small coal stove.

It was already light outside, and we were approaching the railway station of Y. I looked out the window. A number of factory chimneys sent large clouds of greyish black, sulphur yellow, or white smoke belching into the sky. The landscape seemed to be dull and grey. Everywhere there were uncompleted new buildings of several storeys, the bamboo scaffolding looking like cages. Next to them stood small brick dwellings, looking as if they had been deliberately set into the landscape. Crumbling walls, sandy paths, dust, and dirt completed the picture.

Arrival at Y. Railway Station took place to the accompaniment of the loudspeaker giving instructions as to how passengers should conduct themselves in order to ensure smooth disembarkation from the train and exit from the station via the windows where tickets had to be handed in. I really don't know how many of the travellers took the long monologue to heart. Everybody just streamed towards the exit from the carriage on the basis of first come, first served. There was a lot of pushing and shoving near the exit door, and unfriendly words could be heard. I found repeatedly in China, not only on this occasion, that instructions as to proper conduct of individuals usually only applied to others. One had to act and think quickly and force one's way through almost brutally or be left behind. Any hesitation meant that either one fails to get on board the overcrowded bus or else one has to endure the torrents of abuse from the conductor. And so the only thing to do is to follow everybody else's example and urge one's way along. If there is any cursing or harsh words, these are then always intended for the mass at large, not directed at any individual.

Once the train had finally come to rest, the two gentlemen in my compartment insisted on helping with my luggage, despite my protest; they not only carried it to the carriage door, but even took it down and onto the platform for me. I thanked them very sincerely and wished them all a pleasant continuation of their journey and, above all, a particularly happy and healthy Spring Festival, i.e., Chinese New Year. The Year of the Buffalo was to commence on the twenty-first of February.

Whilst I was getting out of the train I noticed a wildly gesticulating small woman outside. It turned out that she was the leader of the bureau for foreign affairs of the institute, Mrs. Z. Barely had I been able to take care of my two pieces of luggage when she was already tugging my sleeves, turning me around, and exhorting me in a staccato voice to say farewell to my fellow travellers and wave good-bye several times. Above all I was not to forget to say *"xiexie,"* thank you. I finally became quite angry and made it clear to her that I did know the rules of behaviour and politeness.

Somehow the reception in Y. did not go well, and a feeling of foreboding crept over me. I recalled the prophecy of my helper in Beijing, who had suggested that it might be better to arrive in Y. before the festival. It seemed that the leader, this excited little woman before me on the platform, had indicated politely but firmly to him on the telephone that my plan to spend the festive days with my friends in Beijing did not suit her at all. We all regretted this very much, but in order to avoid any unpleasantness right at the beginning I complied.

So here I was, standing on platform 2 in Y., and in front of me the little woman, who complained endlessly about my two pieces of luggage and grumbled at my having brought so much with me. The suitcase was much too heavy (twenty kilograms), she said, and why did I need a tote bag as well? It was all very unpleasant. So as not to create the impression that I was going to allow myself to be ruled by her, I countered politely, but firmly, that in any case, I had not come just to stay for the weekend. Both of us got on with the task of dragging my bags, with nonstop complaints on her part, along the long platform, then down the steps and through the underpass, and up the steps again on the other side. She, in fact, could have left me waiting with my bags while she fetched the chauffeur who was waiting by the exit and left it to him to carry the heavy suitcase, but she did not do so. Be that as it may, at long last we arrived at the counter where we had to surrender my tickets. Using her elbows, and in a far from delicate manner, she forced her way

through the throngs of people, motioning to me to follow her
example. The crowd voluntarily cleared a path for me, for which
I thanked them. And in no time a murmur started: "She can
speak Chinese!" This of course awakened their curiosity, and
in no time at all I was surrounded once more. Mrs. Z. had
already got through, whilst I was hemmed in by the crowd, trying to pass with my hand luggage, hopefully intact and unin-
jured. Mrs. Z. became increasingly nervous. Not only did she
scream at me to force my way through more energetically, but
she also hissed and yelled abuse at those around me. At last I
stood before the ticket collector in her little hut and showed her
my ticket, but unlike Chinese travellers I was allowed to keep
it, because I told her I would need it later in order to claim
reimbursement. At last there I was, on the square outside the
station. Despite the early hour, 7:30 A.M., it seemed to be just
as crowded as the station itself.

Mrs. Z. left me standing there, and in no time at all a new
swarm of onlookers had gathered around me. This time I kept
silent and listened to the comments about my fur-lined leather
coat, including: "I wonder if it is real?" One of them was
encouraged by others to feel it and see for himself, but he was
not game enough to try this. Another suggested that I must
belong to the institute in the south of the city of Y., because that
was the only place where foreigners went. But most of the crowd
remained silent. They just stood there and stared at me. Finally,
chauffeur in tow, Mrs. Z. made her way through to me, and
together we fought our way through to the car waiting, once
more Shanghai brand. Once all the luggage had been stowed we
were on our way. While we were threading our way through, I
caught glimpses of the immediate surroundings of the station.

Everywhere I looked there were people standing, sitting,
lying down, smoking, with bundles, carrying loads or holding
children by the hand, or carrying them in their arms. People
trotted past in whipping gait, carrying shoulder poles with large

baskets full of vegetables or other goods at each end. The rhythmic way they moved gave the impression that the baskets at the end of the bamboo pole were quite light. I have always been an admirer of the way a Chinese can run with a heavy load, almost harmonic in the way he moves. They looked balanced and at ease even when carrying two or more full bags or other heavy loads on their backs or shoulders.

It was a picture familiar to me from my childhood. The people still had to work so very hard and must labour away at doing their day's work. However, compared to the old days, their faces looked more relaxed, their eyes more cheerful, and often there was a smile about their lips. The first impression I gained of these people, in passing, was that they seemed to be very much peasant stock. Their skin was darker than that of their paler and more sophisticated brothers and sisters in Beijing; they were not dressed as well, but neither were their clothes patched. Also, their facial expressions were more open and straightforward. Many of the women had coarse woolen cloths wound around their heads, and their clothes consisted of padded cotton pants and jackets. In Beijing it is common to see down jackets in a more modern style, made of synthetic material. What is already commonplace there is still exceptional here. Shanghai is said to be even more "elegant and modern."

The streets we drove through were still largely empty, with few people. There were bicycles here and there, an occasional car, and some two-wheeled mule carts loaded with bales and baskets or materials for construction such as logs or bricks. A light haze hung over the city, as smog was not limited to the very large cities. Accompanied by a lot of tooting and at a speed of around sixty to eighty kilometres per hour our driver sped through Y. with us. I noticed that many of the streets were tree-lined and, in comparison to the eight-lane thoroughfares of Beijing, of normal width (one car in each direction and pedestrian walks). We passed through streets lined with a large number of small businesses and shops of various trades, mostly still with wooden shutters over their windows on account of the early hour. On the other hand, I did not see many multi-story buildings in the inner city itself. For a while we drove straight ahead, then left, around a square with a tropical-looking tree in the middle, and straight ahead again. Reaching an intersection meant first of all constant sounding of the horn, after which we turned right through a red traffic light (traffic rule in all socialist countries) and straight ahead we went. Gradually the surroundings became more rural. We drove out of the city proper and then passed on our right the memorial park to the fighters and fallen of the Huai Hai Offensive (a 1948–49 civil war action between troops of the Kuomintang [KMT/nationalists] and the People's Liberation Army [PLA], about four hundred thousand killed on both sides). On our left were fields and here and there small houses. A block of low-roofed dwellings, built at ground level and surrounded by a wall, was home to a small rural community. Here we saw a middle school, there a work unit of some kind, and somewhere in the distance between the hills some barracks and military training fields. At this time of the year everything had a dull ochre colouring about it, with fields and trees looking grey and bare. As we came closer to our destination I repeatedly saw many tall, boxlike buildings with square holes in them through the leafless branches on the roadside. One particular building, yellow and flat-looking against the hills, attracted my attention. As we were approaching it I saw the rectangular holes were, in fact, windows.

The only road leading to this cluster of buildings was in very poor condition, with sandy footpaths on either side. The bitumen was badly warped in places, whilst elsewhere the road had large holes. Our driver negotiated the many potholes at full speed. My poor head!

One more turn to the left, and there we were outside the institute's main gate, a wide and solid-looking metal affair. The gate opened, and the first glimpse I had of the institute was of the yellow building with an overly large wide stairway in front of it. This was the building I had viewed during the ride. Before me lay an almost unbelievably clean campus, compared with the mess and filth outside the rail station. A few minutes more of driving along a boulevardlike street, lined with many trees, shrubs, and bushes, now all bare, a turn right up a small incline, and there we were outside one of the six two-story red brick buildings by a bitumen road. I had arrived at last.

Impressions of the First Few Days

So, here I was. After the driver had carried my luggage up the stairs for me and driven off, Mrs. Z. accompanied me into the building. I had been allocated the upstairs apartment. On the ground floor, I was told, an American couple were living. We climbed the few concrete steps, and in front of us was the two-door entrance to my future home. The wooden doors, painted brown, with three small glass panes on either side, could only be opened with difficulty. Inside, the stairwell, concrete and stone, reverberated dully to the grating sound of the door being dragged over the concrete floor. The lower left pane of glass, held loosely in the frame by a few nails, rattled, and I could not help wondering how long it might last. Then up some twenty-five uneven concrete steps, and I stood outside the door of my flat. The door was hanging in a wooden frame, around which the concrete masonry had mostly crumbled away. I was afraid to slam it shut, so I closed it very gently. There was a lock on the door to protect me from unwelcome visitors, and now my future home was proudly presented to me by Mrs. Z. Here was the "public" living room (for the time being the word *public* in this context puzzled me), there the kitchen, a generous hallway, and two balconies, one outside the kitchen door and the other accessible from the hall. A door in the hallway led to the bedroom, another to the bathroom; however, two of the three doors leading from the hall were locked. Also, I could not get access to the balcony off my bedroom. There was also a storeroom.

Once Mrs. Z. had shown me everything she handed me the keys, with strict instructions to always lock all doors, including those in the stairwell. I was even to lock my bedroom door. I soon discovered that all "private" doors in fact had security locks. Mrs. Z. talked to me constantly. I cannot recall the details; it was mostly about various rules and regulations I was expected to adhere to. In the meantime a young man had joined us who introduced himself as Xiao D. (Little D.) and was one of the German-speaking interpreters attached to the foreign affairs bureau. He gave me the impression that he was a faithful vassal of the all-powerful Mrs. Z.

My head was spinning from so many new things. Here were the keys to the refrigerator, there in the hall the red telephone, the shower worked like this, Xiao D. would show me, the TV worked like this, two women would come every day to clean up and to refill the five thermoses with boiling water, etc. And should I have any questions or problems, the foreign bureau was always at my service.

Of course I had a question. Was there a shop somewhere where I could buy something to eat? (I had had nothing to eat since the noodle soup in the train the night before.) Xiao D. was willing to show me immediately to the dining hall, but Mrs. Z. insisted that I should first meet the American couple living downstairs. By this time I was willing to go along with anything, as long as I got out of the company of Mrs. Z. and got something to eat. The introduction was brief. Mrs. Z. then left us, and after a five-minute walk Xiao D. and I arrived at a single-story building with two swinging doors and huge windows.

The dining room resembled a railway station hall. On the right, partitioned off with three movable folding screens, was our eating nook, just next to the main entrance. There were two round tables, each covered with a somewhat grubby tablecloth and with four chairs. The table decoration consisted of two glass vases with tall plastic flowers, chrysanthemums, carnations, and other products of sheer fantasy. Salt and pepper shakers, toothpick holders, and a box containing paper napkins completed the table utensils. Our dining area of some twenty square metres was illuminated by three huge windows, each some three to four metres high. Over each of them, hanging from crude iron rods, hung pale blue cotton sheets that moved gently in the draught. During my entire stay I never once saw these curtains opened.

The cook, who had been instructed previously to serve the new expert from Germany breakfast at the late hour of nine o'clock, had a cup of cocoa waiting for me, plus two fried eggs swimming in oil and two cakes resembling rocks. The eggs were cold, the cocoa so sweet as to be undrinkable, and as for the cakes, I did not even try them. I caused Xiao D. a great deal of embarrassment next, when I carefully asked for some bread. Bread? No, such a thing did not exist here. Well, I suggested then, if they did not have Western-style bread, I would be quite happy with a *mantou*, a steamed yeast bun. Sorry, the *mantous* would not be ready until noontime, but why not eat my eggs with the cakes? This was awkward, as I had assumed that bread would be just as readily available here as everywhere in Beijing. Jam and butter were also out of reach, as Xiao D. told me jokingly. Well, not to worry! I had something in my stomach, and after Xiao D. had explained the mealtimes to me, lunch at 11:30, dinner 5:30, and breakfast 7:00, we parted and I returned to my domicile.

Having arrived back within my four walls I looked about me. Quite lost I went from room to room and just did not know what to do next. I was quite alone, without even one familiar human being anywhere near, everything new and unaccustomed, strange. I felt cold; the apartment was cold and very sparsely furnished, bare concrete everywhere, dust everywhere, toilet, basin, and doors filthy. I was overcome by howling misery and wanted to leave again straightaway. There were still two whole hours until lunch, when I would see another face or have someone to talk to. Somehow, if I was not to dissolve into tears, I had to occupy that time. And whilst cleaning never has been my favourite activity, here it fulfilled its purpose and became occupational therapy. In the storeroom I found some old worn jeans and shirts, evidently left behind by my predecessors, together with large heaps of cartons, copied papers intended for exercises in grammar, newspapers, scraps of cloth, and so forth. For the purpose of cleaning, these things were just what I needed. Months later these very items led to a most unpleasant argument with Mrs. Z., who wanted to know what had happened to some of the rags. But for the moment I just helped myself and immersed myself in work. My first task was to tackle the evil-smelling refrigerator. Before long I had warmed up from the physical activity, and in no time at all it was time for lunch. On my way down the American couple joined me.

The first time, a few hours ago for my nine o'clock breakfast, I had only noticed the sheer size of the hall, but now I discovered that the main part of it began just beyond our partitions. There were countless round tables, each with eight to ten folding chairs. At the end of the hall a row of serving windows divided this large area into two parts. Situated behind the glass wall lay the gigantic kitchen, partitioned into a number of working areas. On the left of the hall, past the collection of chairs and tables, a sort of a corridor had been left to give access to the clientele. During mealtimes it was possible to buy various foods from the serving windows, such as *mantous*, roasted peanuts, smoked chicken meat or feet, sausage, and sometimes fresh liver. If the kitchen staff had been able to do its buying at special favourable prices, one of the many cooks would sit in the free corridor with his offerings of fish or pork and wait for customers. I often had the feeling during our meal hour that I was sitting in a transit station. There was a constant coming and going, a constant hum of voices offering this or wanting that, and occasional peeps into our "foreign section" from some nosy pokies.

In time I got used to keeping my overcoat and cap on at

mealtime. It was bitterly cold; there were draughts from every-where, and the swinging doors did the rest. Once we were seated, a young girl served the food. Every one of us was served two dishes with rice, and to drink there was cold boiled water in a teapot. The glasses always had to be cleaned with a paper serviette before usage. They usually were greasy, and this had been a constant cause of complaint to the serving girl. But it seemed this did not bother her at all. As I learned later, wash-ing up was done only with cold water, with cleaning sand being used to remove grease. Tea towels were unknown, and freshly washed crockery was placed back in the racks still wet and left to dry in a stack.

My first lunch consisted of mashed potatoes, very tasty, two large meatballs in a sweetish tomato sauce, and at the end of the meal a watery pepper-flavoured soup with a few pieces of car-rots and potato cubes floating in it.

The surroundings did not encourage me to linger. We ate quickly in order to escape the cold. In the summer we also hur-ried, so that we could get back to our rooms, which were "cooler" by means of ventilators. Mealtime was evidently not intended to be an occasion for a pleasant social chat, but rather as a means of taking nourishment as quickly as possible so as to have as much left as possible of the afternoon break and leave time for a nap of nearly two hours.

If one of us arrived at the table a little late, the serving staff became quite unpleasant (it shortened their midday nap); if one did not leave the table immediately after swallowing the last bite, preferably still chewing, one was again likely to incur looks of censure. In general, our waitress was rather a friendly girl with a sense of humor. A little joke, a suitable quip or two, and a friendly grin, and she would be all smiles again.

I found time and again in China that apparently a bad mood or unpleasant situation could be turned around again quite easily with a little humor or showing human understanding. The Chinese have a ready ear for spontaneous humor or repartee, and many a time a heated argument or verbal duel was directed back into calmer waters in this way. I always enjoyed being able to listen in as an observer.

Already on this first day I hurried with my meal, because I had been invited by the American couple living below me to a cup of hot tea, and I noticed they were finishing their meal rather fast. During the next hours I learned much about the facts of daily life in Y., enough to confuse me even further. First of all, I was warned about Mrs. Z. I was told that she was a dictatorial, quarrelsome woman who barely tolerated arguments or opposition. She could be friendly to your face; she was then nasty and treacherous behind your back. The best thing, I was told, was not to even go to the foreign bureau without good reason. At the enumeration of so many negative qualities I started to feel quite trapped. The couple surely did not leave even a small good trait to her. Mail also ran through this so important department, and an English-language newspaper, *China Daily* (usually a few days old), was made available by them, too, for foreign teachers. Further information concerned the Japanese teacher, who was on home leave still and not expected back before March. He was a very nice elderly gentleman but, unfortunately, only spoke Japanese and Chinese. Regarding the teaching activities themselves, I was told, it was supposed to be very enjoyable and satisfying, but there was virtually nothing available in the way of teaching materials. My German predecessors had had to improvise a great deal and do their teaching as best they could under the circumstances.

So, there were no books! Fortunately I had brought a complete teaching syllabus with me, intended for my own use and as a basis for my teaching. Well, I thought to myself, this could turn out to be quite interesting, and what a challenge! But at this stage I had no idea as to how many students I was expected to teach. I had written many letters concerning number of students and availability of teaching materials, but until this day I never even received a single reply to this. (It was to come just a few days before the school term began.)

Now sitting in the living room, I was informed that there were still almost four weeks to the beginning of the semester, with the New Year/Spring Festival first, so that there was no way I could make enquiries or prepare myself in any way. The libraries were closed, the language department only managed by a skeleton staff. Those responsible were fully occupied with preparations for the festive days.

Why couldn't I have stayed in Beijing then and enjoyed this big feast with my friends? Well, the orders of leader Mrs. Z. had to be obeyed, and it seemed quite boring days were coming ahead.

In China there is no occasion celebrated so grandly, so joyously, so noisily, or with such all-embracing enthusiasm as the New Year Festival. At that time the shops are almost bursting with offered merchandise and markets are flooded with meat and fish, sweets, and fruits. Old debts must be settled and new clothes bought, preferably bright red for the young ones. But as for how my future students would fare as far as books were concerned, I was told not to worry: "It will be all right; we'll talk about it after the festival." Such and similar were the replies I received to my enquiry: "First settle in." Well, I would certainly try my best to do so. Nevertheless, my head was spinning after all the information I had received. I was starting to feel a little disheartened, with a fear that I might not be equal to the tasks ahead of me. But this attitude was not encouraging, and I certainly had no intention of simply packing up and going home, and so I just surrendered myself to circumstances and took the risk, jumping into cold water, so to speak.

After leaving the American couple, I went back to my flat and continued with my cleaning. A few hours later, surrounded by now-dirty rags, I had managed to get the toilet, washbasin, and shelves in the cupboard reasonably clean. My bedroom was about fifteen square meters in size, with a three-meter-high ceiling, with a medium-sized window to the north and a window door leading to a balcony in the south, which, unfortunately, was locked. Simple crude iron bars were fitted above the windows, and hanging from them by means of plain iron rings were two baby blue sheets of cotton, which served as curtains. The department for furnishing interiors must have got a good bargain on blue cloth. The curtains in the dining hall, the curtains and the coverings of the couch arrangement, and not only in my flat but everything seemed to be decorated with this colour cloth.

There was also a bamboo pole, almost two metres long and as thick as a thumb, which served as a means to open or close the drapes, because trying to open or close them by simply pulling would have meant not only tearing them on the iron rings, but probably also tearing the whole apparatus out of the wall. Every room had such a bamboo rod, for which I also found other uses. For example, on rainy days such a pole laid across the hooks of two clothes racks served as a clothesline. In China there is no common object that does not have more than one use and it does not take long to become resourceful and practical. Appearances do not matter much.

My room contained a big blue iron bed, a desk with several drawers and shelves, and a kind of sideboard with glass-fronted movable panels. The glass panes had simple cut edges, not smoothed or polished. There were also two armchairs concealed under baby blue covers and a clothes rack. The plain concrete walls appeared as if they might have been whitewashed at some stage, and a neon tube hanging from the ceiling provided illumination in this otherwise drab, dull room. A worn, reddish-looking wall-to-wall carpet covered the stone floor, and various pipes for the heating system ran along the walls and the edges of the ceiling. The radiator itself was under a stone sill beneath the northern window, painted brown. There were ends of pipework sticking out of it, and the whole object looked like a squashed accordion. Somewhere, about halfway up the wall, I even managed to find an air vent for ventilation. The radiator and associated pipework had also seen better days, judging from the peeling, dirty silver grey paintwork on them. The other two rooms were no more appealing, and the less said about the kitchen and bathroom the better.

In any case, there was no warm water to be had from the simple taps. The shower was an electrotechnical monstrosity, which for the time being I only looked at from a distance. Xiao D. had explained the way it worked earlier that morning, but I had little confidence in the contraption. On the wall above the bathtub there hung suspended a rectangular plastic box measuring twenty-four by thirty-three by seven centimetres. Sticking out of the top was a thirty-centimeter-long movable shower head, also made of plastic. Supply of water to this device was by means of a plastic hose connected to one of the taps via an additional small tap. Next to the plastic water container, which was about two and a half metres above the floor on the wall, there was a power point, a number of strange-looking power boosters, a switch, thick cables, and a multiple adapter. Nothing was insulated or earthed, despite being situated in the very close proximity of water. Xiao D. demonstrated: first open the small tap; then set the switch on the plastic box to the desired position of the three available heating levels. While this was being done there must be a bang; otherwise the shower was broken. Voilà, warm water! But no warm water came out; instead the apparatus gave off a shower of sparks, and the demonstration came to a sudden end. It was not only I who received a fright. Xiao D., also a shade paler, suggested, "The shower must be out of order. Your predecessor did not report this to the foreign bureau; otherwise we would have had it fixed straightaway."

Now he would see to it that the matter was attended to immediately. In fact, it took several months with lots of vain pushing and visits to the bureau, and at the end the shower still malfunctioned. Be that as it may.

Tacked to the back of one of the doors there was an English "house rules for foreigners." These rules were divided into several sections, some of which read as follows:

- Rooms for foreign experts, teachers, and guests have been furnished in a uniform style by the Bureau of Foreign Affairs. It is forbidden for guests to change the rooms themselves. [This probably referred to rearrangement of furniture, because any rooms not allocated were locked in any case.]
- Please behave quietly in the apartments, and do not disturb while working or resting. Please be careful with the furnishings. Do not waste water or electricity. Please notify the Bureau immediately should there be faults with items such as heaters or electrical appliances. Since there is only limited electricity available, no high performance implements should be used. In special cases the Bureau will give special permission.
- No overnight guests are permitted without authorisation from the Foreign Bureau.
- If you wish to invite guests, you must inform the Bureau well in advance.
- Bed linen and towels are provided by the Foreign Bureau. They will be changed regularly and washed without charge. [In fact, it never happened once.]
- Should you require a car for business purposes, please contact the Bureau. For private journeys, as long as a car is available, half the regular fare will be charged.

So these were the rules and regulations, which I had heard from Mrs. Z. early in the morning but forgotten.

Around four o'clock my two domestic helpers appeared, an older woman and a young girl of peasant appearance. They brought hot water with them in a zinc sprinkling can to refill the five thermos flasks. In total astonishment they asked what I had done with all the hot water. The two women just could not understand that I had used precious hot water for cleaning. Such waste! I found this quite embarrassing, not having been able to cast aside my Western habits as yet. Boiled water was intended for drinking, maybe for washing oneself, but cleaning? In any case, the older woman said, they had "thoroughly cleaned" my apartment before my arrival and had also washed the towels and changed the bed linen. I had the feeling that she was slightly offended, but once I explained that I had found it necessary to kill time and keep warm, her face lit up again, her smile returned, and totally satisfied, they both departed with a *"Mingtian jian"* (see you tomorrow). I was already learning. Many things I took for granted. Many small pleasures and comforts would have to be replaced by different types of conduct if I was to find the local lifestyle and everyday existence, so primitive and frugal by our standards, a little more bearable. The future would bring the answers and show me the way.

Gradually my first day became night. There I sat, in my glaringly lit but otherwise cold and bare apartment, feeling a yawning emptiness about me. I was overcome by a feeling of having been deserted; that familiar emotion of childhood days crept up. There was no one with whom I could discuss my many and new impressions. I was completely left to my own devices, and I had to ask myself whether I would be able to handle these conditions, which I knew would be repeated many times in the coming months. I had got through childhood and, somewhat "steeled," would certainly be up to this, too. What did it matter if there was no hot water or if you did not have a warm, cosy room? How often were you cold as a child because there was not enough money to buy coal? Put on more clothes; it is much healthier and helps to make you tougher. *Make this year, the Year of the Buffalo, a successful one for your own self*, ordered myself. Such were my somewhat last thoughts on this sixteenth day of February 1985 before I switched off my little bedside lamp. At some stage my thoughts slipped away and I must have fallen asleep. I awoke the next morning feeling fully rested and wonderfully refreshed, a feeling I had not known for quite some time.

Settling In and Getting to Know
My Way Around

The next few days passed at an even pace, without any special demands on me. As the winter holidays did not end until March, I did not have to start teaching just yet.

Two days after my arrival, it was Sunday, 17 February. We received cinema tickets from the foreign bureau for the theatre owned by the institute. They did not cost us anything. I was to learn later that the foreign bureau would, from time to time, hand out tickets to its foreign teachers to enable them to see films that, in the view of the bureau, would be of special interest or were particularly good. And so this film, too, was intended as a feast for the eyes, because the subject was fashion, with a show of beautiful clothes. There was no way the tenor and lesson of the film could be missed. At the time of the Cultural Revolution and the "Gang of Four" such things as fashion and cosmetics were considered bourgeois and reprehensible. But now it would be different. Ideas would now be listened to and even developed, and not everybody who was interested in fashion or beauty was decadent, antigovernment, or against the party. The film was designed to encourage young people to seek to better themselves—for example, to become a fashion designer rather than a mere tailor. The crowning reward for hard work, industriousness, and endurance, overcoming all obstacles, was acceptance to the school of fashion and thus entry to the elegant world, such as fashion shows in hotels reserved for foreigners. And at the end of the film came a real feast for the eyes in the form of a half-hour presentation of the most magical designs, starting with suits, pants, blouses, and dresses of silk, velvet, and brocade up to and including flowing evening gowns, furs, and at the end a symphony in white and gold bridal gowns. It was intoxicating, with the graceful young models and their delicate rounding-off effect. I did gain the impression that the fashion show was intended mainly for foreign fashion buyers, tempting them to buy Chinese designs or to have them made in Chinese silks. The audience, consisting of young and old, simple peasants and more educated people, seemed to find the film quite amusing, but I had the feeling that the majority of them saw the pictures more as an exotic fantasy rather than something real for them. An old, almost toothless woman next to me, bundled up in padded pants and jacket, with her formerly bound feet in padded cloth shoes, whispered to her companion, "How can anyone work in such clothes? Anyway, they look untidy and poor." She was referring to the "beggar look" of Western fashion, seen at the time as the dernier cri of elegance, which had also found its niche in the Chinese film.

After two hours the film came to an end, and everyone returned to their normal everyday life, mainly concerned with the many preparations for the Spring Festival, which was to take place on the nineteenth of February. This coming event fully occupied both young and old. The campus was alive with merchants and itinerant pedlars. Everywhere one looked, various merchandise was on offer, spread out on the ground. In order to do business within the campus it was necessary for each merchant or pedlar to obtain a permit from the institute's department for internal affairs. On some days large loads of frozen fish were on sale from the trucks that had brought them in, which caused a tremendous crowding and a great deal of noisy haggling. Quite apart from the familiar smell of fish, remnants of fish would be left lying on the ground in the sales area for days afterwards. The reader must not imagine for a moment that the fish on offer was all hygienically wrapped and attractively presented. By no means! Instead the various fish lay there, not cleaned, frozen together in clumps. The fish came from a port nearby.

On other days the merchants might unload countless baskets of apples and oranges from their trucks. Everything was sold by kilo weight. The buyers, both men and women, would crowd around the seller with the scales, children would run around among the crowd, and adolescents would be there as spectators. Huge quantities were bought, and it was not unusual for one individual to buy ten, twenty, or even more kilograms. At that time a kilogram of apples cost around sixty-five fen, with oranges costing about 1 yuan.

Just before New Year's Eve the chicken seller arrived with his truck. His wares, deep-frozen plucked chickens, uncleaned but still with feathers on their heads and feet, found a ready and eager market. To me the chickens, which had black feet and a bluish skin and were probably some special breed, did not look very appetising, particularly as the sales counter was, as always, the bare ground.

Pork was sold in just the same way. Rather than having been previously segregated into the various cuts and individually wrapped, as we know it, the meat was simply hacked from the carcass, fatty or lean meat; if one was willing to pay a little more one got the better cuts. Most of the meat was only fatty.

Whether the food was covered in dust or other contamination did not seem to matter. In China it is customary to thoroughly wash everything and then cook it thoroughly. Fruits are eaten raw, meat and fish never eaten raw.

I sometimes wondered, as I looked at the way in which food was sold, that I was still able to thoroughly enjoy with a hearty appetite the various tasty dishes on offer in the dining hall. All of my hosts were excellent cooks, and never once did I eat anything that did not agree with me.

It was very busy on the grounds of the institute, and it was while out shopping that people would get together for a little chat or gossip. It was the same in the institute-owned general store, where, among other items, veritable mountains of sweets, including lollies, were sold. A chat enlivened the waiting. Shoppers would lug home many kilos of purchases, wrapped in coarse, brittle brown paper and carried in nylon string bags. Someone, an expert in the starch industry, once told me that developing countries, once they achieved a certain level of prosperity, tended to place their first emphasis on their sugar industry, and what I saw here seemed to prove the point. Apart from lollies there were hundreds of kilos of various biscuits, with or without icing, arrayed in large wooden boxes behind the counters. Also displayed under the glass-topped counters were many kinds of candied or preserved fruits, as well as sesame or peanut bars in various sizes, made with honey or molasses. The preserved fruits included mandarin oranges, pears, pineapples, peaches, apricots, lychees, and cherries. There was plenty of everything, and the salesgirls were kept very busy.

Even we foreigners, few of us as there were, were included in the festive whirl. It was not possible to spend the festival alone, even had one wanted to do so. One at a time the language teachers of the older generation were encouraged to invite us and play host to us. We were to take part in this happy event and enjoy ourselves just like the Chinese.

On the Monday after the film, the vice president of the institute gave a New Year dinner, which also doubled as an occasion to welcome me. The president himself, as mentioned in the chapter "Eventful Days in Beijing," happened to be absent. I was not yet able to fully understand the hierarchy of all the various people present, all of whom I was told held important positions. Here was a vice president, there another, this one was a senior or lower party secretary, and so on.

It was quite confusing until I was able to obtain some information from one of my students later as to what the story was with all these vice presidents. There were one president and two vice presidents for each of the major faculties, such as education, research, and teaching, and a vice president for housing and board, and in addition a director of administration heading up the whole. A large number of subgroups with equally competent leaders completed the internal bureaucracy of this institute. It was run like a small community. If on occasion I did succeed in remembering some of the names and the important positions they held, I often found that this one or that one had been replaced by yet another, usually as part of an exchange, so that in the end I was no wiser than I was at the beginning. So I gave up keeping the names in mind.

But let's get back to my first days and weeks on the large campus. After the welcome feast, another New Year reception was organised for us foreign teachers by the foreign bureau of the city of Y., which took place within the campus. The deputy mayor and the head of the foreign bureau, as well as many department heads of the city administration, used this as an opportunity to meet us. We had to make our appearance as one group at nine o'clock in the morning. Small talk was encouraged, courteous and friendly, but meaningless speeches were made; and we were offered sweets, dried fruits wrapped in edible cellophane, tea, and peeled apples. I was freezing cold in the unheated rooms, and only the hot tea helped a little to keep me warm. One was expected to sit nailed to one's chair and only answer politely when spoken to. The conversation dragged on very slowly, mainly because every sentence had to be translated for those who did not speak Chinese, and similarly the answers from foreigners had to be translated back into Chinese. After about two hours the deputy mayor announced, "So, that is enough; the reception is over." We all stood up abruptly, shook hands all round, gave thanks for the kind invitation, and wished everyone a "Prosperous New Year," *gong xi fa cai.* Everyone went back to their daily tasks, as the ceremonial obligation had been met and courtesy satisfied. During the rest of my stay I was to take part in many more such receptions, all with similar speeches about friendship between nations and major development programmes, together with minor speeches on various topics.

According to our Western wording, it was New Year's Eve. All day and even before that we had been listening to the rattle of fireworks and the hissing of many rockets. The climax of the celebrations, however, came at midnight, which triggered an earsplitting cacophony of noise and exploding fireworks from every window and balcony and from the streets as well. The sky was illuminated with a sea of colour and light, and loud whistling and hissing accompanied the giant rockets as they sped upwards. It was really a tremendous spectacle, and I found myself infected by the joy and spontaneity all around me, so that I joined with enthusiasm in all the clapping and cheering.

Together with the American couple living below me I had been invited to dinner by the head of the foreign bureau. We had been asked to arrive earlier than usual, as we would be able to take part in *jiaozi* making and thus celebrate New Year's Eve in convivial company. The leader, Mrs. Z., and her husband really did us proud. The husband, who worked in Sichuan, some three days' travel away, had been given some days off for the festival. As for Mrs. Z., she appeared just as hectic and frantic in her home as she did at work. Her daughter, some twenty years old, made no attempt to cover for her mother's nervousness and impatient conduct in front of the guests. As for the father, he said very little. He was a leader of a school for cadres and a loyal party member. While we were eating, around 9:00 P.M., Mrs. Z. told us that there would be a very good show on television at ten o'clock, which we should not miss. But we had time to finish our meal in plenty of time, and then we could watch the show in our own homes. Half an hour later we were all back home. That was the one and only invitation I received to her home, and I had done my courtesy duty. Actually, I preferred the invitations to visit much nicer people, but they advised me I'd better go to the "leader's."

Back in my room I switched on the TV, and indeed, there really was a colourful programme. There were dance sequences, in which a group of young girls in fairytale dresses flowed to and fro in a round dance like grass in the wind to a mixture of modern tunes interspersed with old Chinese melodies. Much of it sounded rather soothing to my ears. Then there were large scenes of singing men and women in uniform, evidently belonging to a military or paramilitary work unit. There were also female soloists in Western dresses of tulle, organza, or nylon, fashionably made up with flowers in their hair and rather too much facial makeup. A large revue staircase played a major role, even though it was not as elaborate or as elegant as those of well-known American musical shows of the 1940s. Much of the show reminded me of Hollywood in the day of the "glamourous touch." A lot seemed naive and smacked of Hong Kong show business. Small amusing sketches and a witty two-person dialogue served to entertain the audience spending New Year's Eve in the studio. The audience attend shows like this dressed the same as any other time. Some of the women wore padded jackets made of colourful cotton or woolen jackets with long pants. The men, mostly wearing warm caps, sat there in similarly padded blue jackets and applauded wildly. Here and there, particularly among the younger generation, one might see a suit of Western cut, with a tie in the most garish colours. If the trouser-legs happened to be a little short one might catch a glimpse of the wearer's long johns, also brightly coloured lilac, green, or wine red. I even spotted the long knit undies on one of the female singers as she walked elegantly, singing, down the staircase in a long evening dress with long side slits. Even though the legs of these pants had been pulled up somewhat, the dark brown underclothing did not go at all with the white and pink silk and brocade of the dress. But this did not distract in the least from the festive mood. The first duty of everyone is to make sure not to catch a cold, and I imagine that the studio, like everywhere else, was poorly heated, although it might have been a little warmer on the stage from the lighting. The programme was transmitted until well after midnight, but I was too tired to watch all of it. The Year of the Buffalo had begun well, and I hoped that it would be a good year for me also.

Shortly after the New Year—it had been snowing and the landscape looked enchanting—I decided to undertake an exploration of the campus. I made my way past the eight red brick houses to the main street of the campus, Road Number 1. Descending from our hill, I saw on my right the many uniform grey boxes of five storys where the teaching and other staff belonging to the education and research departments lived. The house numbers were painted on the exterior walls in large numerals. Opposite, situated a little higher, lay the hospital, a three-story *L*-shaped building, which I was told could also undertake small operations such as a normal appendectomy. At the intersection where the letterbox was situated, I turned right and walked along the very long Road Number 1 towards the southern gate. Looking past the above-mentioned grey houses I spotted many wooded patches of ground, the trees now without leaves at this time of the year, but covered with snow. There was a system of clean paths leading in all directions, made of flat stones.

The many balconies attracted my attention, and I did not see one empty. On most of them all the kitchen supplies were stored, together with associated utensils. Boxes, chests, and earthenware pots were stacked everywhere. I soon discovered that every apartment had at least two balconies. One of them was always used for cooking, summer and winter, because kitchens as we know them were nonexistent. Cooking was done on a bucketlike stove, without a chimney, with a hole at the top for adding fuel and another at the bottom to remove the ashes. Small balls made of coal and clay dust were used for fuel, and in order that no one suffocate from the combustion gases all cooking was done outside, in the fresh air on the balcony, so each flat was provided with one. These "bucket stoves," lined with fire-clay inside, were used for the preparation of the most delicious meals, and this has been true for many generations, at least in the so-called normal households. Cooking for a group of invited guests is a slow, laborious business, which is why the housewife rarely joins her guests at the table, as the various dishes have to be cooked and brought to the table one at a time. Devices for keeping food warm, such as hot plates or ovens, are not commonly known.

The sky was overcast, and the snow remained on the ground, as it was several degrees below freezing. And so I strolled down the Number 1 towards the south gate. The footpath beside the car road was lined with poplarlike trees at short intervals, whereas the meridian strip had been planted with shrubs or trees, which were devoid of leaves at this time, snow covering the bare branches. The road had two traffic lanes on each side of the meridian strip, but was rarely used by cars, unless there happened to be a market of travelling merchants driving by in their trucks, as it was prior to New Year.

I stopped at a round garden bed just before the south gate and looked back along the Number 1 to the north, where at the very end stood the ten-story yellow edifice I had already noticed on my arrival. I walked out by the south gate, viewed with curiosity by the two gate watchers, but they did not say anything. Immediately outside the campus I discovered the free market. A bitumen road, not very wide, ran past the institute campus in an east–west direction. A few peasants were squatting on the ground in front of their spread-out wares waiting for customers in the cold. Sitting there, rigged up in their padded blue jackets and bulging padded pants, with fur-lined caps and lowered earflaps on their heads, they seemed to me to be a cheerful lot. The range of food-stuffs on offer at this time of year was meagre. There were carrots, cabbages, cabbages, and more cabbages, peanuts, wrinkled apples, and large whitish-looking fungi. Much of the merchandise was in large baskets covered against the cold with a thick padded rug. I bought ten eggs from a peasant woman for 1.30 yuan, and in no time the fact that I spoke Chinese attracted a swarm of onlookers. There were amused and slightly mischievous faces all around me, but they were all friendly and of course very inquisitive about my Chinese.

Finally I took my way back to the south gate and went on Number 1 straight to the yellow edifice. I was to learn later that it was the teaching building and generally referred to as the "main building." Strolling along, I passed five rows of the same grey houses to my right as on my way out. A small road to the right led to the campus kindergarten, school, and other administrative buildings. Farther along, up a few steps, was the hairdresser and the bank. Diagonally behind was an open paved square, with a large general store and the dining hall I described previously.

On reaching the crossroad again with the mailbox and way leading up to "our hill," I turned right. On the left I saw four living "silos" for young members of the faculty and young teacher couples, with or without child. Their dining hall lay opposite, together with a shop where one could buy beer, lemonade, sausage or salted vegetables, plus a small room where food tickets were on sale.

Farther ahead lay a large building site, where the new guest house for ninety-nine visitors (traditional lucky number) and experts was to be completed in September for the big international symposium on mining and technology. The old one, situated in front of it, was no longer adequate and was intended for students coming from Tanzania, who were to commence their education in the winter semester. The new building was to be a structure of superlatives. Each room was to have a bathroom, TV, telephone, and wall-to-wall carpet with particularly well made furniture and the most modern aluminum windows (dust- and noise-proof), as well as modern faucet fittings. I was told proudly that all the technical innovations had been imported from Hong Kong. I was quite curious how things would look at the end. For the time being only the foundations could be seen, with the men busily at work even though the New Year had only just taken place. I was told that the budget for the new building was estimated at over 1 million yuan.

From here I went back to the crossroad and along the Number 1 towards the north. On both sides of the Number 1 the buildings were raised, and if I wanted to take a look at the higher areas I had to climb a series of steps. The way there took me in a zigzag manner through the living quarters for single teachers of both sexes, as well as students who were awaiting their final examinations shortly. Down along a winding path, there was the sporting area with cinder track, football field, and on the right the outdoor swimming pools of Olympic dimensions. The road alongside the sports fields led back to Number 1, so that I found myself back in the centre of the campus once more. The yellow main building lay before me and in front of it quite a large fountain installation. The pools at this time of year were empty. A statue of a stone girl absorbed in playing a violin served to decorate this parklike area. Wherever I looked I saw bare, ochre-coloured earth. Nowhere was there even a little evergreen or even a blade of dried grass. Ochre, brown, and grey, these were the dominant colours.

I decided to continue along Number 1 and passed the theatre I had visited, a little farther on the scientific museum for paleontology, then a computer centre and next to it an audiovisual centre, also the buildings for physics classes, laboratories, and other teaching buildings. The broad road narrowed slightly, and turning to the right I found myself in front of many accommodation blocks for the five thousand or so students, a large dining hall, and the bathhouse for students. I went on in the direction of the north gate, which was called the main gate and which I had passed on my day of arrival, and came across a huge open square with now-empty flower beds. This gate was flanked on either side by small houses, the gatekeepers on the left and the letter distribution centre for the entire campus on the right. (The function of the latter I was to learn about only later.) Opposite the main gate was that huge yellow edifice, the main building, with a staircase of some ten metres' width leading up to it. The ground floor, situated under the staircase, was always kept locked. A side entrance led to the elevators, which was only to be used by the professors and foreign teachers. During my entire stay I only used it once, and then only out of curiosity. Heading away from the main gate, I walked around the yellow edifice and came out at the fountain display again. And then I saw another huge building (everything appears to be of gigantic dimensions in China), which turned out to be the pride of the institute, its library of some six hundred thousand volumes awaiting readers and researchers. The total floor area of the four-story building was 11,000 square metres, and again access to this was by way of wide stone steps. At first I felt very small every time I stood in front of one of these huge stairways as described above. It was quite easy to feel somewhat lost among all these large buildings and huge squares. Later on I became acclimatised quite well, and the many stairs I had to manage every day did not cause me any difficulty after I had been there a few weeks. For the fun of it I counted them one day, and on some days I had to negotiate the 140 steps to the lecture room three times. With so many steps I soon got into practice, no more shortage of breath and heart jumping. It is worth noting that none of the many wide rows of steps had any handrail or other means of support.

Having thus passed the two largest buildings on the campus, I next directed my steps down a smaller side street, and this led me to the western gate, with the imposing administration building on my left where the foreign bureau was located, together with the offices of the president, the first party secretary, and a number of other high functionaries. A narrow terraced lane on the left of the building led uphill to the winding bitumen road where our apartments were. Halfway there I came across a walkway covered with a kind of framework supporting various branches and plants, which led in a straight line directly to the top of the hill. This was where the water reservoir was located, a small, rusty affair I would never have believed could possibly be working, if I had not been earnestly assured that it was fully functional.

From the top of the hill I had a magnificent view over the entire campus and found that there were still much I had not yet seen. There was also an open-air cinema, several factories belonging to the institute, and various sporting areas for basketball and volleyball. The tall chimney that towered over the campus was part of the furnaces that supplied heat to the campus heating system. It was coal-fired, and thick clouds of unfiltered smoke were constantly rising into the sky. When a number of German coal experts happened to be visiting the institute a little later and one of them asked whether there were any means of filtering the black smoke, the answer from a senior institute spokesman was: "When the cat's away [referring to the president] sloppy habits come to the fore. I will see to it that the filtering system is switched on again." But the smoke remained black. Did the campus have a filtering system ?

So there I stood on top of the hill and looked around me. From here I could not even see the broad outlines of the city Y., which was situated some seven kilometres to the north, with a number of small hills obscuring the view.

I learnt later that the city had been compelled by government edict to sell the site of some ninety hectares to the institute. Twenty years ago there had been nothing but hilly countryside to the south of the city. These hills, some large and some small, had been partially levelled, which explained the somewhat uneven topography of the campus itself. The institute and associated campus buildings had been built by soldiers of the PLA over a period of five to six years. It was completed in 1978 and now numbered some ten thousand inhabitants. As a consequence of the government edict there was still some animosity between the institute and the city government.

I had explored my physical surroundings. My next step would be to become part of everyday life in this community and share the joys, sorrows, and thoughts of my new fellow citizens, a task I was not to find too difficult.

After the outing around the campus, I decided one day to get to know the city as well. So I borrowed a man's bicycle and set off. It was a very cold day; the wind was blowing sharply into my face. The snow had gone, the sun was shining, and dust was whirling through the streets. I could feel myself chewing sand again, and my eyes were watering despite the fact that I wore glasses. I planned to do a little shopping in the city, as I needed a pair of pliers in order to repair my electric heater myself, having been waiting in vain for days for the tradesman to arrive. I soon found myself becoming not only an electrician and a plumber to fix my toilet, but I was becoming quite proficient in the art of survival.

I had to become resourceful as well. Apart from the pliers I wanted to buy some drinking glasses, unlined writing paper, and airmail envelopes. If there was some good-quality fruit to be had, I also intended to buy some apples and oranges. So, one day I set out shortly after 2:00 P.M. and some forty minutes later I arrived in the main business district.

There was a mass of people everywhere, and not only pedestrians. I had to be extremely careful not to be run over by other cyclists. By comparison to Beijing there were very few cars in Y., and there were no bikeways; also, the streets were much narrower.

One particular cyclist attracted my attention. A male rider was astride a bicycle much too low for him, dressed in a flowing black overcoat of Western cut with long tails flying in the wind. A multicoloured scarf was fluttering behind him; an artist's hat sat on his head, white gloves and long trousers with the usual knit underpants showing at the bottom, this time in beige. His feet, clad in burgundy high heeled men's shoes, were calmly working the pedals. I just had to catch a glimpse of his face and rode past him. A cheeky lock of hair poked out from under the hat over his forehead, and his eyes were covered by large dark glasses. It was quite a sight to see this young man, absorbed in himself and obviously keen to create an impression with his appearance, calmly pedalling away along the crowded road.

The first large store I came to looked inviting. I left my bicycle locked on the sidewalk and was about to walk off when I felt a tugging on my sleeve. It was an old woman, although I thought at first sight she was a man, with a long cigarette holder dangling on the edge of her mouth, the green winter cap with lowered earflaps, and the usual padded clothing. Anyway, this person tugged my sleeve and informed me that this was a watched security parking area for bicycles. She had already handed me a slip of paper for which I had to pay two fen, which was a very cheap price for her to watch my bike. She went on tugging my sleeve, felt my leather coat, and asked whether it was genuine leather and fur and how much such a coat cost. I answered as truthfully as I could, but there was no way I could expect her to grasp the true price. She would have thought I was joking or making fun of her regarding foreign prices. Just before the end of this little conversation she suddenly asked whether I was a native Chinese or one returning from abroad.

Shaking her head, she went away satisfied, and I had the impression that many of the onlookers would return to their homes and families that evening enriched with interesting news and a topic for conversation.

Inside the store there was a constant coming and going. I asked for directions to the household goods department and was disappointed to find that neither pliers nor glasses were to be had. Everything was sold out, but perhaps in a few days there would be new stock. Indeed, I could see that the shelves had been plundered for the festival.

Things did not look much better in the other departments either. Evidently it was a bad time to go shopping.

Back to my bicycle, where the old woman bid me a very friendly farewell, and then I made my way to the next store. This time I was lucky. There were still two pairs of pliers available, but glasses of uniform shape were no longer to be had. There were a few odds and ends left, with no two alike, all with colourful motifs painted on them such as a fairytale landscape with the character for "long life" or red and blue spiral patterns. I bought four glasses, all different, and went looking for a stationery store. There was one in the main street, which I was told would have sheets of white unlined paper in larger quantities, but when I got there the shop was closed. I was told that it was not likely to reopen for some time on account of the New Year holiday. I next tried to buy some fruit from a street vendor, but what he had on offer was very poor. The apples all had bruises and looked shrunken and unappetising. But I managed to buy a few edible oranges and some bananas in a shop. Fruit here is smaller than that to which we are accustomed but make up for their lack of size with more flavour. With my purchases in a bag I cycled along the street looking for a photographic shop and discovered one on the way back to the campus.

As I entered, I suddenly suffered a violent coughing attack and felt I was choking. The people inside looked up, startled, and came to my aid. One immediately brought me a cup of hot water, and another asked what the trouble was. I rushed outside again, regained my breath, and calmed down. I then discovered that the warmth in the small room derived from a bucket stove and the gases of combustion left me with hardly any air to breathe. Our business was therefore concluded outside on the footpath. I remained outside, the shop assistant bought out the ticket I would need to pick up my photos, and as we parted she offered that next time, when I came to collect my photos, she would see that the stove was put away.

It was on that afternoon I discovered that the staff in small shops was always much more friendly and obliging than the salesgirls in large stores. It was not only that the staff was concerned about me on account of my coughing attack; it was simply that they tried harder to satisfy their customers. The salesgirls in the big department stores really did not care whether a client bought anything or not or whether he was satisfied with his purchase. Dealing with their own countrymen the salesgirls were even more unfriendly than they are to foreigners, and a Chinese customer, generally very choosy and particular, would become justly annoyed at the unsatisfactory and reluctant service, as I often did. The client is really at the mercy of the shop assistant; if the buyer is not satisfied with an item shown to him or if he wants to look at something else or make a comparison as to quality, then I often saw how the salesman/girl would simply not show him anything else but rudely send him on his way, sometimes with remarks such as "make up your mind what you want." Indeed, the personnel who, according to a party slogan, are supposed to "serve the people" were, generally speaking, bad-tempered, reluctant, and sometimes arrogant and cheeky. In this context I noticed that it was usually the younger members of the staff who were unsatisfactory, whereas the over-forties tended to be polite, helpful, and more reliable. The Cultural Revolution had left many unpleasant traces, especially noticeable in the service industries. A number of my older friends also complained about the unrestrained and rude behaviour of younger people even towards their parents' and grandparents' generation.

When I arrived back in my apartment the yawning emptiness of the many bare and cold rooms struck me as anything but cosy. They were just not getting warm at all, and even the radiators felt cold to the touch. After dinner I went down to the couple's flat to warm up a bit. They had additional heaters, one for the living room and one for the bathroom. Above all, they had bought a quantity of material for a curtain, which they had hung between the living room and the one adjoining to ward off the constant draught seeping through from everywhere. The windows were dripping wet, because an electric kettle full of water was slowly boiling away, in order to maintain a reasonable degree of humidity in the room—apparently it was terribly dry during the winter months.

I was waiting for my parcels sent away in December and which were still on their way by sea to Shanghai. I had packed a combination barometer, thermometer, as well a hygrometer, so that I would be able to set up a simple "weather station" for my own use, but at this stage I had no way of knowing whether the relative humidity was really as low as I was told. I know that Beijing could be terribly dry, somewhere around 40 percent, but in Y. I did not feel so dehydrated.

Be that as it may, I complained to them about my nonfunctioning heating system, my useless shower, the cold in my rooms, the fact that my rooms facing north were too dark, the absence of a cupboard, and the problem of where to put the additional things I was expecting to arrive shortly, particularly books. Also, what did the term *public rooms* mean? In response they offered to have a look at the heating system for me, because my predecessors had apparently also had their share of problems with the constantly cold rooms. But in their case, once the air had been drained from the pipes, the radiator core had once more had hot water flowing through it. No sooner said than done. The husband knew which valves had to be opened. I searched on my balcony among the many bottles left behind by the former teachers, in order to find a few with a larger opening, which I then held under the appropriate valve. It hissed, and oily pitch-black water came out. Gradually the bottles filled up with foul-smelling water, which I poured out over the edge of the balcony rather than risk pouring it into my toilet. But despite all our efforts the heater only became less than warm. Later I found out that the supply of heating was reduced during the night and that the boilers were not reactivated until 5:00 A.M. Well, sleeping in a cold room is certainly much healthier than sleeping in an overheated one. But as for washing in the cold and then climbing into a cold bed, that was another story entirely. Nevertheless, with a little determination and getting used to it, both circumstances did not harm me severely.

I need to explain why I poured the stinking water over the balcony into the open. At certain times, especially in the morning, I noticed there was a very unpleasant smell flowing through my apartment. In sniffing where it was most smelly, I landed in the bathroom. On my enquiring of the couple as to the cause, the husband told me that all drains emptied directly into the sewage system without the use of "goosenecks" to prevent odours from coming back up the pipe. If I aired the place thoroughly, I froze, and it always took quite a while before the rooms were sufficiently warm again so that I could sit at my desk without overcoat and cap. It is a dreadful thing to be so sensitive to cold as I am!

Despite all the efforts, the apartment remained uncomfortably cold. The couple were so kind as to offer me an invitation to stay in their place as often as I liked. These visits usually consisted of a great deal of "gossip," and I obtained quite some useful information. For example, the answer to my previous question: what was meant by the term *public rooms?* According to the regulations, each of us foreign teachers was entitled to the sole use of a bedroom, kitchen, and bathroom in one of the red brick buildings; this was our private domain. But the two adjoining living rooms could also used by others for discussions and other purposes (watching TV, for instance) if there was no other room available, and without any need to inform me first.

In fact, we regularly used these rooms for our evening conversation groups. The rooms were furnished with a lounge suite, a television set, a large rectangular table, and eight folding chairs. A blackboard on the wall gave one the feeling of being in a classroom. So this was the explanation of the "public rooms." During these conversations in the home of the couple it turned out that my predecessors had, in fact, lived in the locked rooms, which faced the south and were much brighter, and to a certain extent also warmer. It was suggested that I should talk to Mrs. Z. about changing rooms, also about the defunct shower. The former German teachers had additional heaters as well, so why not me?

I had already asked my cleaning woman, who came daily, to make enquiries on my behalf, but gradually got the impression that she made no effort at all, even though she promised to do so. Later I found out that she was terrified of Mrs. Z. When I told the woman that I would have to go and see Mrs. Z. myself, she heaved a sigh of relief and said, "Surely she will listen to you. I would not even have got as far as the office door." At the next opportunity I expressed my desires to some clerks of the foreign bureau to forward the message to Mrs. Z. Unfortunately, she was out of town on business for a few days. So I had to wait for several days, uncertain whether the message had been given and whether my proposed move would be approved. But one day my cleaning woman appeared beaming with joy, the keys in her hand. I was permitted to move, and she was to help me with the cleaning. What a day! We scrubbed and swept the carpet flooring as best we could, although at the end it did not look less dusty. But all together the room was larger and much brighter, and due to the presence of two big wicker chairs it had a friendlier feel to it. There was even a built-in cupboard in one corner and an electric heater standing around, unfortunately not working, but I had my pair of pliers! It did not take long before I had somehow rejoined the brittle ends of the broken coiled wire, and lo, it worked! It was by no means the only repair I had to perform on it, but I did not mind having to patch the wires from time to time, as they used to burn out at regular intervals.

By late afternoon I had taken possession of my new abode and felt very pleased with myself. The room was really warmer, and the view over the hill covered with thuja trees gave me a cheerful feeling. The sun was shining, with warmth in it, the sky was blue, and my cleaning woman and I reviewed the new arrangement of furniture with satisfaction. She had been really enthusiastic in her eagerness to help me. From now on I no longer had to trouble the couple downstairs with my problems of "freezing."

Unfortunately, the joy was not to last for long. Around nine o'clock that evening there was a knock on my door. Mrs. Z., the leader, stood there. Without saying, "Good evening," with Xiao D. in tow, she stormed into my new room, stormed out again, sat down on one of the armchairs in the "public room," and started to bawl me out:

How did I dare to just move rooms. What was I thinking when I engaged the cleaning woman to help me move? Why had I not informed her (the boss)? And in any case, I was not entitled to any room except the one allocated to me. Why had I not asked for a cupboard and a heater? Both would have been made available, but acting on my own initiative was against the rules. The cleaning woman had received no instructions to unlock the room, nor to help me!

And then I had to listen to accusations about my expensive train ticket from Beijing to Y.: that was not as per agreement, and so I would have to bear the additional cost myself!

For the time being I was just listening to her tirades, because in her anger there was just no reasoning with her, and I gave no comments or answers whatsoever. Gradually she got around to other complaints, which bordered on getting to uncontrollable insults. She objected just as vehemently to the fact that the president in Beijing had given me an overfriendly welcome and such an opulent dinner as she did to the fact that the foreign teachers were accommodated in the red brick buildings. "Every foreign teacher is given a welcome dinner here on the campus; why should you have that honour twice? In any case, you foreigners have absolutely no right to live in such large apartments. These were intended for our functionaries, for high-ranking party members, and for our president, who all live in much more modest accommodations. These are the rules determined by the state!"

It all became very confusing, and I suddenly had the feeling that here before me was a person who had come from a humble background but somehow made the right party connections during the Cultural Revolution and managed to gain promotion by virtue of good personal contacts, which were necessary in order to survive in those days. Perhaps she merely came out of the cadre schools well trained. Who knows? In any case, she did not like foreigners; that much was clear.

I still did not interrupt her torrent of words and noticed that my continued silence made her uneasy when she finally stopped for breath. She probably put it down to my not being able to understand her and promptly started urging Xiao D. to translate it all for me. He evidently felt very uncomfortable about the whole situation and was much relieved when I told him I understood everything quite well. As I was talking to Xiao D. in German, she interrupted him the whole time with, "What is she saying? Come on, translate!" so that he barely had the chance to utter a word. When finally I made it very clear to her not only that I was quite capable of making myself understood, but also that I had fully understood all her accusations, she left Xiao D. alone at last.

During a pause I then asked calmly if I might be permitted to say something. I had to struggle hard to contain my own inner annoyance, because the way she had spoken to me was abusive. I then told her relatively calmly that these accusations she had made against me were in no way correct. I asked her to refrain from making any comment, because that way we would get nowhere, but hear me out. I then countered every accusation in turn, one at a time. The fact that the railway fare system was so complicated was not my fault, and would she kindly take this up with the railway directly? It was not up to me to tell the president what he should and should not do. I had been in her foreign bureau and fully informed her of my problems and, in fact, discussed when, first, the shower repair and, second, the move were to occur. She knew as well as I did that employees never handled anything independently, without instructions from above, much less handed out keys. And if we foreigners were not to live in the red brick buildings, then where were we to live? We did not make the rules. In any case, if she objected to my presence I could quite easily leave again on the next train, but abuse such as she had been heaping on me was something I would not tolerate. Quite abruptly she stood up, indicating to Xiao D. to do likewise, and with a slight indication of a nod both disappeared as quickly as they had come.

I was extremely annoyed and upset, particularly because such a person as Mrs. Z. was always to be consulted as an intermediary between non-Chinese-speaking foreigners and the local people. It was considered proper to only conduct negotiations with these intermediaries' "help." And their "help" most of the time resulted in a kind of instruction on how things had to be understood by the foreigner but seldom led to a satisfactory outcome of the problem discussed. It surely was difficult in regard to cultural differences and understanding of negotiations to make both opinions meet, but abusive treatment was certainly not the possible way. What a blessing that I could speak for myself and get the answers, "unfiltered," without the need for an interpreter.

So, Mrs. Z. and I were certainly not favourably disposed towards one another, and this situation was to remain unchanged through the coming months. Whilst we were polite to one another, where at all possible I avoided discussing my affairs with her, nor did I make any effort to disguise the tension between us. This in turn had the unexpected result that many of my fellow teachers and even my students confided in me that they, too, had never been able to get along with this woman. Some did not even exchange polite forms of greetings with her. For example, one of the language teachers had been singled out by Mrs. Z. by being forbidden to visit my predecessors in their apartment. Her every step was observed and reported, and she was denounced to her superiors by Mrs. Z. Getting out of such character assassination, especially in regard to the past political conditions, involved taking on a truly titanic struggle, and I was very glad indeed that I was not dependent on Mrs. Z. In the course of time I was able to find that various back doors opened for me here and there, enabling me to direct my wishes and any problems to the appropriate ears.

And I continued to live in my new, larger room until we all moved to the new "Experts Residence," a section in the hotel for ninety-nine guests, in the following October.

On one morning I was to travel to the city with one of the employees from the foreign bureau in order to visit the photographer. Three passport photos were needed for various documents: one for the "white card" already mentioned, one for the work permit, and one for the residence permit.

We departed for the inner city at around eight o'clock in the morning by means of the campus bus, got off downtown, and walked a few steps through the misty streets, the air filled with a smoky smell due to the many chimney outlets from the windows. At the front counter in the photographer's shop I first had to pay for the three photos and then was given a receipt I was to hand to the photographer. We then started to climb the stairs to the studio, which was located several floors higher up. With every step I found it more difficult to breathe, and once again the bluish biting air, saturated with smoke and combustion of gases, caused me to have an attack of coughing. The photographer, a charming older man, consoled me very sympathetically by assuring me that I would become used to the smoke and the smell if I stayed in the country for a few years, just as they had all become used to it. I was to hear the term *xi guan le*, got used to it, many more times during my stay. In trying to help me get back out into the open air he tried to hurry proceedings as far as he was able to do so with the huge and ancient camera. The first plate did not fit, the second one must have been used already, but the third one met all requirements. He turned my head, first to the right, then to the left, now, "Hold still please," and zzzzzz bash, the long cable release did its job, and my image was in the box.

Whilst looking for the photographer on the upper floor we had passed through a number of photo studios. There were partition walls everywhere, screens, stands with vases, tables, garden chairs, artificial flowers, rocking horses, huge balls, and other similar articles. Hanging from various hooks were some grubby bridal dresses with veils and flowers, jackets, and trousers. There was even a bearskin among the collection of requisites. Somehow it had a very special atmosphere about it, and I am sure I would have seen more if I had not felt unwell. As it was, I left the building for the fresh air outside as soon as I could after the click, leaving

Mrs. G. to arrange for the photos to be picked up.

Whilst the so-called fresh air outside was certainly better than that inside the shop, I was still glad to be back on the campus, where I was able to breathe freely in real fresh air once more. What a difference it made to be seven kilometres south of the city in what was by comparison an idyllic rural setting.

My sensitivity to coal smoke derived from an event experienced in my teens, when our family had nearly perished due to a closing up of our chimney during the night and it was good fortune that my father and his guest were still up so late to wake us up. Abruptly as the smoke found its way into the rooms through the iron stove, it went through the chimney again many hours later. The windows were frozen tight, and it was impossible to open them. We could not get any draught through the rooms. Whoever had the intention of killing us was never brought to daylight. But my sensibility to smoke became a very part of me.

Part of the reason for the relatively clean air on the campus site may have been the fact that the buildings there were heated by means of the campus-owned district heating, so that there was no need for the use of open coal heaters apart from the small bucket stoves used for cooking. I found out later that there was no regulation making it obligatory to provide heating in houses. There was a government regulation that decreed that the area of northern China where heating was required ended at the northern bank of the Yangtze River. In the northeastern provinces (formerly Manchuria) buildings were provided with heating. All other provinces up to the Yangtze might have heating, but it was not compulsory, such matters usually being determined by household edicts on the part of individual work units. The homes of workers attached to small factories or firms could not afford heat in any case. And so the ordinary people got warmth by the use of bucket stoves or sometimes enclosed stoves with smoke outlets poking through the windowpanes.

This also explained why the air pollution was so bad, especially in the mornings, when the stoves were relit or stoked back to life. All the smoke, everything, poured into the air without any form of filtration. In areas where a lot of people lived close together, such as industrial centres or overpopulated cities such as Beijing, the situation was exceptionally bad. It was not unusual to hear of poisonings, sometimes with fatal consequences.

Back to the morning after leaving the photographer shop. Together with the foreign bureau employee I boarded the public bus for the trip back to the campus. The fare was two fen each. There was a dreadful shoving and pushing, but we got on the bus. Due to the broken windowpanes it was rather breezy, and the bus rattled and shook from every corner. The people stood there crammed together so tightly that there was no chance of anyone falling over if the bus should suddenly swerve or brake. Some of the passengers with their traditional mouth protection of cotton muslin looked like surgeons straight out of the operating theatre. I noticed also that a number of bus riders sat there bundled up in padded blankets and supported by friends or relatives. A few of the women were carrying small children or babies in their arms, also heavily rigged against the cold. There was even an older man carrying his little old mother piggyback. A stop brought the answer to the riddle, because all of a sudden the bus was empty. I learned that this stop was the hospital. Later on I often saw sick people being transported, always wrapped up in blankets, even in summer when it was very hot. It was not unusual to see a patient lying covered up on the bare boards of a two-wheeled cart being calmly pulled along to the hospital by the relatives.

Two weeks after the New Year came the Lantern Feast. Everybody, young and old, carried their bought or homemade lanterns through the sparsely lit streets to the campus square in front of the theatre. The lanterns came in all sorts of shapes, from fish and balls to temples and other fantasy objects. There was to be a farewell fireworks display to conclude the New Year celebrations at 9:30. Like New Year's Eve, this evening was to become one infernal spectacle. To begin with, the long chains of small crackers were lit, and then the larger rockets shot into the air with a great deal of noise, only to give off another ear-shattering bang just as they reached their zenith. To give the show its crowning touch the whole square was bathed in Bengal fire. A number of tables taken from the lecture rooms and placed together served as a launching platform for this purpose. Any rockets that happened to misfire just shot sideways through the crowd, which stood in a circle at a suitable distance from where it was all happening. And yet it was not without danger if a large rocket decided to shoot into the multitude rather than straight up. Now and again sparks would fall on someone's clothing or into the hair of a child, which would give rise to a lot of shouting and hectic activity to beat out any flames. The mood was jolliness. One exchanged greetings with acquaintances, had a little chat, admired the lanterns, or discussed a number of topics; I really felt great at being part of all this, almost as if I were already a member of this community. Here and there I would be greeted with a friendly: "Oh, also here, Teacher Shi? Have you settled in a little better yet? Aren't you cold in those thin woolen pants?" All this also helped to involve me in the festive spirit. Unfortunately, I was not able to stay right to the end, because I had been invited to a *yuan xiao* eating. This is a sweet delicacy only made at the time of the Lantern Festival. Small balls are made out of glutinous rice flour and then filled with almond paste, pureed dates, pieces of candy, candied cherries, and other green-looking substances before being placed in boiling water and boiled over a low flame until well done. One cannot eat too much of these sticky little balls, because they are very filling, but they sure are delicious!

I had now been in Y. nearly four weeks. Details such as the

timetable, how I was to conduct the lessons, how many students I would have, from which books I was to teach, etc., were no clearer than at the beginning. I knew nothing. The official start of the lectures was on the eleventh of March, and I still had a few days before that date. So I decided to go downtown again.

When I travelled into the city the first time I only made a few purchases and got to know the means of transportation and the main thoroughfares. I had heard that Y. also had a museum, an old Buddhist temple, and various places in lovely country-side where one could make excursions. To begin with I bicycled to the museum. There among other exhibits I saw a small copy of the famed figure made of platelets of jade held together with gold wire. According to the attendant the original was located in Nanjing. There were numerous old stone rubbings, a num-ber of colourful painted clay figures depicting monks and tem-ple guardians, domestic articles from the Han dynasty (206 B.C. to A.D. 220), jewellery and small vases of jade and gold, scrolls of beautiful calligraphy, etc., all somewhat dusty and stored in simply made racks under glass panes, some cracked. The pieces on show differed very little from those displayed elsewhere, for example in Beijing or Hangzhou. In these major centres the dis-plays were of course more comprehensive, largely originals and more valuable than those in a small provincial town. The museum in Y. was housed in what was once the residence of a wealthy person. There was a prettily laid out garden with a small pond, a few artificial "hills," and a round opening in walls lead-ing to little pavilions, which would have been tempting to stroll through had it not been so bitterly cold at this time of year. There was nowhere even a little bit of warmth. The rooms were lined with stone blocks, with windows of carved latticed wood-work situated rather high and very draughty. Not all of them had windowpanes. In summer this must be an oasis of coolness, and not only on account of shade from the trees.

The Buddhist temple site was situated directly opposite the

museum. I crossed the busy "Street of Peace," climbed up a few steps to the front of the imposing arch of white columns topped with a blue-tiled roof, and started the somewhat strenuous climb up to the individual temples along the worn steps of stone or plain earth. There were also prayer houses and other items of interest. There were large blocks of stone everywhere, set into the hillscape as if by nature itself, all bearing red or black lettering in harmonious calligraphy, representing proverbs or sayings taken from Chinese philosophy. Here and there hidden among the bare deciduous trees and pines there were clay igloos, as high as a man, with small openings, standing on the ground. On closer inspection and after making enquiries I was told that these were former Japanese air-raid or defensive shelters. The hill on which the monastery is situated was once a strategically important point for the Japanese occupation forces. Today only the bunkers remind one of the terrible years of war from 1937 to 1945.

The arduous climb was worthwhile. From the top of the hill, where individual long buildings, arranged in a horseshoe shape, with red columns and carved wooden windows, stood awaiting visitors, one had a marvelous view over the southwestern part of the city. To the right there was a large lake, from which delectable carp were harvested for official banquets. I heard that freshly caught fish could cost, depending on their weight, up to twenty yuan each, which means that a normal consumer could only afford them for a very special occasion. Generally a pound of fish cost around four yuan. I was to have the opportunity during various official dinners to find out for myself how delicious the flesh of these fish was.

The city of Y. is surrounded by numerous chains of hills, which have names such as Sleeping Buffalo, Camel Hump Mountain, Nine-Mile Mountain, Cloud and Dragon Mountain, Phoenix Mountain, and so forth. The monastery complex is located on the ridge of the Cloud and Dragon Mountain, which is made up of nine rows of hills. The "head" is visible in the distance to the south, the following range adjoining it is named the Seven Parts of the Body, and Buddhist monks have built their refuge on the "dragon tail."

A bust of the Buddha, more than ten metres in height and made of gilded wood, is located inside a temple specially built to house it; it has been somewhat restored following the Cultural Revolution. Today it is again worshipped with incense sticks and sacrificial gifts such as small sums of money, which are thrown in front of the statue. The faithful bow reverently. The small children, mostly boys, were taught the correct forms of ritual behaviour by their grandparents, mostly their grandmothers. It was a picture of peace and of calm being radiated by the people as they went through their slow ritual movements or walked slowly in a calm way. Next to the temple stood a small house built of grey tiles, and inside, suspended from heavy ropes, hung a large bronze bell. A long wooden striker stuck out through a largish opening in the wall, and by pushing it forcefully at the bell a heavy "duuuuung" sound could be evoked.

Slowly I made my way down again, not using the same direction as coming up, but via a series of winding paths. Now and again old steps would lead one to small enchanted spots, which I imagined would be quite delightful in the summer. Having reached the bottom, I had to make my way through a series of narrow lanes, which belonged to an older part of the city not yet demolished. People here lived very close together in a square consisting of three low grey single-story houses at ground level, each having two or three small rooms, without kitchen or sanitary installations, built around a tiny open area. A high wall would have prevented me from seeing inside at all, had some of the large double wooden gates not happened to be open. All the buildings looked neglected. Some of the courtyards contained water several centimetres deep, while in others it was frozen. Odd bricks set into the puddles here and there served as means of negotiating the courtyard without getting wet feet. In one corner of a courtyard there was a huge pile of rubbish in a heap, suggesting that the corner in question was indeed intended for the disposal of garbage. Chinese household garbage looks different from our consumer society rubbish. One does not see packing material or bottles or cans. Nevertheless, ashes, bits of paper, vegetable waste, and fruit peelings did cause an unpleasant smell problem, particularly in the hot months. Despite these surroundings, little children, looking like balls in their thick padded clothing, played and ran around happily. The bare bottoms poking through the open seats of the pants did not worry anyone. During my childhood we used to call these pants, worn by children up to the age of three or so, rapid-fire pants.

I continued my stroll through the lanes. Fireworks were still going off. Chickens with red paint on them ran around looking for anything edible. The red paint on the back feathers is intended so the owner of chickens can recognize his own. Now and then I saw red paper cuttings with "good luck" characters, which had been newly glued to the pillars on either side of a large wooden gate. Evidently a wedding must have taken place behind the grey stones recently, and the characters on the red paper would continue to tell of this happy event for a long time to come, until rain and the weather eventually washed the wall clean again. A pedlar was slowly pushing his heavily laden bicycle along and praising his oranges in a loud singsong. Despite the cold weather there was a lot of activity in the narrow streets. In the summer every stone on the paving would be occupied by sitting, squatting, reading, or playing humanity, all keen to escape their claustrophobic homes to look for space, fresh air, and a little coolness. On my walk I came across nobody who wanted to remain outside at this time of year. All were hurrying home with nets or bags containing shopping. Gradually I got to the end of the lanes district and found myself on the little open square once more in front of the arch, the entrance to the monastery complex.

Later in the summer I would see a small corner of the square fenced off, where a brown horse and occasionally a mule or two were waiting for customers. The owner of these animals would offer interested parties colourful costumes from past centuries, inviting them to put them on. He would then photograph them as proud generals high on horseback or common soldiers astride one of the mules. The donning of the costumes and mounting of the horses would take place to the accompaniment of much cheering and laughter by the onlookers.

Leaving the small square, I headed back in the direction of the inner city, because I wanted to have a look at the old riverbed of the Huanghe. The Huanghe, the Yellow River, has since time immemorial been China's great sorrow on account of the recurring and devastating floods, but it has also been the cradle of Chinese culture. Here, standing on secured banks, one did not even suspect the enormous quantities of water this river pours into its new bed, which was situated farther to the north and was several hundred years old. The Huanghe had changed its bed many a time. This river here, also called Huanghe, was now a tributary stream, looked dark in colour, and was not very wide, just flowing lazily along. On it there was not a single boat or other sign of life. On the other hand, the narrow street by the riverbank was a colourful picture of small business. Here one could select knit items in the most garish colours to one's heart's content, all made of synthetic yarn. There were glowing lilacs, violent reds, poisonous-looking greens and strong oranges. Jeans, the latest fashion in pants among the young, sold well. In Chinese translation the word *jeans* means "cattle-killing pants." There were also many other stands where one could buy mandarins, oranges, apples from Shandong Province, peanuts in their shells, and other items such as sesame bars and nuts in "Turkish" honey.

During the summer, as long as it was not too hot, old men

would sit along certain stretches of this street, smoking pipes and chatting with one another. They would sit and enjoy the singing of their feathered pets, who would be singing and twirping away in their cages hanging from the branches of the trees.

Gradually I found that it was simply getting too cold to wander around on my inspection tour in this time of year, and I rode back to the campus. There were many months ahead of me I intended to use for additional trips and more exploration.

Joys and Sorrows of the First Semester

The official start to the semester was on the eleventh of March, but the language department started a week later. A few days earlier, on the eighth of March, it was "Woman's Day." On this occasion all working women, young or old, were given a half-day off. All female employees received from their employer, in my case the institute, a small token, such as cinema tickets, fruit, or sweets. We campus women received cinema tickets. Young and old, with or without a child, streamed into the campus theatre by the hundreds. The film showing was a recently made colour film that had as its subject the time before liberation, i.e., before 1949, dealing with child labour, exploitation, suppression, and finally liberation by the PLA from poverty and suffering. It was one of the usual films, painting everything black or white and saying nothing new about the old system. The people exploiting their fellow citizens, corrupt and treacherous officials, denunciation, spying, everything one could imagine as having been part of a decadent form of society caused by the KMT (national party) was packed into the film. There was plenty of action, shooting, children being used or misused as agents by one part or the other, dramatic death scenes, tragic family histories, tearful sacrifices, all for the glorious liberation that at the end of the film promised to carry China into a happy future among the noise of exploding bombs and shells. Finis! While the women were watching this film on the time of KMT rule, their husbands or adult sons were taking care of the household, which generally involved shopping and the preparation of food.

After I had returned from the film, the dean came, in order to discuss with me the timetable and the number of lessons I was to give. I was to work a six-day week, with two lessons in the classroom every day of fifty minutes each, the first lesson from 7:30 to 8:20 and the second, after a five-minute break, from 8:25 until 9:15. Once a week I had to give a third lesson after the long recess, which was from 9:15 until 9:35, and teach until 11:20, with a small break at 10:25. Apart from the lessons I would conduct conversation practice on three evenings per week and give advanced lessons to my two Chinese teachers of German. Thus, with a workload of almost twenty hours per week, I would be quite busy, as the dean said. As there was very little opportunity for leisure activities, either on the campus or in the city, this suited me quite well. But when I asked for teaching materials, course content, and course objectives I was met with embarrassed silence, then: "There are no instructional books available at all. We thought you would bring everything with you!" I was quite speechless but not too surprised at the way it was taken for granted that foreign teachers would bring with them everything they needed, preferably free of charge.

Long before my arrival I had asked the foreign bureau to give me information about this very point. In their replies I received lengthy details about my duties, my salary, room and board, reimbursement of travelling costs from the point of my arrival in China to the institute and back to the point of departure, the laws I had to obey, and reasons for and terms of terminating my contract. Once I had sent back a signed copy of the preliminary contract my letters were not answered at all. As I knew China also from my previous visits, everything would be arranged face to face on the spot. Discussions usually began with apologies for their own negligence, with lack of time being the excuse. It was regretted, and there generally was a lamenting undertone to the fact that such a good opportunity to inform me of what was needed had slipped away. Well, such was the situation!

As mentioned before, I had brought with me a language programme, intended as a source of ideas and a precaution. This programme consisted of a textbook, a workbook, test sheets, and a Chinese-German glossary. I had selected this material for use as additional or complementary references, to be used with the basic books that I assumed would be available. In the end there was no need for me to ask what the syllabus for the lessons was, as the dean told me he would leave everything in my hands and felt confident I would work it all out. He, being a professor of machine construction, had no idea, in any case, how a language course might be conducted. The objective was that the students, all graduate engineers in fields like geology, mining, machinery construction, electrical engineering, etc., learn to master the German language sufficiently for daily use and learn as much as possible about daily life and culture in West Germany. At an appropriate time they might wish to continue their studies in Germany, assisted by a stipend from the German government or some organization; for most of them the wish to obtain a German Ph.D. was paramount. The institute had excellent working relationships with a number of various technical universities in Germany.

I was able to learn all these things from the dean, but when I came back to the question as to where I was to obtain teaching materials he was not able to offer any solution. My suggestion to order the necessary books, some thirty in number for my ten students, direct from the publishers would not be implemented, as the necessary foreign exchange or foreign bank account was not available. On the other hand, I was reluctant to agree to his countersuggestion to handle the transaction via my personal bank account. It involved more than one thousand deutschmarks, plus postage. What would my reimbursement in RMB have been worth? The Bank of China will never convert RMB to foreign currency, even in the most unusual circumstances. It is only possible to return FECs, accompanied by the needed documents, when larger amounts are involved.

Whilst I am not normally a devotee of photocopying, in this instance I thought that it might provide a way out of the dilemma; however, this avenue was foiled by objection on the part of the dean. The equipment or paper was not available for this purpose, and in any case the students were probably not in the position to afford the considerable costs, so it would be better if I were to turn to the appropriate departments concerned with student matters, was his view. "But who is to undertake this task?" I asked. He replied that he did not know the engineers who would learn German himself, nor did he know the circumstances where they were working; however, in the case of his own two candidates (I would call them protégés) there was no problem.

I had simply not reckoned on encountering this many difficulties and decided that it might be best to appeal to the president of the institute. The conversation with the dean lasted almost two hours, but the end result was no different from what has been described. Instead he explained to me in detail just how free I was to move about within the rural area in which the institute was located. I was not to travel more than twenty kilometers from the campus in any direction. Also, the many barracks and military training grounds, as well as the military airfield, were taboo in any case. Should I wish to visit a place beyond this region for sightseeing, I must first inform the foreign bureau and obtain permission. If they considered my request "acceptable," then they would "find a way." Of course I was permitted to travel to the city at any time, but preferably not at night or at late hours. The streets were poorly lit, and the institute could not be responsible for my health or well-being.

Oh, how concerned they all were about us foreigners, but I often had the feeling with many of the "officials" that they were worried not so much over our well-being, as over our desire for independence and ability to make our own decisions.

On the following evening the deputy head with the principal secretary of the English language department came to see me, in order to discuss anew the syllabus, timetable, and manner in which lessons would be held. The number of lessons was unchanged; however, there was a slight rearrangement of the days on which I was to give either conversation practice or advanced lessons. New times were fixed for the students. Instead of three evenings there would be only one, the other two being moved to the afternoon. Instead of four hours of advanced lessons there would now only be two. The deputy head, a very pleasant lady of about fifty-five years, suggested that the lectures should include some introductory course about everyday life in Germany, such as culture, some geography, customs, manners, social conventions, and the like. I was agreeable to her suggestions, once I had been able to establish where the main emphasis was to be.

Since I was employed by a technical institute, it was my impression that I was to teach German engineering terminology, although there had been no mention of this in the preliminary contract. But one had to be prepared for anything. It was widely believed, as I learnt later from a number of people I spoke to before the semester started, that once one had a good command of the language, both spoken and written, one was automatically able to explain the most complex expressions correctly and clearly from a technical point of view. And this doesn't only happen in China.

And so the timetable was confirmed, as were the number of hours and the number of students. I knew what was expected of me, and so it seemed that nothing could now go wrong. Those responsible had discussed everything with me, and all details had been ironed out. At the end of this meeting I asked why the English department had undertaken the task of informing me. It transpired that they were responsible for all foreign languages, as language was not an independent faculty and languages were not taught per se; language here was not regarded as science. The system was that students, teachers, and graduate engineers from any discipline could be selected via a specific process to undertake a course in a particular language important to them, either as a basic course or to further their command of that language. It was a most interesting discussion, and we all understood one another very well and established a good rapport.

A few days later I had another visit, this time by the secretary on her own. The reason was yet another change to the timetable. The afternoon lessons were to take place in the evening after all. I still do not know to this day just what the causes were for the decision to again change the "final" timetable. Once again we came to an agreement, and I pinned my "unalterable" schedule, the "absolutely last alteration," to the wall above my desk.

I was not a little surprised when, some three weeks later, after I had started teaching already, one or another student began to criticise this afternoon or that evening as not being convenient to them. Had the students had their way I would have had to arrange individual lessons for each one, as there was so little agreement among them as to what times were suitable. Nevertheless, we finally agreed by a mixture of voting and compromise, very democratic. We were all satisfied and did not bother to inform the administration of the changes, as nobody would be concerned as long as the whole arrangement worked. Much later somebody said to me I should not have let my students "put me under pressure," as a teacher's word is *law*. Once, when I mentioned this during a conversation class, one of my students commented very truthfully, "If it was not for the fact that you speak Chinese we would not have dared." From then on we no longer had any problems with orders from above. Arrangements made at lower levels worked very well indeed for all concerned.

It was a puzzle to me as to why it had been the dean, who was a professor of mechanical engineering and not a representative of the appropriate department, who came to discuss the topic of language teaching with me.

Gradually I came to understand the structure and inter-relationships of the various sections and individuals by putting together fragments of information gleaned from my students. It appeared that this particular dean was responsible for the foreign teachers who had to consult him as coordinator on any topic at all. The same applied to the Chinese side, if they wanted to talk to us officially. Since he had his office in the main administration building, right next to the foreign bureau, he also had considerable influence there and a related function, although I was never able to establish clearly just what that was. This may have been at least partly due to the fact that I was able to fend for myself when I needed something, without having to involve him. Be that as it may, I did gain the very strong feeling that relations between the foreign bureau and the language department were not the best at all. The many enquiries I had made before my arrival concerning books and so forth had not even been passed on and were never dealt with. Settling everything in person was preferred. Later I happened to mention during a conversation that my questions had never been answered, to which one of the language teachers replied, "The best thing is to have nothing to do with the foreign bureau. They are totally disinterested. For them the only thing that matters is the party identification."

The days passed and the eighteenth of March arrived. There were still no teaching materials for my ten students. I could not help feeling that they were all looking to me, expecting me somehow, like a *dea ex machina* (*dea* being feminine of the Latin *deus*), to perform a miracle and solve the problem. I had also heard by various means that my students were not all beginners, far from it. Some had been studying German for two years, others were taking a refresher course, having originally learnt the language some thirty years ago, and only two or three were real newcomers. Above all, my first objective was to look for means and ways to obtain books, i.e., to gain access to photocopying facilities.

I decided to join forces with my Chinese German-language teacher, Mrs. S. She was very helpful and knew all the back doors and how to get things done. A few days later I had a talk with the president arranged through the foreign bureau, which I had to use as intermediaries this time. The president and I had met already in Beijing, and in the meantime I had acted as interpreter during a visit by a German industrial delegation, so that we greeted one another almost as old acquaintances. The conversation took place in Chinese, although Mr. L., another German-speaking interpreter in the foreign bureau, was also present. The atmosphere was pleasant and relaxed. The very charming president offered his help without any hesitation, and the interpreter was sent to fetch the officer in charge of the photocopying room from the administration section. He was instructed to ensure that someone was seconded to make the copies I needed from the books I had brought with me. To begin with, we would work our way through to lesson 6, and then we would talk over this matter again. I was even given an assurance that the copies for each individual student would not cost anything.

And so cheerfully I made my way to the copy room with a young woman. We spent nearly three hours there. I was not allowed to operate the machine, which was a Japanese brand, in case something went wrong, and in any case she was the only one authorised to work with this copier. My job was to sort and collate the various pages and instruct her as to what was to be copied. It was a rather laborious and lengthy business, and the cool temperature in the room—I estimated it as being not more than ten degrees Celsius—did nothing to make the task more enjoyable in the poorly lit room. The outside temperature was around two to four degrees above zero. I was frozen through when I eventually left this uninviting place after we had finished. Instead of the authorised six lessons, the good woman copied twelve. She took the view that one never knew when another opportunity might present itself, as the copier often was inoperable for extended periods. Well, that was fine with me. Joyfully Mrs. S., who had come to the copying room to assist me, and I carried the pile of paper into my apartment.

It was like this with almost everything. What you have, you have. Whether you can use it straightaway is rarely debated— sooner or later there is always a need for things. Presumably, this is why Chinese homes often look "so untidy," because they are crammed full of boxes, cupboards, and chests of drawers stuffed full of various objects.

On the eighteenth of March, which was the day of my first lesson, I was greeted with great deference by my ten students, men and women. As I entered the classroom they all rose and a unified chant of "Good morning, teacher," in Chinese filled the room; word must have passed around that I understood Chinese. I found it embarrassing to encounter so much discipline and respect from adults, some older than I was. The class consisted of three young women aged between twenty-three and twenty-eight years of age and seven men of various ages. One was in his midfifties, one around forty-five, and the others between twenty-three and thirty.

I used the first day as a means of getting acquainted, and also to explain my concept of how we would tackle our common goal. On the first day I spoke only Chinese, partly to remove any shyness that might exist, but also to give them the feeling that it was acceptable and desirable for them to address me in Chinese, in order to solve problems related to the lessons or to other difficulties, which could not otherwise be discussed fully due to language barriers.

I also found out a good deal about their backgrounds, professions and occupations, family and origins, as well as why they wanted to learn German, and what their aim in that language was. With the exception of three women, all had technical backgrounds and training. Two of them had never seen a university from the inside, much less heard a European language or learned the alphabet. These two had been instructed by their work unit, in this case their factory, to undertake a course in German so that they could evaluate technical literature and undertake correspondence in connection with business conducted with Germany. This was what was expected of them. Quite a high goal! Each of these two had mastered the alphabet in their spare time already and knew something about the language. This meant that I did not have to start right from the beginning, which would have been a problem for the more advanced members of the class. Most of them spoke a little English, one very well, and two of the women knew a little broken German. One was a teacher of mathematics at a pedagogical institute in downtown Y., while the other was from Beijing and employed by the publications section of a research institute. Both could stay only for one semester, not being able to obtain permission for a longer term. The third young woman worked as an English teacher at a factory in Y. All the others were working either as teacher's assistants or scientific employees in the areas of research or technology in the institute. Three or four of them had either a bachelor's or master's degree. Four of my students came from the city Y.; the young woman from Beijing was living as a member of the institute for one semester and had a bed in one of the students' dormitories. Her work unit in Beijing had had to pay a not insignificant sum to the institute in order for her to spend a semester here. Similarly, the factories had had to pay their tribute before their candidates were accepted. As for the exact sum involved, I was to find this out only after some time. The cost of teaching and accommodation for one student was 580 yuan per semester, which covered a stay in a four-bed room without board. The factories, though, continued to pay the salaries of their candidates.

Then each of my students told me something of their private lives. The mathematics teacher was married but, unfortunately, was living apart from her husband. He was working in Nanjing, while she had been transferred to Y. The other two women were not married. All the male students were married, and some of them were young fathers with children one or two years old. The son and heir was mentioned with considerable pride, while one father referred apologetically to having "only a daughter." And so on that first day I learned a good deal by the usual game of questions and answers, and they, too, learned something about me. The two hours passed in no time at all, and almost before I knew it I had completed my first day's work.

Before I start relating my observations and experiences of day-to-day life as a teacher at the institute and giving details on specific topics as they arose out of the conversational evenings, I would like to give a brief description of my classroom. As I have already mentioned, all the classrooms were located in the ten-story building, namely, the yellow main building that towered over every other structure of the campus. The language department was situated on the fifth floor. Each morning I had to conquer the 140 or so steps so that at 7:30 sharp, as the bell rang, I would punctually face my students. In the beginning the constant climbing of steps caused me considerable trouble, and I was always out of breath. But with practice it became fun to race up the steps in competition with the others, feeling fleet-footed and fit. Once I reached the top I had to turn right and walk along a long, bare, and not always clean corridor to room 501, which was the first of the rooms numbered up to 519. All the rooms with odd numbers faced north and were, therefore, less sunny. The windows afforded a splendid view over large fields, still brown and bare at this time of year, and distant hills. The classroom itself, on the other hand, offered nothing of beauty: light-coloured concrete walls, a grey stone floor, and the most basic tables and chairs roughly hammered together, draughty because of ill-fitting window frames with thin panes of glass, without curtains of any kind. Bare neon tubes on the ceiling gave a glaring light, and there were also two ventilators for the hot summer months, painted baby blue. In front of the students' desks was a slightly raised podium with a table for the teacher, but no chair. On the wall behind it was a large blackboard of stone with a smaller white metal board hanging in front of it. There was a considerable selection of felt pens in various colours, green, blue, lilac, and black, but without exception they either had dried out or were broken. Only on very rare occasions was I able to write a whole sentence in the same colour, and a search for fresh pens was usually unsuccessful. If one of my students did find some, they would always disappear again the next day, presumably because they were just as badly needed elsewhere. In the end I gave up the idea of writing with felt-tipped pens; I had the white board taken away—it was a new acquisition on the part of the department—and from then on I used chalk quite successfully, again in a great variety of colours. But wiping the blackboard caused a lot of difficulty. It was impossible to obtain a sponge or even a piece of rag. There was a dry brush made of velvet velour material (for wiping the felt-pen writing), which did not absorb water, and while it would certainly serve to wipe away what had been written, there always remained a layer of chalk dust. But one becomes accustomed to almost anything, *xi guan le*, as the old photographer predicted, and it was really not the end of the world if something did not function quite the same way as one had come to expect in a fully functioning state.

I was able to come to terms with many inadequacies and defects, but not with the rule that a teacher was not allowed to sit down during a lesson, which explained the missing chair behind the teacher's desk. Many weeks later I heard about this rule and from then on was no longer surprised every time my chair was "misplaced" again. But my stamina was stronger, and at the end someone must have given up moving the chair every time.

The audiovisual equipment in my classroom consisted of a television set (black-and-white) and a tape recorder/radio of local manufacture. The room was allocated only for German lessons. One of the students had a key, as he had got permission to use the room also in his spare time so as to have a quiet place for study.

Every door on the floor was numbered. If a room had two entrance doors, this in turn meant two numbers. Only the toilets did not have numbers, and instead their doors were resplendent with the characters for *nan* (gents) and *nü* (ladies). The interior fittings were always identical, as one egg resembles another. The door for gents was usually open, so I could have a glimpse on passing by. Two small cubicles were divided by a central wall, each with a Chinese toilet bowl set in the centre of the floor. There was also a rectangular basin, with a constantly dripping tap, for washing hands and other uses. It seemed the ladies' room was equipped with some kind of "sprinkler system," because the room was always wet, from dripping taps, dripping pipes, or wet mops left lying across the washbasin. The rubbish that had been swept together previously was usually piled in a corner, waiting for some day when a cleaning staff would eventually take pity on it.

One thing I found particularly revolting and very unhygienic was the constant presence of phlegm that had been spat out against the skirtings (at least not in the middle of the floor). This repulsive custom incurred my displeasure again and again, a fact I made no attempt to conceal from my class. It always required a lot of willpower on my part when I walked past somebody who was busy with coughing, choking, and retching in order to eventually bring up the phlegm and spit it out, all accompanied by a lot of noise. Women seemed less prone to this habit than men and simple people more than the more enlightened, but there seemed to be no difference between young and old.

Despite several major campaigns to address this evil, nothing much had changed. The many articles that appeared in the newspapers on this topic were read but did not seem to find their way into the readers' minds. So, for example, the following event was said to have occurred: In the capital the "anti-spitting campaign" was running as an example for every other town in the land. In the streets stands had been erected by schoolchildren, under the guidance of numerous doctors and other medically trained personnel, where they handed out information leaflets and worked hard at explaining to passersby and other interested people how spitting was unhygienic and caused illness. Health police were patrolling the streets, and anyone who spat was immediately fined fifty fen. One peasant spat with gusto, was caught, and was asked to pay his fine, which he did with a one-yuan note, and waited for his change. The health police had no small change. The peasant replied that it did not matter, heaved deeply, and spat again with relish before going on his way.

It is proving difficult to educate the common people in these things, unless they can be persuaded by sound arguments and good example. Old traditions are firmly entrenched, and "modern fads," especially those from abroad, are not accepted readily by the rural populace. This includes some of the vitally important hygienic necessities that have to be adopted and to which the government is committed because they concern matters of life and death and are viewed as unimportant by the majority of the people, especially in rural areas. It is a slow and painstaking task to arouse a consciousness for unavoidable reforms or changes in a population of more than a billion people.

The wave of educational zeal about healthy and unhealthy behaviour swept over our campus, too, as evidenced by the flowing inscriptions in white or blue chalk on all kinds of steps: "Please do not spit," or, "Antispitting campaign." In this context I am reminded of a remark once made to my father by a Chinese friend of his: "The foreigners have some odd customs. Instead of spitting out phlegm and getting rid of nose secretions, they save everything in their handkerchiefs and keep it in their pockets. Is that healthy?" Unfortunately, he did not live to see the advent of paper tissues.

Back to class again. Working with the copied materials turned out to be better than I had thought it would be. However, the originals incorporated a number of extra pages with pictures designed to help the reader understand the content that I had not copied, as I only concentrated on the text. I had copies for the twelve lessons, but the first volume encompassed twenty-four and there was no guarantee that I would be allowed to do more copying. In my despair I wrote to the Goethe Institute in Munich asking for some kind of help out of this dilemma. My joy was great indeed when, after some time, several packets arrived by airmail, consisting of the entire teaching material I needed for all my students, all as a gift to them. This most generous gesture was something I had not counted on, and my students, too, could hardly believe it and spontaneously wrote a letter of thanks to the publisher.

From then on it became a real joy to teach, and their enthusiasm to learn assumed almost frightening proportions. In my opinion we were progressing too quickly, which was caused by the fact that my students were always extremely well prepared for lessons. In order to check whether this rapidly acquired knowledge was soundly based I interspersed occasional quick tests on grammar, vocabulary, and idiom. On the average, test results were around forty points of a possible fifty. When it came to knowledge that could be tested, they all learnt without great difficulties, and all were outstanding when it came to learning by heart and memorising rules. However, my aim to motivate them to become fluent in conversation and progress beyond mere repetition of standard phrases was not so easily achieved.

It was my observation and also experience that most of my students were passive learners. It was very difficult to get them to form their own opinions. A Chinese student does not ask questions during a lesson. The idea of having something they did not grasp clarified and explained during a lesson was something the students considered quite impossible. It was, according to their understanding, impolite for a pupil to interrupt a teacher. For this reason, during the first few weeks of my teaching I found my table besieged with enquiring students every time there was a break. I resolved to change this situation and made a suggestion to the students that they should ask questions related to the topic at hand straightaway, during the lesson. This, I explained, would overcome the problem of the question being forgotten by the end of the lesson or, at best, being no longer pertinent. I did not accept their objection that such a question might be boring for the others or lead to loss of face for the one asking. I again had to explain to them that a particular question might interest the others also and that asking a question denoted neither stupidity nor loss of face, but rather that it made for good cooperation if something not fully understood was brought out into the open, where we could all address the issue together.

They even had to be taught to make notes of specific points or key issues. In order to encourage speaking freely, which I called "juggling with words," by way of illustration and drawing the comparison to Chinese acrobatics, I introduced short, simple discussion exercises. In the beginning it was a laborious task to try to obtain an opinion on anything, and I was always finding myself forced into the role of an arbiter. By the end of the first semester most of the class had overcome their shyness and begun to enjoy the discussion sessions, so that at times I had to call a halt in order to not get behind with the teaching syllabus. They had understood that a discussion can and should occur without the need for evaluation on the part of the teacher or the leader of a round and that any opinion expressed would not be interpreted to the disadvantage of an individual.

I came to realise what an enormous advantage my Chinese was for me. With it there were no barriers to communication from the start, unlike those reported by my American colleagues. Many misunderstandings and unpleasant arguments they encountered due to this during the first six weeks or so of the semester.

Also, I was able to correct typical student behaviour without incurring their disapproval. In Chinese schools, apparently any Chinese educational institution, it is a tradition that a student, no matter what age, has to stand up in order to answer a question put by the teacher or stand up for a respectful greeting, as I experienced the very first day. Once I was able to talk about this custom with my students and put to rest their concern about any lack of politeness, I felt much more relaxed with them and gained the impression that they, too, liked it this way. During the coming months a most sincere and hearty relationship was to develop between us, which was to last until the end of my stay and, indeed, beyond. Despite the familiarity and mutual trust between us, neither side ever trespassed beyond that certain distance needed in order for a teacher/student relationship to function smoothly and without friction. I thoroughly enjoyed teaching them, and the months simply flew past.

The days were becoming warmer. The fields had already been planted, and green started to appear everywhere. But a gradual transition between the seasons was not to be. Lilac blossoms, mere buds one day, were already spent a few days later. The mimosa tree, with its countless deep pink blossoms looking like small soft brushes, attracted hundreds of butterflies. Myriads of them were all over the blooming tree, and it was a splendid sight to watch these colourful insects *(papillo macháon)* swarm about. Numerous coloured and shiny beetles crawled about the earth, some with long feelers, lizards, including geckos, rushed over the warm stones, and various grasses and small flowers unfamiliar to me blossomed modestly by the wayside. June brought swarms of swallows. There was a constant chirping from the many overhead wires they had chosen as resting places. On one occasion I even heard a cuckoo in the nearby "forest" of thuja trees.

The institute had its own nursery, where the workers were having a busy time. The greenhouses had to be cleaned out, and all plants were placed in the open, in the sun and fresh air. Here and there seedlings were being planted, and large fields planted with nothing but peonies had to be watered. The glorious spectacle offered by all the blossoming flowers was indescribable, with colours from deep red through pink to pure white. The many flower beds around the campus were planted with pansies and other summer flowers. Entire columns of young women were distributed all over the campus, busily weeding, planting small trees, or protecting already-existing trees against insect pests by painting their trunks with a lime mixture.

All of this work was being done almost exclusively by rural women living beyond the university gates, who were employed for the seasonal work. On more than one occasion I was quite shocked at the heavy work these women had to perform. Large quantities of earth were moved with simple hoes and spades, and huge areas were dug over and the soil loosened and aerated. When it came to transporting huge quantities of earth, the women were always near at hand. They carried the rather heavy, rich clay soil in large baskets, and when I asked one of the women one day how much such weighed, I was told that a full basket usually weighed more than sixty kilograms. It seemed inhuman to me that women had to carry such heavy loads, but they merely laughed and commented that it was something to which one became accustomed, again the *xi guan le*, got used to it. Their male fellow workers only gave me a tired smile—their job was to supervise!

I found it very difficult to digest the huge discrepancy between the positively archaic implements being used in the fields and the modern, computerised technical apparatus I had seen in some of the laboratories. On the one hand some people had to perform very heavy work with prehistoric tools, and on the other hand there were a privileged few pushing buttons. It seemed that it was just as difficult as ever for someone from lower levels of Chinese society to attain an advanced education. Often during conversation I found people making derogatory comments about their peasant countrymen. If someone from the lower classes did manage to make the jump to becoming an educated person, he or she tended to very quickly assume an exaggeratedly superior attitude. My impression, gained from a large number of discussions with many people, was that not much had changed in normal social intercourse. The "scholars" looked down on their "uneducated" fellow citizens just as much as they ever had.

My fondest memories and most pleasant experiences I owe to the many vegetable farmers who offered their wares in the free market (in contrast to the state-run markets) just outside the university gates. Not once was I ever taken down or treated unpleasantly by even a single one of them. For instance, there was one old woman who sold eggs. Among all the eggs I bought from her over a period of months I never found one that was rotten. She would always choose the freshest eggs for me personally and then charge me the same price as everybody else, never once taking advantage of the fact that I was a foreigner.

The vegetable farmer, too, would always advise me in my selection of tomatoes or cucumbers. Once I needed a little parsley—I intended to cook tomato soup—which was only sold by the kilo. The farmer gave me a small bunch without charge and wanted to know what I was going to do with such a wee bit of parsley. When the melon season arrived I was never once sold an unripe fruit. It was usually a jovial revelry when the seller, with a selection of sliced melons before him, tried to convince me of the quality of his goods. One can never shop alone. Wherever one goes, a crowd soon gathers, with people offering advice and expert opinions. On one occasion when "my" vegetable farmer was picking out particularly good tomatoes for me, his neighbour (or perhaps merely an onlooker) advised him against doing this. His reasoning was that if I was not satisfied with the goods I bought this way, then I had the right to bring them back later. However, if I picked my own then I could not blame the merchant if I was not satisfied. It certainly was logical.

The advent of the warmer season not only brought more colour into the landscape and to nature generally; it also meant that children and the younger women wore more colourful clothing than was usual in drab, grey everyday life during the cold weather. Furthermore, this time of year, June to July, also signaled the arrival of the rainy season with its heavy thunderstorms, fierce lightning, crashing thunder, and violent storms. A sky coloured sulphur yellow was invariably the forerunner of a typhoon or a similar storm, and with temperatures of forty degrees in the shade. It really meant a major mental and physical effort to go to classes in this heat. It also meant that my students and I showed each other a good deal of understanding if someone's attention lapsed or if we all decided it was just too hot for strenuous mental work and opted instead to spend the lesson time watching an English- or German-language film.

The language department had a number of American films, such as *Oklahoma*, *The Godfather* (strongly censored), *True*

Grit, and *To Kill a Mockingbird*; even *The French Lieutenant's Woman* could be found in the constantly locked cupboard. German films I was to show included *Die Brücke* (The Bridge), *Die Verlorene Ehre der Katharina Blum* (Katharina Blum's Lost Honour), and *Johann Strauss* (1950). In order to help my students better understand the more demanding films, I prepared some content descriptions beforehand. The brief summaries of past and present German history contained in these were also intended as a trigger to find out how much my students knew about Germany. It was not much; however, they all knew something about the Third Reich. The atrocities of that regime seemed to have little meaning for them; on the other hand, most of the younger people were fascinated by Hitler's "magnetism" or "charisma," and they spoke with great respect of the way in which he conducted the war and of the deeds of the Wehrmacht. Comparisons were drawn between the Hitler Youth and the Red Guards; on the other hand, their likening of the KMT "Blueshirts" to the SS was an indication of how pleased they were to be living under a Communist regime and not under the fascism of a Chiang Kai-shek. Most of them knew very little about the Federal Republic of Germany today, but they did know exactly which German chancellor had visited China: Sh-mi-de (Schmidt) and Ke-er (Kohl). Once when I showed pictures of a number of German composers, scientists, politicians, etc., I found that Beethoven, Einstein, and Goethe were known, but Brandt (ex-chancellor) meant nothing to any of them. After all, he had never visited China, and thus his name never rated a mention in the newspapers. Also, the geographical situation of Germany in the middle of Europe did not strike a chord. On the other hand, they had some knowledge of the major political parties. They knew that Franz Josef Strauss and his party were somewhere near the top and the SPD and CDU had been or were still part of the government. The FDP was totally unknown, and the Greens were not taken very seriously. Apart from F. J. Strauss the names of the other party heads meant nothing to the Chinese I met, and Kohl was known only as the current chancellor.

During the winter months the campus streets were deserted in the evenings and the few streetlights gave a dim glow. Everyone was glad to be sitting comfortably in a warm room. Not everyone who lived in Y. could count himself so lucky as to have central heating. Those who lived on the institute campus were certainly a privileged few. They had clean surroundings, reasonable accommodations (not if measured by our standards), school, a kindergarten, and even a small hospital. Indeed, conscious of being part of an elite institute, they tended to be quite snobbish in their day-to-day relations with the ordinary people of the city, as evidenced by some of the remarks they made. For example, when one day I asked some students about shopping opportunities for silk and other beautiful things I received as a reply: "I have never been in the city. What is there to buy? The people there have no taste, and the goods on offer are ugly and of poor quality." Others suggested I should do my shopping in Shanghai, which was the most modern city there was. Even the capital, Beijing, paled by comparison, and anyway, everything there was so bureaucratic! I found it difficult to believe some of the things they told me about fashion, cosmetics, and hairstyles. However, in the coming months, particularly in the warmer part of the year, I came to agree that Shanghai did indeed have better fashions than I had seen in some of the cities in China and that these were meant for the local population as well and not solely for the export market.

The streets deserted during the cold months became very busy in the warmer seasons. Families would calmly stroll along, complete with grandmothers, fathers, uncles, aunts, and offspring, in short, the entire "clan." Grandmothers would use a large fan made from dried lotus leaves not only to provide cooling for themselves and their descendants while walking, but also to keep troublesome mosquitoes and other insects at bay. The clothing was lighter and more colourful. One saw many fancy fashion accessories, such as glittering brooches, colourful barrettes, necklaces, and earrings/clips with coloured stones. Brightly coloured socks adorned the feet of young women and girls. Transparent blouses made of nylon or some other synthetic material, complete with puffed sleeves and bows, rapidly sold out whenever a delivery arrived from Shanghai. Similarly, miniskirts, pants suits, skirts with shoulder straps, and dresses with frills and flounces quickly went over the counter.

The production that stemmed from the local clothes factories in Y. invariably looked homemade and even childish. If I happened to spot a pretty blouse or a fashionable skirt, it came from Shanghai. Shoes were really an area where fashion was nonexistent. In my estimation, the only attractive form of footwear was the cloth sandals with tapered heels. All other shoes looked clumsy and were roughly made, and the leather was of poor quality, not to mention the garish colours. Whether they were men's or women's shoes, whether the heels were high, low, or flat, the heel itself was always a shapeless clump. It was not surprising that the women acquired a waddling gait like "Daisy Duck." I could not have walked any more elegantly on these heels either. The men, especially the elderly ones, did not find the way the women walked esthetically pleasing either, as one man of about sixty confided to me one day. The younger "half of heaven" (a phrase by which Mao Tse-tung described the women of China) tried hard to break away from the so-called Mao style of blue jacket and pants and often dressed in a manner the cadres and functionaries would find provocative. The older generation, it seemed, remained true to the uniform fashion of long black or blue cloth trousers with white shirt or blouse, which was generally worn over the pants. Once, when I suggested to a young woman of about thirty years of age that she might like to tuck in her blouse or wear a pretty belt, she replied that she would not mind trying it but was afraid of the criticism she would incur from the older people. This fear went so far that she would wear the pretty and fashionable clothes she had bought in Shanghai only in her room. One day, with some embarrassment, she showed me a photo of herself. A pretty young woman, nicely made up, with an attractive hairdo, which made her look an entirely different person, smiled at me. Whereas another young woman about twenty-four years old took no notice of any criticism on the part of the old guard. She would come to classes powdered and made up and often wearing a fashionable new hairstyle; however, in winter she wore padded pants, several jumpers, and warm jackets, plus a man's overcoat. There was nothing smart about her appearance in winter, but during the summer she put on a mini fashion show almost every day. One day she came in an aubergine silk suit; the next she would wear knickers with a sloppy blouse. Then again she would turn up in a tight skirt with inverted pleats, a pale blue blouse, and a necktie. She really looked chic. When I asked her one day if she had bought her wardrobe in Shanghai she replied quite proudly that her mother had made it all for her. This young lady, in comparison with the other just described, had more self-confidence and was by no means dependent from any disapproval of the cadres, as she was not an employee or student of the institute. Whether she would work in that stylish outfit in her work unit I was not able to say.

There were many pleasant aspects of life here, such as the enjoyment of my teaching activities, the sunny weather, the nice people around me, and the sincerity of my students and my Chinese colleagues. But there were also less pleasant things, like a red thread (red tape) right through summer. For one thing, at least two or three times a week, on unpredictable days, there would be no water, no electricity, or sometimes neither. There was never an advance warning or ever an explanation. In order to have some independence from the unpredictable water supply I soon got into the habit of keeping my bathtub full of water; however, it was not suitable for drinking. Small grains of sand, bits of iron, or rust particles normally contaminated the very hard and milky-looking water. My drinking water I drew from the tap in the kitchen, if normally supplied, but I had to let it run for some while to get all the rusty-looking water out of the pipes.

In China one does not drink unboiled water, and I never did. My large kettle was big enough to fill two and a half of my five one-litre thermoses. This in turn meant that, depending on my rate of usage, I was forever boiling water. I got into this routine once I found out that my domestic helper had to carry hot water at some eighty degrees Celsius from the public campus boiler in large sprinkler cans all the way to my apartment, and I had to boil it again before using it, for instance, for tea, in any case. Every two weeks or so I had to scrape away the kettle fur and let the remaining deposits soak in diluted vinegar. It was a very messy business. The lack of water taught me, however, to use this precious liquid sparingly. I soon got into the habit of thinking twice before I used water, to make sure I did not waste it thoughtlessly.

While it was possible to lay down a reserve of water up to a point, there was no way to store electricity. If one failed to acquire a bunch of candles and a supply of matches, then it was quite likely one would have to spend considerable time in the evening sitting in the dark. This is what had happened to me the first time. In later months the many candles burning in my apartment gave me a feeling I otherwise only had during the time of Advent, the four weeks leading to Christmas, and certainly never before in the summer months, much less at thirty or more degrees. But there was nothing for it; all of us had to endure this trial. On many evenings the lessons in the lecture building had to be abandoned because of this, or else we would sit in my apartment by candlelight with perspiration pouring from us and held our conversational exercises despite every-thing. Mosquitoes, moths, and other insects were constantly fluttering about the lights. Somebody would then kill the insects, either with a flyswatter or with their bare hands. There was constant commotion, but it also was a good deal of fun; everybody would watch, fascinated, as someone or other would go after an insect in an unceasing hunt.

In early May my two domestic helpers arrived with a large mosquito net for my bed, as well as two upright electric fans. One was for my private and one for the "public" room. Four long bamboo poles, tied to the bedposts, held the closely woven pale blue net, which fell down right to the floor. The curtains were divided on one side and held open during the day by means of two gold-coloured metal hooks hanging from pink tassels. It was not only food for the soul to have such a cosy little "cave," but the net also gave me effective protection against various flying invaders as well as falling beetles, centipedes, and other insects, which were exploring the ceiling constantly in search of some-thing edible. There was one variety of beetles I treated with a special respect, very cautiously, and only if armed with a sheet of newspaper. The Chinese called them stink beetles. If one touches them or crushes them, they give off an utterly repulsive strong smell, which drifts away only very gradually.

If I saw such a beetle on my balcony, where I would rest during the lunch hour if it was too hot in the room, then in the beginning I would pour hot water over the greyish brown little creature with its long feelers, armoured body, and spotted wings, in the hope that this would kill it immediately without allowing it to exude any of its "perfume." But how mistaken I was! In death they stank all the more! And so I learned not to try to kill them, but rather to avoid them if I saw this species fly or crawl in my direction. Should one wander into my apartment, I always approached with a sheet of paper, in order to carefully coax it onto the paper and then out the window. As it grew warmer, however, I gave up these efforts. I was no longer able to maintain the upper hand against these hordes, and so I went on the retreat and abandoned the offensive. Nature indeed was much stronger!

The countless cockroaches no longer bothered me either. The kitchen was the El Dorado of these crawlies—as soon as I switched on the light they would vanish with incredible speed into various cracks or else play dead. They ranged in size from about two to five centimetres. Anything edible, such as sugar, noodles, or even salt, had to be kept in jars with screw-on lids. Since these insects were only a nuisance and not dangerous, I spared most of them.

But it was a different matter with the scorpions, which turned up one day in my kitchen and bathroom. I still remembered from my childhood how one had to deal with scorpions if confronted with them in a room. This one I saw one morning was some fifteen centimetres long in attack pose in front of my rubbish tin. Several baby scorpions were crawling around the big one. With boiling water poured over them they did not stand a chance. From then on I developed the habit of giving shoes and clothing a good shake before putting them on.

One day I heard a ceaseless rustling from the bath, from one of the straight pipes covered only with a metal mesh strainer. A rat was making his way upstairs. In the apartment below mine, the American couple were used to occasional visits from rats. So they advised me to place a large stone on the strainer, and from then on, though I heard the rats scratch, I could rest at ease that they would not be able to get into my rooms that way. In fact, I never had any rats in my room.

Despite the relatively better living conditions on our campus, rats lived in the thousands in the homes. Even in daylight, and much more so by night, they would scurry around the floors, over corridors, and crawl into cupboards, under and into the beds. On a number of occasions when I visited somebody I saw the rats vanish under a shelf on which saucepans with food in them stood or where other edibles were stored.

The rat problem is an almost insurmountable challenge in the everyday life of the population. There were and are rats everywhere. Cramped living conditions, inadequate hygiene, a poor drainage system, and inadequate garbage removal all helped the plague to multiply. A major campaign against these animals seemed to have met with little success. Rat poison and similar means were ineffective. Once I read in a Chinese newspaper how in the newborn section of a hospital four babies had been attacked and bitten to death by rats. And so the last resort was adopted, or so it appeared to me. The populace was encouraged by means of many articles and advertisements in daily papers to catch rats and add them to the daily diet as a source of protein. Rat meat, it was said, was tasty, easy to digest, and cheap, because you caught them yourself. A number of recipes accompanied the lengthy article.

Indeed, China suffers from lack of protein in the diet. If you take a good look at the various dishes that appear on private dining tables or on sale at various ordinary cookshops in the streets, you cannot help but notice that there is very little meat present. In the more expensive restaurants one finds the most delicious meals and wonderful menus. The normal consumer, Wang, and his family, like the great majority of the plain population, eat frugally and simply. The exception for more luxurious feasts would be weddings or other celebrations.

I personally experienced, for example, how one of my teachers and his wife breakfasted on rice gruel with vegetables preserved in salt and vinegar; others might breakfast on one or two steamed yeast buns with preserved vegetables. For lunch it was usual to fry fresh vegetables, flavoured with tasty soy sauce and served with rice. Occasionally a shredded omelette with dried shrimp or only the shells of them for flavouring might be added. The evening meal generally looked much the same.

It therefore became much easier for me to understand why the Chinese needed their midday nap, not just as a result of habit, and why a number of short breaks were necessary during the working day also. When I asked one of my students about this, he informed me that lack of protein affected concentration and endurance, and this was the reason people needed so much *xiuxi*, rest, revival. The relatively monotonous diet gives one little energy, and indeed vitamins and tracer elements are also in insufficient quantity. The man also told me that one of his colleagues sent abroad to the USA felt much stronger and endured working without feeling easily fatigued, since he stayed there for a lengthy time.

By comparison the food served to us foreign teachers was almost in the luxury class, although not always to our taste. Sometimes quite unrecognizable dishes appeared on the table, so I often asked what it was before helping myself. I was not always convinced by the answers I got, particularly where meat was concerned. On a number of occasions I had the feeling that the piece of meat on the plate quite easily could be dog meat. And so, despite assurances that it was "the finest meat from a suckling pig" or, on another enquiry, it was meat from a "large unnamed bird," I left the much-praised piece on the plate. Whether it was supposed to be pork or poultry, somehow the meat looked different from what it was described as, and the bones seemed to come from quite the skeleton of a quite different animal. It was certainly edible and, in fact, did not taste too bad, but in my eating habits there was no place for dog meat or fancy birds.

We did not have to pay for our meals. The foreign bureau paid 3.30 yuan per day to the kitchen for each of us. If, by prior arrangement with the kitchen, we did not take the meals we were entitled to, then the above-mentioned amount was refunded to us by the kitchen. However, no refund was paid if we only skipped one or two meals on a given day.

After an initial period of becoming accustomed to the various inadequacies already described, I found that I managed quite well in coping with everyday life in China. The circumstances in which I found myself compelled me to change my attitudes, and very gradually I was able to adjust.

Whereas in the beginning I would still try quite actively to change something, even though it would not fit in with the day-to-day routine, later on I developed a more relaxed viewpoint and so I discovered that life under the prevailing meagre conditions had some quite positive aspects as well. Instead of becoming agitated about the many insect pests, I just left them in peace; I found ways and means whereby I could live with the lack of electricity and lack of water; the bureaucratic obstacles were overcome by learning to operate the little back doors. And so I found myself slipping more and more into the Chinese way and reacted accordingly. There was one particular circumstance I found difficult to accept, but in the end I had to concede to defeat.

After the many beautifully coloured butterflies had hatched and started fluttering about the trees, shrubs, and flowers, one day a small motorised lorry with a large tank drove onto the campus. A spraying team was about to spray all flora with an insecticide. And from that day on not a single butterfly was to be seen fluttering. I have no idea how many other, and equally useful, insects were destroyed in this way. I only know that the fine spray from the jets did not agree with me at all.

Quite by accident I happened to stumble through such a shower as I was walking past a man who was spraying busily. The wind blew the fine droplets over in my direction. A few hours later I found that I had little red pustules on my arms and legs. My fear that these were caused by the spray was not shared by the Chinese, and one young woman doctor thought that I must be suffering from lack of vitamin B. Thoughtfully she brought me a few little bags of vitamin B_6 and B_{12} tablets from the clinic pharmacy, plus some vitamin C as an added precaution.

During the entire summer until well into October the spraying column thoroughly drenched every tree, shrub, or other plant at least once a week. As soon as I heard the sound of the engine in the distance I would close all my windows. In spite of this, the penetrating chemical smell came through every little opening and always left me with a throat irritation and slight cough.

I enquired about the composition of the fluid and was told that it was certainly not poisonous DDT. They said that they use DDV. (Whatever those initials stood for they could not tell me.) In any case, they assured me, it was entirely harmless to humans. "We protect the flora and guard the environment," they said. On my asking a higher-ranked person concerned with the campus administration about it, he conceded that in past years major campaigns from the air had led to devastating consequences for the bird population. Whole flocks of birds had fallen dead to the ground. But "Today we use DDV." The fact that butterflies were killed off by the thousands was not regarded as so serious: "After all, they will be back next year." So, there I was.

Was this particular insecticide really harmless to humans? Was it only coincidence that I developed a rash, cough, or throat irritation? The workman handling the insecticide wore no protective clothing of any kind, nor did he have eye goggles. But everything came down to a matter of habit with the populace, whether it concerned toxic waste gases from burning coal, insecticides, or other impairment. The concepts of resistance, rebellion against something, and working together in order to achieve something were not in the current vocabulary. Since it was all in vain, there was no point doing so.

By and by I, too, had to learn that my view or attitude led nowhere and that it harmed only myself being angry or feeling annoyed, because it was I who became upset and not the others. And so my attitude changed. When I was asked whether I had settled in I would simply reply, "It is a matter of getting used to it." Indeed, I found that I did get used to many things, and my reply was not so ironic as it might have appeared.

To cope with all the bureaucratic procedures and resulting delays, this, too, I had to learn. It took an incredibly long time before anything at all was accomplished. If one lacked the patience to handle this, then the only alternative was to face the consequences by doing it oneself. Everybody was most helpful in such a situation. The Chinese I had to deal with themselves didn't want to take any responsibilities, but if somebody else was willing to take it on then they would side with the person enthusiastically and help as best as they could within their ability, mainly by torrents of words against the bureaucrats.

In fact, I found it sometimes most enjoyable to battle with seemingly boneheaded administrative employees. On the other hand, if I was subject to time pressures or something really important was involved, then it was anything but pleasant. For example, the language department had at its disposal two well-equipped language laboratories with headphones, microphone, a switching device, enabling each individual learner sitting at his or her own table to use various techniques. The teacher also had the use of a screen with the relevant switching gear in order to record or reproduce the various texts, plus an illuminated pointer to use on the monitor, on which the desired portion of the text could be programmed to appear. Two speaker boxes on the wall provided stereo reproduction. Surely all this equipment had to offer other possibilities besides just listening to the text via speaker or headphones. Unfortunately, nobody was able to explain how it all worked. I asked for user instructions and was told by way of a reply that the other teachers used only the one programme. Towards the end of the semester I discovered quite by chance that there was a manual in the departmental library. I tried to borrow it and thus familiarise myself with the many techniques one could use with the equipment. But the mere thought of having the manual out of the library on loan was unthinkable. However, I could read it in the library, and since the language lab was right next door surely it would be no trouble to run back and forth! With a lot of effort I finally managed to persuade the woman department head how nonsensical this was and was handed the booklet at last, but only for one hour. This got me nowhere. In the end I abandoned this idea and went back to managing with the very simplest measures. It was a real pity, because the equipment was never properly utilised and I imagine that such imported Japanese electronics did not come cheap. The mere fact that I was permitted to take the booklet into another room for a whole hour almost bordered on the miraculous!

I was able to strike up quite a good relationship with the female head librarian, who belonged to a Korean minority from the northeast of China. Once I got to know her a little better and understood the way she worked, I soon learned how I had to go about achieving the desired result with her. To get anything done immediately, such as photocopying, was quite impossible, even though she was only sitting at her desk reading the newspaper. Operating the copier myself was not an option, because that would have interfered with her rights. So I adapted myself to her way of doing things, bringing her my work in plenty of time and discussing with her when I would need the copies. She never let me down, and our good cooperation was to continue during the following semester also.

I discovered that as long as I gave one of my Chinese coworkers sufficient time, then I could usually depend on it being done. Just as I had to battle with the bureaucracy, the Chinese staff had to do likewise, and in fact I found that I was more likely to be granted some minor concession than they were. For example, my fellow German teacher often asked me to borrow a special book for her from the library, because she was not allowed to do so. Students and younger teaching staff (say, twenty to thirty) would use one of the more influential older teachers in order to obtain a particular book from the department library. Whether it worked the same way at the main library I could not tell, for I was never in need of a book there.

Trivial and Unusual Occurrences

Soon after my arrival I gave up taking my breakfast in our teachers' eating nook. The cook, who considered himself my compatriot, as we both came from the same city, Tianjin, suggested that surely it would be more convenient if I took my breakfast with me on the previous evening and then fixed it myself. He would supply me with an eighth of a litre of milk, butter, and eggs, and a *mantou* could also be found just for me. I must add at this point that the cook had learnt his trade in the early years, i.e., before the Communist takeover, in one of the best hotels in Tianjin, the British Astor House. After that he had worked for a number of European families as number-one cook before being allocated to the institute after 1949. He treated me with every courtesy, asking my favourite dishes and often sending his assistant over to ask me if I was enjoying my meal and was it enough? The assistant also came from Tianjin. One day I ventured the question whether by chance he had also learned to bake bread. Lo and behold, he had indeed, and from that day we were given bread. It was baked from unbleached flour and baking powder, but it had a light brown crust and tasted quite different from the yeast bun *mantou*. Breakfast became a delight! Each evening I would receive milk and two eggs, butter, and bread sufficient for a week or so. The only thing he could not help me with was jam. Such a thing was unknown in Y. But I was not to be fussy, being delighted to have what was almost a normal breakfast for a European. Later on it was sometimes difficult to obtain a butter ration. I was to learn that the kitchen bought butter in Beijing for the exclusive use of Western visitors to the institute. In Y., butter was unavailable. If a member of the kitchen staff happened to be travelling north, then he would bring back the desired quantity of butter at the request of the chief cook, my compatriot. Actually, according to the regulations, we were not entitled to butter, but who was going to control the *chef de cuisine?* The Americans had been living on the campus for six months already and had not "tasted such delights for ages." They were issued neither milk nor butter, and milk was not to become available to them in the future either. Milk was rationed. Only infants, the old, and the weak were entitled to it. A doctor's certificate was needed in order to obtain 125 millilitres of milk daily. Next to the dining hall was a wooden structure with doors that were always locked, at least the times I passed it. For a long time I did not know what it was for, until one day the cook told me about the daily handing out of the milk ration. Each day the device was opened between 7:00 and 7:30 for this purpose. Nobody was entitled to more than an eighth of a litre. He, as chief cook, was issued several bottles for use in connection with his "foreign cooking skills," of which he gave me a bottle every day. As this was far from being a normal entitlement, I used to show him my appreciation by way of giving him foreign, usually American, cigarettes, which I would buy in the city in the hotel for foreigners, much to his delight. And so we were all quite content, and life was somewhat enjoyable under this arrangement in what was otherwise a very sparse everyday life in China.

Until now it had never been customary in China to drink milk or eat dairy products. Yoghurt and cheese had only very recently started to find their way into the Chinese diet, but there were few consumers—they could be counted on the fingers of one hand. One of my students came from Inner Mongolia, although he was careful to point out that he was Han Chinese and had been used to milk and cheese since childhood, his father having been in charge of a "dairy factory." Thus cheese was known to his family, and his two-year-old son had to drink a daily quantity of milk, albeit made from powder. Dried milk was readily available, although only heavily sweetened, and could only be dissolved in hot water. A 5,000-gram pack cost some four yuan, which made it a luxury for most people. But major campaigns aimed at educating young parents have done much to improve the nutrition of infants. Even the simple man in the street today knows that milk is a source of protein and that animal protein is an important component in a balanced diet. But so far they still avoid butter and cheese, although young people in the cities and students who have returned from Western countries have developed a taste for such products.

Soon after my arrival one of my household helpers brought me an electric boiling ring. It was actually forbidden to cook inside the apartments, except by special arrangement with the foreign bureau. This meant that one had the food and sustenance money paid out in cash and from then on must provide for oneself. In any event, my "pearl" brought me the hot plate with the comment that I might want to cook something different occasionally. The hot plate was just the thing for toasting *mantous*, because cold ones are difficult to digest. Up until now I had been toasting slices of *mantou* for my breakfast impaled on a fork between the heating spirals of my large room heater. Now I could do my toasting on two forks laid across the ceramic surrounding the heating spirals of my hot plate. Unfortunately, this method would cause a short circuit from time to time and I would have to play electrician. The spirals were really quite brittle and gave up the ghost rather easily. Repeatedly pulled apart and patched, they gave off less and less heat with the passage of time, and it took an incredibly long time to boil water or even make toast. And so one day I asked my houseman if he could help. And indeed, he succeeded, after much trying, in obtaining a brand-new spiral for me. With it he repaired the boiling ring, and from then until the end of my stay it never failed again.

As already mentioned, I had two domestic helpers in my one-person household. The older woman did her work without much enthusiasm, preferring to stand around and take every opportunity to converse with me. The younger girl stayed nearby as much as she could in order to make quite sure she did not miss anything. It was the older woman who gave me the keys to my new room and helped me with the cleaning after, with much effort, I got the "green light" to move from the northern to the southern room. But after that event I never saw her in my apartment again. I heard that she had wanted to visit her family somewhere north of Beijing and had gone away to do so. Many months later I met her again while shopping outside the main gate. I asked her why she had not been coming and why there was also a change of the young girl some weeks later. She told me that the head of the foreign bureau, Mrs. Z., had caused her a lot of annoyance, had abused her and accused her of acting without instructions because she had not only given me the key to the room, but helped me with the cleaning as well. Such treatment and loss of face was more than she could bear, and so she had given up this job: "The pay was two yuan per day, meagre enough, and then to be abused!" As for the young girl, she could not say anything, as she came from the rural district outside the gate.

Looking back on it, I suspect that she was dismissed on of account of her "incorrect conduct" towards a foreigner. The young girl told me quite openly that she came from a peasant family in the vicinity and her wages were one yuan per day. Her family consisted of her parents and several brothers and sisters. The older ones were mostly married, and she, as the second youngest, was thinking of getting married, but it was quite difficult to find a suitable man. Her parents would not let her out of the house and were trying hard to find her a suitable husband. At home it was "dreadfully boring"; she had to look after her youngest brother and do her share of the housework. That was already one reason why she would be happy to be married, so that she no longer had to take orders from her parents. When I asked her how old she was, she said, "Twenty-two." I would have thought her no more than eighteen. One day she accompanied me to a nearby market held outside the gates of another work unit, in this case a petrochemical plant. We pedalled away together, leaving the campus via one of the guarded gates. We went shopping together, too. She cycled along, head held high and greeting acquaintances left and right, happy at her special status accompanying a foreigner, or so I had the impression. I am sure the Cerberuses at the gate must have reported our trip to the foreign bureau.

I was so sorry that she also did not come anymore, not only because she had promised to introduce me to her parents and her entire family, but also because she was just a nice and open-hearted young girl, unspoilt. She wanted to show me the farm also—she just wanted to invite me to her home. My concerns were dismissed with a casual wave and her innocent comment was: "Who could have anything against that?" Her good and close contact with a foreigner was to be her undoing, and this was an experience I was to have a number of times. "Friendships" were tolerated as long as they served some purpose and had been sanctioned. Whenever I had social contact with people, simple people outside the campus, there was usually just the one meeting, sometimes two. Sooner or later it fizzled out to nothing. If I happened to meet them again somewhere, they would politely look the other way or avoid me with a quick nod of the head. In order to avoid causing them any more trouble I acted the same way.

My first two female helpers were replaced by a man of thirty and a woman of about fifty years. I got along quite well with them both. The houseman obtained the heating spiral for my hot plate, repaired my defective shower, and made himself generally useful with heavier work. The woman did the dusting, which meant that she used a dirty-looking moist rag to distribute the grimy layer uniformly over the furniture. For very little money I bought some towelling cloths and asked her to use these instead, but to no avail—I could not persuade her to do it. She continued to use her rag, sparing the "good" little towels, so everything remained as it was. After that I would wash the rag now and again in the hot used suds of my washing machine, which at least gave me a feeling of acceptable cleanliness. She would not understand this peculiar quirk on my part, but during the course of our association she got used to it. Sometimes she would even wash out the used rags on her own initiative, and she beamed with pleasure as she told me about this. She was really a good soul, kind, helpful, and always ready to gossip. I had the feeling I could rely on her. It was she who alerted the woman doctor when I took ill a few days after the start of the semester with a slight fever and the beginning of a touch of bronchitis and was in bed when she came to fix the rooms. She bought apples for me when I had an appetite for fresh fruit. Much later by chance I found out that the apples were from her own supply; in March good apples were no longer available. I was not able to repay her the cost of the apples, as she would have been offended. When I went on vacation that summer she tended my plants and looked after my apartment. For my birthday she staged a big spring cleaning, including the corridor and the staircase, sweeping the balconies and mopping out the whole apartment.

But I had to resign myself that I could not get her to abandon her habit of rinsing the mop in the toilet bowl. I had to be satisfied that she no longer used the kitchen sink for this purpose, leaving the dripping wet mop draped over the taps to dry. We agreed that the kitchen balcony was a much better place for drying. During the summer it was sometimes impossible to retrieve the mop from the balcony, because torrential showers would turn the balcony into a pool in seconds. During the construction of the building somebody had forgotten to provide a means of draining it. A rusty dustpan served its purpose here, and repeated emptying of it over the edge of the balcony would eventually enable us to get to the mop without getting our feet too wet.

A Chinese mop is made of countless strips of rag tied to a broom handle. It is neither wrung out nor soaked in a detergent of whatever kind. By dunking the mop into the toilet bowl and dragging it back and forth over the stone floor the woman managed to distribute the dust evenly into all the corners. The remaining dampness spread a sharp, penetrating smell. A further dunking to rinse the mop completed the cleaning procedure. In order to let the mop drip dry, she laid it diagonally over the balcony railing—a long trail of water from the bathroom to the balcony showed the way. During the hot and humid summer I stopped this method of cleaning, as the apartment was moist enough as it was.

One day I had visitors. The cook's assistant had been charged with inspecting the kitchen cupboards of the foreign teachers. Allegedly there were a number of items missing from the teachers' eating nook, such as plates, bowls, and cutlery. We were suspected of having taken the items. We had noticed that the salt- and pepper-shakers had disappeared from our tables, also the container with toothpicks, the box with paper serviettes, and the plastic flowers in their vase. When we asked our serving girl about this she just shrugged her shoulders. So the inspection by the foreign bureau was to be understood in this way, but it was also possible that the head of the bureau was annoyed about something concerning the foreign teachers, and thus this was her little revenge. We gave the cook anything we could spare, so that he would not have to go away empty-handed and risk further trouble with Mrs. Z. by not having found anything belonging to the eating nook. The cook's assistant thought the whole operation rather silly, saying, "I don't think you would

steal these ugly cheap things or the blunt knives." It is probable the whole haul failed to satisfy Mrs. Z. A few days later she
not only stormed into my apartment in person, but without saying much she raced to the kitchen cupboard, tore open the
doors, and grabbed everything movable to be stowed in the large
bag she had brought with her. I had to order her to stop, because
she was also taking the glasses and other things I had bought
myself. I very firmly forbade her from ever entering my apartment again without advance notice and a good reason. Quite
strangely, from then on she was very careful in her relations with
me and avoided me as much as she could without seeming too
impolite. I was very glad that I no longer had to argue or negotiate with her over day-to-day matters. We both kept our distance and observed the rules of polite behaviour, but beneath
the surface there was little love lost between us.

A few days later, we took our plates, cups, etc., from the
main kitchen. They were part of the apartment inventory, and
any major shortage would have meant problems on departure.
The chief cook indicated by touching his temple that he thought
Mrs. Z. was not quite sane. He made no secret of his annoyance
over arguments with her over alleged overexpenditures for our
meals. If she had had her way we would have had only rice gruel
and salted vegetables. Oh, what the heck!

Somehow the president must have heard about the incident, and a few days later he bade me see him in his office on
the pretext of making a regular report. I told him that I did not
want to bother him with such trivialities, but he insisted on
being fully informed about the smallest detail. He remarked
that the private affairs were not his concern, but we were there
as guests and put up with so much inconvenience in order to
help China. He therefore felt obliged to help make our stay as
pleasant as he could. He gave a hint that I should talk to such
and such a person; he also told me that management had the
intention of appointing a joint head of the foreign bureau to

work alongside Mrs. Z., of the same rank as she. He was a man "of good education and good manners, who also understands English." This finally occurred in June. Mrs. Z. was allowed to travel to the USA, and then the new appointee visited me. Mr. Y., a very likable and pleasant man, was a physics professor, and his wife was the language department's section head for English—we already knew one another. Both of them were particularly delighted people, and during my stay a most sincere relationship was to develop among the three of us, finding expression mostly in mutual visits and telephone conversations. We tacitly agreed to adhere to an unspoken rule that we would keep our official business and private friendship quite separate, which served the latter well.

In mid-May an excursion to the Mount Tai in neighbouring Shandong Province was "ordered." Without any prior arrangements or even notice, we all had to be at an appointed place at a specified time on the day in question, and a 100 percent roll call was taken for granted. We foreign teachers, with one exception, were not at all happy with the arrangement. For example, I had fixed that day to hold a test for my students, and postponing it would necessitate a major rearrangement of our timetable. The teacher below me had to make recordings in the language laboratory and her husband was busy with a term assignment on that day, whilst the Japanese teacher, Mrs. S., had to complete some urgent preparations for some examination. We four requested a postponement, but the foreign bureau would not budge. They did offer, if necessary, to arrange "leave of absence from duty" for the day with the head of the language department.

Certainly by Western understanding it would have been no problem to postpone the recording work or the other preparations, if possible. But the teacher had been waiting for weeks to do her work in the language lab, and she was not ready to give up an available time slot, obtained after weeks of wrangling, for a "command" excursion. Her husband could not postpone his assignment either, because his coworkers had to come from outside the city and anyone who understands the distances in China and the deprivations the Chinese take upon themselves for such a journey will not act irresponsibly and let people come on such a trip for nothing. Ordinary citizens do not have telephones, so there is no way of letting them know either. We therefore presented a united front and refused to budge. This firm stand on our part must have made the foreign bureau feel somewhat unsure, and they realised that they could not just order us about at their whim like that. Yet our stand had no effect as far as future arrangements were concerned, and we were to find again and again that we were faced with a fait accompli.

We did, however, manage to negotiate a later departure time, and so on the appointed day we five teachers took off into the mountains, with two companions from the foreign bureau. One was a young woman who spoke not a single word of any foreign language but was considered a more suitable person for any potential "women's problems," i.e., in search of the toilet, etc., the other a male interpreter for German and English. The rail journey to Tai'an, a town at the foot of Mount Tai, was about two hundred kilometers and took some three and one half hours.

Tai Shan, or Mount Tai, is one of the nine holy mountains in China. Climbing this mountain, which is some two thousand metres high, constitutes part of a fulfilled life according to Chinese thinking. Confucius meditated on the top of the mountain, and his thoughts on philosophy are said to have matured there. He admired the sunrise and sang about the passing clouds and heavenly white mist, as countless poets and writers have done after him. The many thousands of pilgrims do the same thing. They undertake the difficulties of the climb so that once they have reached the summit, they can allow the beauty of nature and the cosmos to have its effect on them. Young and old alike tackle the many thousands of steps to the peak.

We arrived around 7:00 P.M.; it was already getting dark. The mountain was covered in low clouds. After we had been put up in the hotel and had our evening meal, I took a walk to the start of the climb, already coming across many people. Everybody was streaming towards the mountain, the young with rucksacks, the older with bundles on sticks over their shoulders. It was about 9:00 P.M. I asked one young family with a boy of about seven years where they were all going in the dark. The woman answered very cheerfully that they hoped to reach the summit in time for the sunrise at around 3:00 A.M. I was impressed. The black darkness did not seem to worry them, and there was not even a suggestion of light to be seen anywhere, except the few flashes now and then from flashlights. They climbed the mountain in pitch-darkness, oblivious to the slippery steps (it had been raining) and the many damaged sections. I wished them success and went on my way down the street and came across an old woman, hobbling along on her lotus feet (as the bound feet of olden times were poetically called), in a stooped position, using a bamboo stick as support. She wanted to get to the top. "Before I get any older and die I must climb Tai Shan," was her comment to me, delivered with a southern accent. She was with other members of her family.

Next morning we, too, were expected to climb the mountain. I was in no mood for this, and in any case, I prefer to admire mountains from a distance rather than at close quarters. The couple felt no desire at all to break their legs in the attempt, and neither did the Japanese teacher. The interpreter thus went up alone with the only remaining teacher, an American. The young woman for "women's problems" left us in the lurch, also wanting to climb the mountain once in her life. The four of us who remained behind contented ourselves with a visit to a nearby monastery and a stroll through the small city. As it was not too hot that day, it was not unpleasant being outdoors.

Other than the cost of meals and drinks the excursion had cost us nothing. The foreign bureau organised everything, handled the daily problems of foreign workers in their care, and arranged for entertainment to break the monotony of everyday life, including excursions, supply of cinema tickets, etc., regardless of whether one wants to go. What was ordered was ordered. Individual wishes or points of view might be, but not necessarily, considered if they did not happen to suit the foreign bureau.

For some weeks the couple living below me had wanted to visit a Chinese theatre downtown. She had heard that a group of young actors was performing *The Prince and the Pauper*, by Mark Twain, in Chinese. Repeatedly she asked the foreign bureau to obtain tickets for her. Time and again she was offered various excuses, until eventually, in desperation, she turned to one of her Chinese friends, asking her to buy the tickets on her behalf. But the woman tried in vain. She was told that the performances were only for young people and perhaps the foreign bureau could help, i.e., she was back where she started. Her friend was so thoughtful as to buy tickets for a Chinese opera instead and invited the couple to this spectacle. The foreign bureau somehow got wind of this and was not to be outdone, so on the next day, without informing us at all, tickets for an acrobatics show were bought, and we were expected to go to it. None of us had the time for this, and the show was not so interesting that we would have cancelled our classes for it. The organiser left, obviously quite offended, not understanding why we would not comply with their arrangements. For the remainder of the semester they left us alone then.

Campus life was regulated by the loudspeaker. Every morning at six o'clock it blared us from sleep. A marchlike piece of music, then news, the weather report, and a melody for morning exercises took up most of the thirty minutes at the start of each day. The remaining thirty minutes brought one or two advertising spots in the form of a Chinese operetta–style dialogue and many quotations of important party secretaries and similar personages. Generally these were exhortations to increase production in the spirit of the Communist and party ideology or to develop technology faster and better so as to enable China to overhaul Western industrialised nations. A local weather report and a time signal concluded the transmission, which occurred throughout the semester at this time.

The university, like all major public institutions, had its own radio station. Until 7:00 A.M. each day they relayed the early news from the city broadcasting station, and at midday (11:45) the campus station broadcast local campus events. Here was where one heard about good films the theatre was offering or that the management for "domestic affairs" had bought a large load of oranges for the campus population, which could be bought at such and such place for a fixed price. On another occasion the loudspeaker announced that two young ocelots had escaped from the nearby zoo and were hiding in the mountains. Parents were advised not to let their children play there without supervision. But mostly the content was party quotations and propaganda about following political guidelines for achieving success in one's studies, thereby enabling one to better "serve the people" in the future. Any meeting called at short notice was announced this way, as were honourable mentions of particularly industrious and exemplary teachers and workers. At 2:00 P.M. the loudspeaker started again to wake everyone for work, which began half an hour later. At this time only a few pieces of music of Western origin were played. "YMCA" and other disco songs were hits at that time and came over the air almost every day. It became somewhat wearing. At six o'clock in the evening came the last news bulletin and political indoctrination. After that one could be assured that the transmitter would take a well-earned rest unless something extraordinary happened. For example, at nine one evening, I heard that there were isolated cases of meningitis in downtown Y., an unusual report at such a late hour. One should avoid unnecessary visits to the city, especially with small children, and listen to further announcements, we were told.

When I asked my students whether they listened to and followed everything that came over the loudspeaker all I got in reply were tired smiles. I was told that people in Y. were particularly backwards and that in other major cities, especially the big "Western" cities like Beijing, Shanghai, and Canton, this evil had long been abolished. When I discussed the weather report with them one day and mentioned the temperature—thirty-eight degrees Celsius according to the broadcast—one student remarked that I should not pay too much attention and I would do better to rely on the thermometer I had brought with me from Germany, because false information was often transmitted. There happened to be a rule that work might cease once the temperature went above 40 degrees, so "deliberate misleading" ensured a good roll call in the workplace. In this context I recall another discussion, which had occurred some time previously. I was told that during the great earthquake in northern China in 1976 the needle on the Richter scale went well past the recorded value of 7; however, the strength of the quake had been reported internationally as 6. There allegedly was an international agreement to the effect that once an earthquake exceeds a specific value, then various international aid organisations would become active. China however, according to my informant, would not allow anyone to enter its territories for such a reason, and therefore the reported value had to be under the critical figure, agreement or no agreement. At the time at least 1 million people were said to have lost their lives. Be that as it may. In my class I had a young man who survived the earthquake as a twelve-year-old child under a collapsed house. Several days later—or was it hours; he could no longer remember with certainty—he was dug out and rescued.

In mid-June a national football (soccer) competition for

juniors took place. Since the city Y. did not have its own playing fields, the games were played in the sporting arena of our institute. Despite the heat, the stadium was packed with sports fans at midday. On that particular day a team from Beijing was to play against Jiangsu Province—and Beijing lost. There was absolutely no end to the cheering, as everybody yelled themselves hoarse with delight, as the city of Y. is one of the cities in Jiangsu. I could hear the thousands of cheering voices all the way to my apartment.

Football fans react in much the same way everywhere, and two students got into a violent argument over the victory and defeat, which deteriorated into physical violence and gave the game so cheerfully begun a dreadful twist. The other fans who witnessed the confrontation were able to separate the contestants with great difficulty, and each eventually went his own way. Unfortunately, the two of them met again later that evening after dinner outside the students' dining hall. The young man from Beijing pushed his adversary so suddenly and unexpectedly that the latter lost his balance and fell on the stone steps head first. Blood started to seep from his ears, and the young man lay unconscious. Frightened by this, the other ran off to get help, but as it was quite late there were few people about. After a while the patient was carried to the clinic. However, it was decided that he could not be treated in the campus clinic and he was transferred to the main city hospital, where he died a few days later without having regained consciousness. The student from Beijing who had caused this tragic accident was arrested the same day and imprisoned in solitary confinement. Although none of us teachers or students knew either of the two young men the matter continued to occupy our minds for several days afterwards. The wife of one of my students was a doctor and had rendered first aid immediately after the patient had been taken to the hospital; even after that she received details of the affair as it continued. According to her information, the accused was in poor mental condition and it was feared that he might attempt suicide. He was the son of a highly respected academic family, of which many members were well-known doctors. One person predicted a sentence of nine years' banishment, and the young man's career was finished. The deceased was the son of a peasant family and was the only surviving son; the family and clan had thus invested a great deal of money and effort in the career of their promising progeny. Whether any legal proceedings between the two families ever took place I was never able to find out.

The weeks passed and soon the summer holidays were to come. The test papers had been written, the marks recorded on a large special form, and that form locked up in the office of the responsible officer who held the function of a subordinate leader. My students heard nothing of their marks. As already mentioned, we had spent the last few lessons watching foreign films. We were all tired and exhausted from the long semester, which had started on the eleventh of March and, except for Sundays and the May 1 Labour Day, continued without a break until the twenty-first of July.

I wanted to get away. The heat was becoming ever more unbearable, although according to one woman, with forty degrees Celsius in the shade and relative humidity of about ninety percent it had not yet peaked. Between the end of July and mid-August the weather could be described as hot only if the rice straw mat that served as a surface for sleeping on literally stuck to your body and you had the feeling you were sleeping on a hot coal. I was already heartily tired of constantly changing my soaking wet T-shirts, and even frequent showers in lukewarm water, which were supposedly cooling, brought no relief. My ventilators were running at full speed day and night, at least when I had electricity. I longed for a rest, to relax, for pleasant coolness. I also longed to be with Europeans, people with whom I could converse as an equal partner. I longed for a neatly set table. In short, I longed for the Occidental culture and aesthetics to which I was accustomed. In the surroundings where I had spent the last six months I always had to be an example, always the teacher, in a position of honour, and informant about Western know-how. Certain behaviour was expected of me, and this meant that I always had to reply with enthusiasm and selfless detachment to intelligent and not so intelligent questions, lend an open ear to all who wanted something from me, and, if possible, organise a stay in Germany for each individual. I was becoming more and more irritable, and less and less inclined to offer advice or linguistic help. I was exhausted and felt quite burnt out.

On the twenty-second of July I travelled to Beidaihe, a lovely seaside resort on the Bohai (Bo Sea), which I remembered from my childhood and which is situated northeast of Tianjin. With my prior booking and payment of a deposit, the hotel, which was the diplomatic guest house, had reserved a double room for me, even though I had requested only a single one. I had to pay the full price of thirty-six yuan, to which costs of meals and drinks had to be added. I booked for two weeks. It was sheer joy to hear German and English sounds. I struck up a friendship with three American women. Together we visited a Mongolian restaurant, which was located inside a large yurt. The serving girls were Mongolians in their typical dress, alert and very friendly. The kitchen was in a separate yurt, and smoke rose through the open flap in the canvas roof. We had to force ourselves to use the cups and chopsticks, as everything looked so grubby, but the various dishes that filled the plates to the brim tasted delicious. We ate mutton prepared in different ways, stewed in slices, shredded with a spicy sauce, or stuffed into pockets of flour dough and boiled. With the food we drank lukewarm beer from the bottle, having seen how the glasses were rinsed. There was room for at least fifteen diners in the yurt. Seated on low stools around a small round table, we were able to dine very pleasantly. The prices were unbelievably low, and the Mongols charged us foreigners the same prices as the local population. Finally we were farewelled by the entire clan, with great honour and ceremony and with best wishes for the future, as they were hopeful they would meet us again soon. I have rarely experienced such natural and sincere hospitality, taken as a matter of course, other than with friends.

In marked contrast to this stood a visit to a restaurant that once belonged to a German master pastry cook and still carried the German name Kiessling. Around lunchtime—it was just before one o'clock—we tried to order something. The waiting staff, quite attractively dressed and heavily made up, explained that we could not order anymore because the kitchen was closed. When I objected that according to the sign outside lunch was served until 2:00 P.M. a woman replied with rare cheekiness that the sign was from last year. We were the only foreigners. There were Chinese diners at several other tables, who were busily studying the menu and ordering as they wished. After an unpleasant argument, she finally brought a menu and told us to select something. The Americans told me that they had had similar experiences a number of times, but not being able to speak the language, they had always been at a disadvantage.

There was one little incident, early one morning on the beach, I still smile about today. I wanted to take back some small souvenirs from my holiday for my "pearl" and other friends. I knew that one of the things they would much appreciate would be a nice figurine made from seashells, and the itinerant pedlar I happened to come across just about to spread out his wares on the ground was just what I was looking for. Barefoot I stood before him and asked the various prices. Without looking up, he told me. The items I had selected ranged in price between seventy fen and 2.50 yuan. But when I asked him to pack the several items I had chosen together he looked up. For someone to select ten pieces at once, without even any complaints about the high prices or attempts to haggle, was obviously contrary to his selling experience. Quite puzzled by this, he asked me again what I wanted and then, without even blushing, declared that he had made a mistake with the prices and instead of some seven or eight yuan I would have to pay twice that amount. Without any further ado I just left him sitting there, but I could not resist telling him, "There seem to be different prices for feet and face. You can keep your goods," and going my way.

Two weeks later I left Beidaihe and travelled by rail to Beijing, in order to spend a few days with my Chinese friends in their home. It was the first time I had received such an open invitation. It had become possible to have almost familiar personal contacts with the Chinese. If I compare this situation to our first meeting back in 1980 and my subsequent visit five years later, then it was noticeable how much more freely my friend was able to move about and behave. Back in those days he did not even venture into our hotel without first reporting to the gatekeeper with all due reverence and having his name entered in the visitors' register.

The rail journey from Beidaihe to Beijing took some eight hours, and I arrived in the evening at the same sparsely lit railway station I had left from six months ago to go to Y. in Jiangsu. The elder son of the family was there to meet me, and in the midst of a torrential shower we rode by taxi along the wide streets to their house. It was a very hearty reunion. The family would not even consider the thought that I might stay in the guest house operated by the university, and under no circumstances would I be allowed to move out of their house. So I stayed and was able to gain an insight into everyday life of a Chinese family at very close quarters, although this particular family enjoyed relatively high social status in comparison to the majority of the population and conditions in their home were thus probably not typical. Both husband and wife came from well-known families of scholars, who had had to endure a good

deal of suffering during the Cultural Revolution. The couple
found it quite painful to talk about this and must have had some
dreadful experiences. The elder son, who was now thirty years
old, was not permitted to learn anything at all during those terrible years, nor was his younger brother. Like many others from
the same social strata, they were banished for more than five
years to a rural area, where they had to perform heavy physical work. The family was torn apart, their house requisitioned
and given over to strangers, common people with a simple background. Although the family must have endured much during
this time, there was scarcely a bitter word uttered. I found the
same attitude from others, many of whom had fared even worse.
After the Cultural Revolution the family received reimbursement. An apartment of some ninety square metres on the
ground floor of a house for four families, with a small garden,
became their new home. The flat consisted of three and a half
rooms with a dark hallway, a small bathroom, and a tiny
kitchen, but the main rooms were bright and airy. As is the custom elsewhere in China, houses on the campus of this university were built of concrete and in box form. This particular
multifamily house had been built in the 1950s and followed the
Soviet architectural model. These functional rectangular buildings of brick with red hip roofs were intended for Soviet advis-
ers and experts, who came to China soon after the collapse of
the KMT government in order to help her rebuild for a better
future. These houses showed their age by way of various defects
and a neglected exterior. Since the occupants of the houses, who
all belonged to the higher academic ranks, were not responsible for the maintenance of the buildings and management of the
university evidently did not feel responsible for this either, in
effect nobody cared, now or in the past, for repairs and the like.
The bathroom was a permanently damp oasis. Several times a
day the housewife had to empty the various buckets and bowls
she had placed under the constantly dripping pipes running

along the walls and the ceiling. At night she had peace, because the water was then turned off. Mould in a variety of colours adorned the walls. Small items of laundry, washcloths, etc., hung in this moist atmosphere to "dry." The bathtub was made of rust-coloured terrazzo, and the single tap delivered only cold water. In order to have some semblance of a shower, particularly for the hot season, the husband had affixed a long plastic hose to the tap. The bathroom had a Western toilet and a washbasin. A wire basket next to the toilet was intended for used paper. All too often the drain was blocked, and if one chose to wait for the plumber to fix such problems it would mean some strolls into the wilderness. A kind of fan light with several transoms admitted a little light into this dark room, which was next to the kitchen. The family had a two-burner gas cooker, operating on propane gas from a bottle. Thus in many ways this family led a more advanced lifestyle, as they did not have to cook in the open or breathe poisonous combustion gases from burning coal. The kitchen itself was equipped with hanging shelves made from crudely sawn boards, and there was a large cupboard made the same way, with its doors covered with flyscreen. Each room had, hanging from the ceiling, a bare white neon tube, which gave off a glaring white light. However, the kitchen was lit only by a twenty-five watt lightbulb. Several rooms had bare concrete floors, just like my apartment in Y., and the walls were also concrete, albeit with a light-coloured whitewash.

Certainly one did not get the feeling of cosyness, but then Chinese houses and furnishings did not aim to create such an atmosphere, which probably exists more in Western culture. The average Chinese is a very practical person and a pragmatic thinker; what counts for him is bodily comfort. Thus it could well be that the refrigerator is set up in the living room and the washbasin in the hall, because there happens to be a tap there. If there was no side table or sideboard of any kind and the dining table was too small, then the pots and pans would be placed on the floor, where everyone could help themselves, at least in daily family life without invited guests.

I was glad the housewife made no special fuss on my account but treated me as one of the family. There was no special feast, and I ate the same as they ate. For breakfast each of us had a hard-boiled egg (as precaution against salmonella) and one or two slices of white bread or *mantou* from the previous day and some jam. After breakfast each of us would then go about his or her individual business. The housewife would ride her bicycle to the nearby open-air market, whilst the professor would attend a lecture or scheduled discussion about "everything and nothing."

The days in Beijing passed quietly, without fanfare. We had time to chat and visit mutual friends. One evening guests were invited for dinner, which meant more shopping and preparation of the meal. I was somehow to conjure a "Western" dish onto the table. Given the limited resources, I suggested adding meatballs as an adjunct to the Chinese dishes. But ground meat was unobtainable, much less beef. The housewife bought fresh pork. A board was placed over the bathtub to serve as a table for the mincer. I cut the meat into small cubes and removed sinews and gristle.

One day during my two-week stay was washday for the larger items. Using solid soap and a washboard, the housewife laboriously washed and scrubbed sheets and the bigger towels. It was a dry day, the sun was shining, and there was a bit of breeze, so it did not take long for the hand-wrung laundry to dry out on the line in the garden. How well off I was by comparison with my "quarter automatic" washing machine in Y.— at least I did not have to scrub or wring. All I had to do was pour hot water, which I had to boil up first, into the washing drum, and add soap flakes, turn the switch for wash, which meant the drum would turn awhile towards the left and then to the right, and set the time. Yet my method of washing was still physically strenuous, because all rinsing had to be done by hand. The best part of my machine was the separately installed spin dryer. Once it was allowed to rev up it would give almost dry washing after spinning for the set time. My friend had the same kind of machine, but as it was located in the hallway she thought it too troublesome to move it to the bathroom every time and fix all the paraphernalia, such as attaching the hose to the tap, and put away all things piled on the machine. She found that it was much better if she did her washing slowly and in her own way and at her own pace. So that was the day when I witnessed her big washday.

My four-week vacation was drawing to a close. I had to go to the railway station in order to arrange for my return ticket. Considering that it was peak travel time—it was mid-August and China was visited by many foreign tourists at this time—I did this in plenty of time, a week beforehand. The process was similar to the first time, when I went to buy my ticket in the company of my Chinese helper, only this time I was able to present my local worker card and so had to pay the "citizen" price of forty-six yuan. As the sleeping car of the first (soft) class was air-conditioned I had to pay a surcharge of six yuan.

Remembering my rushing to the train six months earlier, I arrived at the station in plenty of time. I occupied a compartment with three Chinese men. Standing in the corridor was a group of foreigners, all men, conducting some form of business discussion in English. One of them came over to me and asked what, by all heaven, I was doing all alone on a Chinese train. We got into conversation, and it turned out that the man was British and on a tour of inspection for his firm. Somewhere in Shandong he, a senior geologist, was to check over a mine in the process of construction and hold discussions with the responsible Chinese officials about inadequate rations for his British construction crew. He complained of nonadherence to a number of promises on the part of his joint venture partner, such as a high-protein diet. His men would refuse to go on working under such conditions, and thus negotiations faced him now.

It was certainly not easy to start doing whatever kind of business in China. I heard from a number of sources how difficult it was to get a foothold in this country; from one day to the next new laws would take effect or existing laws would be abolished, or rents suddenly would be increased out of all proportion.

Another man, a geoscientist from the same group, joined us. Being of Austrian-American descent, he was glad for the opportunity to speak German again. He was travelling with the group and had been sent by his institute in order to take soil and ground samples and undertake test drilling in Anhui Province, looking for oil or other minerals. The rest of the group, all Americans, were on their first trip to China and were having difficulty coping with the humidity and heat. The air-conditioning on the train worked only after a fashion, and after 10:00 P.M. it was turned off altogether, which meant that we had bearable temperature conditions only for four hours. And for that I had paid six yuan extra! The geoscientist, a somewhat overweight man, was dressed in a T-shirt that was a little too small for his height and girth, so that when he sat down it would slide up somewhat. This meant that his back was partly bared, which incurred the displeasure of the railway police travelling with us. He was reprimanded and told he must be properly dressed. As it was already quite late, every one of us returned to his or her own compartment.

After a four-week leave I was clattering towards my work unit and wondering whether there would be anyone to meet me at 7:00 A.M. the next morning, as I had sent a telegram.

When the train came to rest on the station of Y. and I finally stood on the platform after much pushing and shoving, I was met by the new associate leader, Mr. Y., and "Little D." Both greeted me with the utmost pleasure and sincerity, and Mr. Y. and I even embraced. I was quite overcome by so much heartiness, and the pleasure of meeting up again was genuine and mutual. It was not at all typical Chinese behaviour to allow such a public display of emotion. Even Little D. greeted me with something like an embrace. Amidst a lot of laughter and questions about my trip we drove back to the campus together in the campus limousine.

I was almost overwhelmed by a feeling of having arrived home again when a number of my neighbours and colleagues also bid me welcome and inquired about my vacation. I was glad to be back within my own four walls, with the relatively cleanliness of my apartment, especially the toilet, situated as it was in a well-lit bathroom without dripping pipes everywhere, was a real luxury after my long journey.

The second semester brought nothing of particular noteworthiness in campus life. I was by now well integrated, living according to the same regulated rhythm as everyone else, and no longer allowed myself to become annoyed at bureaucratic inadequacies. I was by now able to find my way among the labyrinth of official channels, and I was not subject to any prohibitions, orders, or rules. I could do or not do as I pleased. The Chinese, knowing quite well that I would not step over the accepted boundaries of conduct, trusted me, and I felt that they understood me, just as I had learned to understand them so much better.

My household help, the "pearl," had cleaned my apartment thoroughly; the steps had been swept, the balustrades dusted, and the plants on the balcony looked fresh and green. Before I went on vacation I had placed all of my private correspondence on a shelf in my wardrobe and locked it, also locking the door to my bedroom. The wardrobe lock was a safety lock from Germany and nobody had another key to it, so the correspondence was at least secure.

Now as I returned I had the feeling that somebody had gone through this locked room. Whilst everything was just as I had left it, I still could not be sure it had not been disturbed. In the other rooms, which were unlocked, I could tell that someone had been there because various items of furniture had been moved. It did not look like my helper's work, and the fact that even the little cupboard where my predecessors had left their discarded clothing and cartons, paper, and newspapers suggested that a major action had been mounted here. It all bore the handwriting of Mrs. Z. I asked my "pearl" about it but could not obtain a clear answer. But her demeanour, her uneasy smile, and her comment that everything was just where I had left it said something. She did admit that Mrs. Z. had personally cleaned out the cupboard with the old clothes and so on and was very annoyed when she found that some of the old T-shirts, worn-out men's shirts, and bundles of rags were missing. My helper did not tell Mrs. Z. that I had used these as cleaning rags. However, she told me of Mrs. Z. being very angry when she found that the cartons containing empty lemonade, wine, and spirits bottles that the former German teachers had left on the balcony were no longer there. My helper told me all this with a kind of malicious joy in her eyes and a knowing smile on her face.

It so happened that she and I, some months earlier, had cleared the balcony of all this rubbish. Where had all this garbage gone? To the buyer of empty bottles, of course, who sat outside the southern gate waiting for sellers. Depending on demand, each bottle was worth some .25 to .35 yuan. There had been more than sixty of them on my balcony, which was already a small fortune by local standards.

With the help of the houseman (he was in the picture) and my "pearl" I had placed the empty bottles next to the large rubbish bin that belonged to the house and was emptied once or twice a month. I thought that the garbage collector with his little wooden cart would have been delighted at improving his household finances with the old glass, but alas, my helpers beat him to the punch. Agreed: the left hand did not know what the right was doing. Thus my helpers could say quite honestly that they knew nothing. And when I was asked about it a few days later by Mrs. Z. I could say with a clear conscience that as far as I knew the rubbish had finished up in the bin, and I did not know what happened to it after that.

I must admit that I was quite annoyed at the fact that my bedroom had been gone through, even though I could not prove it. When I happened to meet up with one of my Chinese neighbours, the retired party secretary of the campus, a few weeks later and he asked me exactly when I got back, I was rather taken aback. He told me that during my absence there had always been a light on in my "public" rooms, and did I know about this? It was all rather mysterious, but I did not take the trouble to find out what was behind it; I had already become that indifferent! In all probability I would not have found out much anyway, and as nothing had been stolen, why conjure up a major drama over it?

In the meantime, the new English teacher had arrived from the USA. This young woman, just turned twenty-one, was to relieve the American couple, who had left after completing their one-year contract. At the same time a group of twenty-two students from Tanzania arrived, as part of a Chinese aid programme to that country. Having spent one year learning Chinese in Beijing, they were now allowed to complete their actual training at our technical institute. For many of them this meant study of at least four years' duration. All together they were in China for five years; after two or three years a home visit might be possible. Their life in the "Middle Kingdom" was by no means an easy one. Their every step was watched and controlled. They had to abide by quite ridiculous rules. They were forbidden from moving about freely outside the campus. One of them told me that some of the group had been forbidden by the head of the foreign bureau, Mrs. Z., from visiting any of the small food or refreshment stalls outside our campus more than once. When they ignored this instruction despite several reminders and the head could see no way of enforcing compliance with her orders, she simply caused the stalls and kiosks to be closed by higher orders, i.e., she was able to see to it that the owners of these establishments would no longer serve the Tanzanians, thereby subjecting them to open ridicule. I was told that a policeman, disguised as a caretaker, was always in the house where they lived. Something was afoot on our campus. There was much talk and gossip among the campus population, and the grey everyday monotony was enlivened by many colourful rumours and stories. The Africans had a very difficult task preserving in the face of such overwhelming weight of prejudice and discrimination and had to fight hard against it. Nevertheless, in spite of all difficulties, daily life went on as always.

On the eighth of September the winter semester started, and it was scheduled to continue without interruption except for four holidays (10 September, Teachers' Day; 1 October, National Day; 25 December, a holiday for foreign teachers only; and 1 January) until the twenty-fifth of January, which marked the start of the winter/spring holiday (Chinese New Year). Tirelessly my students continued their studies, expressing regret that my time with them was now soon to end. Towards the end of my stay I received a large number of invitations from everyone around and was most sincerely and hospitably looked after, having presents heaped on me. I also received help in the form of advice and physical aid when it came to assembling and packing my effects for the journey back to Germany.

Selected Discussion Topics

When I think back now to the many evenings of discussion and conversation practice in my "public" rooms, it is difficult to decide which were the most interesting. The participants, most of whom had already completed several semesters of German at various language schools, were able to express themselves quite well and conduct a normal conversation. We usually met once a week for two or at times three hours, depending on how lively and interesting the discussion was. The obligatory time was from 7:30 to 9:30, and it was up to me whether or not to extend this time.

The participants in these conversation practice sessions did not have to prepare themselves with reading or learning any new words. Anyone who had a reasonable command of German was welcome. There was no need to list their names in advance either, as I had enough room in my apartment.

During the course of several months a core group of five participants seemed to crystallise, who also continued to come regularly during the second semester. In the beginning there were more than twenty interested people, of varying ages and levels of education, all very hungry for knowledge and eager to learn, but quite a few dropped out after only a few weeks. I was to learn the reason for this later. At the beginning of the first evening I talked over my plan with all my listeners, which was unanimously accepted by all. I intended to discuss one specific topic, suggested by them, during each session. Since the listeners varied so much in terms of command of the language and vocabulary, I sought to be fair to all of them by giving them a week beforehand to familiarise themselves with the theme. It did not mean studying some kind of terminology or something similar, but just contributing some of their own ideas about the suggested topic. I also had to prepare myself every time, as I am not omniscient. For example, one wanted to discuss computers and their applications, another was interested about our education system, and yet another wanted to learn about our health system, culture, history, etc. In order to ensure that each exercise would not merely be a one-way effort, with me lecturing and the others listening, I always tried to relate each topic to their own country, society, and culture. By doing it this way I hoped that we would have a lively discussion in which various thoughts and opinions would find expression, because the participants would have the opportunity to compare and relate. I also hoped to learn a great deal myself in the process.

But after a few weeks it turned out that the way I had planned was not particularly suitable for a number of them, although everybody had consented to my suggestions. Well, such was the way, and I was to learn not to count too deeply on unanimously given approval. I suspect now that my idea that all should give the special topic some attention really was not all that promising from the start, and I found out that they had never learned to concentrate on a theme, albeit of individual interest, just for the sake of learning how to discuss or express their opinions, thoughts, and ideas in such a roundtable talk and thus were overburdened. Without giving any reason they would simply not turn up on a given day. After the first few times the interested came less and less "prepared," so that I had to improvise more and more each time. And so, after a few evenings had passed, I resolved to abandon the more systematic handling of conversational practice and just let things go. I was curious as to how the session would turn out now. The surprising thing was that once we got away from the sort of schooling system, we always had a stimulating topic to discuss.

If one or the other participant did not arrive punctually, he or she would be asked why he or she was late immediately after preliminary greetings had been dispensed with. Several times the excuse for being late became the discussion theme for the evening, which led us on one occasion into a discussion about sparetime activities for students on the campus. And so I heard that there was certainly very little variety in such activities. Now and again there might be a film worth seeing, worth seeing in the sense that it was not of Chinese origin. Foreign films, my students told me, were always more interesting. Whenever a film deal with action, murder, intrigue, heroes, spies, war, car chases, and the like there was much excitement and everybody wanted to see the film. I was not able to determine which of the foreign countries was the preferred supplier of films to China. I did notice that many old American movies from the 1940s were shown on TV, whereas more recent productions such as *Star Wars, First Blood*, and *Patton* ran in the cinemas. Both East and West Germany were represented, the former mainly by way of films from the 1950s, whose theme was chiefly the "liberation" of Germany by the glorious Soviet Red Army. West Germany exported its evergreen *Sissi*, among others, with great success. Austrian history was falsely regarded by the audience at being that of Germany, and that fact immediately gave me an idea for further discussions.

Apart from going to the cinema, many of my students participated in sports. Volleyball, basketball, and football were the favoured games for those trying to improve their fitness. Every Saturday evening students of both sexes could waltz to the sounds of the "Blue Danube" and other three-step tunes, or else they could sway to the tango melodies of the 1930s and "push" each other over the tightly packed dance floor. They had free use of the student mess hall for this purpose between 8:00 and 10:00 P.M. Music coming from cassette recorders they brought with them provided the right mood. I had one devoted tango dancer in my conversation group. It was expected of me, as a foreigner, that I should demonstrate each and every dance step, and so the young man was quite disappointed that he would not have the opportunity of starring on the dance floor with me.

During the winter semester these dance sessions for the young people were suspended, because it was thought that their studies might suffer from having so much diversion. But behind the scenes there were whispers that there might have been forbidden boy/girl relationships and "excesses of the most depraved kind" at the dances. The depravity probably meant that the young people became a little too close for comfort outside the student mess hall as well. Given the cramped living quarters, it took a great deal of ingenuity to bring about intimate situations. There were usually six students sharing a room with six beds, i.e., three sets of double bunks, plus six chairs, and a long worktable made up the furniture. A glaring neon tube on the ceiling would supply light; concrete floors and bare walls did nothing to make the atmosphere cosier either. This congestion as well as personal preference tended to drive most of the population out of doors in the warmer months, out on the street under a streetlight for a chat with friends or to study. In winter one had to stay in the rooms.

For those of my students who were married or had a child, sparetime activities were much the same as they are for us Westerners. Husband, wife, and child would travel by bus or by bicycle to the zoo, to visit friends, or to go shopping.

Recently there had been a new regulation that forbid an entire family from travelling on one bicycle, with offenders subject to penalties. In 1980, and again three years later, I witnessed more than once how a father would have to pedal away solidly in order to transport his wife sitting on the luggage rack behind, possibly with a floor lamp balanced across her knees, with a child sitting in a basket affixed to the handlebars. Negotiating a busy street this way cannot be easy.

But many of my participants used their free Sundays to prepare for some particular lecture or work on laboratory experiments. Free time outside the campus was rather different. One of my students came from downtown, where he worked in a factory. Often he told of a Sunday spent working in the production plant. Since there was a lack of electricity at least three times a week and there could be no production without it, it was customary to work when there happened to be current to work with. Shop proprietors and others who sold to the public did not have Sundays off either. Shops would open then at around 8:00 A.M.; and close maybe at 6:00 P.M.

One evening only four people turned up for their session. I suppose the others had to go to a political schooling session or a party meeting. It was interesting for me to learn how many of my students were organised. Almost all who had applied for study abroad possessed a party book and were supported and put forward by the leaders. The others had a much more difficult task to succeed. Depending on how an individual was assessed, bureaucratic hurdles for the unprotected were increased or made impossible to overcome. It was certainly a daunting undertaking to try to arrive at a given goal, particularly for those who only wanted to study, do research, or further their knowledge, whilst being skeptical of the party system. Many good scientists have thus been lost to China, and during the Cultural Revolution it is said that conditions in this respect were quite horrendous.

In this small circle I also learnt something of Communist Party membership—who could gain membership, how many were members, etc. According to my sources the Communist Party of China (CPCh) has some 40 million members. The minimum age for membership is eighteen years, and monthly dues are 0.60 yuan. Anyone can apply for membership as long as he or she comes from a family of good repute, does not have any criminal record, and has shown him- or herself to be a model worker or otherwise lead an exemplary life. Members are chosen by the party from the available applicants, and it is considered an honour to be a member. Apart from the Communists, a number of other parties sit in the People's Congress, namely, Liberals, the Peasant Party, the Minority Party, the KMT, and other smaller groups. A strong faction is made up of the intelligentsia, and only senior scientists make up membership of this party. The KMT is said to be a strong party even today. The widow of Sun Yat-sen, founder of the Chinese Republic, Mrs. Soong Ch'ing-ling, was chairperson of this faction until just before her death, furthering the heritage of her husband, who died in 1925. But she joined the CPCh just before she died. Superimposed over all the others is the Communist Party, which is the legislative and executive organ for all aspects of government. The party is organised along hierarchical lines and rigidly structured right to the farthest corner of this big country. Decisions made in the capital, such as new laws or changes implemented there, take some time before they reach the farthest province, such as Sichuan in the far southwest or Xinjiang Uygur in the far west. In the meantime it is quite possible that different laws have already come into effect in Beijing.

One topic that comfortably occupied an entire evening was concepts and opinions about love, marriage, and happiness. The group contained both married and single men between twenty and thirty. In addition we had two women, a single twenty-six-year-old student of mechanical engineering and myself. It was often no easy task for me to lead the discussion away from male utterances such as: "Women belong in the kitchen and are responsible for bringing up the children." The young woman spoke quite openly about her feelings and the expectations she would have of her partner. She wanted to find a man who was intellectually her equal and who, if possible, had an education similar to her own. Of course it would be an advantage if her intended husband was one or two years older than she and if he could bring to the marriage a good position for the future. She stated her views very firmly and with a lot of self-confidence, which earned her little applause from her male colleagues. But the men present disagreed with her quite vehemently and were appalled that a woman should have such independent views. They saw their future wives as being concerned only with the household and the children. The idea that dinner had to be on the table when the husband came home and similar antiquated views were aired. Many said that they would prefer a wife from a lower social level. The tango dancer, for example, said that his girlfriend was a factory worker who adored him on account of his mental qualities and his great knowledge, which she thought would further her social status. A twenty-year-old said he was not looking for a wife—they were always obtainable. A girlfriend, on the other hand, was much more difficult to find, and taking a girlfriend to be his wife one day was for him the epitome of happiness. "Two pillows, one dream; not one pillow, two dreams" was what this young man was searching for. It became apparent from these discussions that many marriages were formed merely for reason of convenience and were still arranged by others such as parents in rural areas or responsible people at the workplace.

The younger men and women wanted to go their own way and make their own arrangements, but this would bring its own problems, as a young woman of twenty told me once confidentially. Her boyfriend lived in Beijing, and she was ordered to the south to study languages. Every day she waited for his letters; no sooner did we call a short recess than she ran to the post office for students to check if there was any mail. If she came back with a letter she would radiate happiness and her performance would improve instantly. She was an industrious and likable girl who wanted to be married. She had never been happy in Y. and wanted to be near him as soon as possible. His recent letters were disturbing, and suggested that he was looking for somebody else. She asked me for eight days' leave of absence from lessons. As a teacher by Chinese standards is "all-powerful," as I learnt when I asked a Chinese colleague about giving leave of absence, I let the girl go. I did not feel too comfortable at being able to act so independently as a foreign teacher, but the girl's academic performance certainly justified my letting her go. She had to promise to be back in eight days. She came back after about two weeks—it was not possible to obtain rail tickets earlier—even more unhappy, but now certain that there would be no wedding. The young man's parents had other plans for their son, who as a good son had to place his own desire after those of his parents. I don't know what came of the romance, as this girl left us after the summer semester.

Another young man, about twenty-two years old, thought that under the still-prevalent attitudes young people had to behave in certain ways, i.e., women were supposed to be reserved and shy, whilst men had to be honourable and disciplined. It was almost impossible even to strike up a conversation with someone of the opposite sex without being compromised.

No one thought anything of it if young people of both sexes met in a group to chat or even flirt occasionally, but this did not appeal to the young either. The result was that young couples met secretly, if possible outside the campus or village, in order not to be seen by acquaintances. People in the cities were already much more tolerant, but very rigid rules remained in effect in the country and away from the major cities. But here, too, as in many other areas, the old order was crumbling, and the generation gap was becoming ever wider.

At that time the Institute for Sociology in Beijing was working on a study concerned with opinions of young people between sixteen and twenty-five on the subject of sexuality and related questions. The young people pleaded for free love after the Western example. They wanted to have the opportunity to have intimate relationship before marriage without being despised or criticised if their actions became known.

There was always something to talk about when we got together, but this chapter would become much too long if I were to attempt to cover each of the numerous subjects in depth. Thus I want to only discuss crime before concluding this chapter.

I was repeatedly advised against cycling into the city late at night, especially alone. Evil characters were said to be on the prowl, stealing handbags, picking pockets, raping women, etc. They made no exception of foreigners, and increasing liberalisation had brought about an ever-growing number of "good-for-nothings." I was told of numerous burglaries, which occurred even in broad daylight while the occupants of the house were at work. Mostly the evildoers were youths, usually organised in gangs. Jewellery and other valuables were not sought after so much as cash. Expensive consumer goods such as cassette recorders, cameras, radios, and television sets, particularly imported models, were still not affordable for everybody even though they were more freely available. Only a long period of saving enabled them to acquire such goods. Purse snatching was on the increase, as we know from our societies. The victim has little chance of recognizing the thief, who usually disappears into the crowd with weasellike speed, or of recovering her possessions.

A young policeman I spoke to about this one day thought that his particular unit was undermanned and that there should be more emphasis on police patrols and policemen on the beat. At this time increasing vehicular traffic posed an additional problem. A lot of police were used in traffic control, placed in the newly constructed shelters at busy intersections, where they had to work the traffic lights. Thus the small number of available police was no longer sufficient to allow regular patrols through the many streets and lanes, many of which were difficult to survey in any case.

Police not only had to concern themselves with theft and robbery; as a result of liberalisation moral standards were no longer enforced as rigidly as hitherto, and so police in addition to traffic control and patrols also had to take care of public decency and standards of behaviour.

Some six months before my arrival the following is said to have happened: A young woman in her midtwenties, "a little stupid, poorly educated, and immoral," was sentenced to death and publicly executed. Her crime? She had had ninety-nine lovers and taken money from many of them as payment for "depraved pleasures." The last three of her lovers evidently had carried things too far. They indulged in group sex. There was no limit to their imagination. Each of three wanted to be the first to take his pleasure, and so a game of cards was organised, with the winner to be the lucky first. The naked belly of the "lustful woman" served as the card table. The game was raided and the four players arrested on the spot. There was no pardon for the woman—"she was no loss"—and banishment for life for the three men was the result of the forbidden "love."

Soon after my arrival a naked newborn baby was found in a shallow drain on our campus. It was a girl. I was told that the mother could have been a peasant woman, disappointed because her firstborn was not a boy. In the country sons still counted far more than girls. The birth control system allowed each married couple only one child, and failure to comply was punished with monetary fines up to one thousand yuan. Many peasants were already so wealthy today that the fines no longer worried them. In the hope of having the much desired son they would even pay the sum during the pregnancy and sometimes earlier. Thus family planners and police were rather powerless to act. However, government regulations were adhered to more strictly in the cities.

I was told that the little foundling was to be taken into an orphanage after initial treatment in our clinic. Despite long exposure to the cold, the child was still alive when found, but no one could tell me what became of her later. This incident brings back memories of my childhood. How often as a child I saw little bodies like this one float down the river, swollen, decayed, and partly eaten.

Postal Matters

The rights of citizens of the People's Republic of China to exchange letters and confidentiality and privacy of the mail are assured. Neither organisations nor persons are authorised, for any reason whatever, to interfere with the process of the mail or with its privacy.

Only in cases where the security of the state is threatened, or where the investigation of a criminal offence is involved, then authorised organisations including the bureau of public security have the right, in strict accordance with the applicable laws, to carry out censorship of private correspondence. (Constitution of the People's Republic of China of 4 December 1982, § 1 of the General Regulations, article 4)

It seemed as if this article had no legal validity where foreigners were concerned, because I often had the distinct feeling that there was something not quite right with the letters I received. The flap on the envelope was often heavily pasted and the contents stuck together from too much glue. But at first I did not take too much notice of my vague suspicions.

Before I go into details, I first want to explain how the matter of the mail was handled as far as we were concerned. All our incoming letters went through the foreign bureau of the university first. Somebody would then bring them to us, or else we would be told by telephone that they were there to be picked up. Depending on when the main post office downtown delivered the letters to the campus and they were distributed to the foreign bureau, we sometimes received our mail early in the afternoon and at other times in the evening. There were also times when we got our mail several days later. This was, however, not the fault of the post office, but due to the slackness of the foreign bureau. They had "regrettably mislaid" the letters and "unfortunately only just found them again." Where packages were concerned we had to travel personally to the main post office downtown. The addressee would be informed by way of a formal postal note, all in Chinese, how long the item would be held and what dues were payable, generally eighty fen.

One day a very angry American teacher living below me came to see me with the conviction that the foreign bureau was deliberately withholding our mail. She asked me whether I would look into this for her. For several weeks she had not received the English-Chinese periodical from the USA to which she subscribed. Together we headed for the foreign bureau. Whilst I was talking to several employees there, asking the reason for such poor postal service, she then interrupted our conversation with a comment made in a terse tone, at the same time holding an opened brown envelope under the nose of the person to whom I was speaking: "And what is the meaning of this? Why are envelopes addressed to me lying about here opened?" When asked where she had found them, she pointed to the windowsill, on which a stack of newspapers and other postal material were scattered. Evidently this incident was very embarrassing to the employees in the bureau, and they apologised profusely with the promise that in the future they would take extra care and that they would deliver mail immediately, even if it was "only" printed matter. And indeed during the following days our letters were delivered, neatly sorted according to recipient, next to our plates on the lunch table. For a while all went well.

Early one evening, as I returned to my apartment, I found a letter jammed in the door. The envelope (it was only the monthly programme for the overseas German broadcasting service) had been opened and not resealed. With this evidence in my possession and the experience mentioned above, I resolved to investigate thoroughly the mail delivery system from the post office to the campus.

Not far from the university was a branch of the main post office. I decided to go there and make enquiries of the supervisor, whom I knew quite well because I often had to seek him out when buying stamps, as the "normal" windows did not handle stamps of higher values. He was extremely obliging but unable to help me, because his branch had nothing to do with mail for the institute, which received its mail directly from the main post office in the city. He suggested I direct my enquiry there. A small, plump older woman was standing beside me. She gave me a friendly smile, and as she did so her front teeth were quite visible. They were covered in silver dental work, which seemed unusual to me because until then I had seen only gold teeth. She had overheard my conversation with the supervisor, and as I made ready to leave she told me that she worked in the mail distribution centre of the university and suggested I come to see her at 10:30 the next morning. Her office was next to the main entrance at the northern gate.

I appeared at the appointed time the next day. After a number of questions as to the why and wherefore, a younger woman showed me the shelf where mail for the foreign bureau was placed. I took our letters out of it and received permission, granted by the woman in a very friendly way, to go through the mail myself in the future. And so, for the next eight months, I would go there each day, sometimes earlier and sometimes later. My relationship with the six people employed there became more and more friendly all the time, and I got along particularly well with the young woman who was in charge of the section.

The mail distribution room was divided into two sections, some twenty-five square meters in all. One section was used to sort postal articles such as books, periodicals, and packets. It also handled registered mail and received telegrams that were then opened and read over the telephone to the recipient at his workplace. If, as often happened, the addressee was not present, then the telegram would sit for an indefinite time in one of the many pigeonholes. In the other room the woman with the silver teeth spread herself with her many newspapers on the floor. All the pages were delivered singly, and collating them was her job, which occupied her for several hours each day.

Not infrequently there was a mood of outright conflict in the room. The silver-toothed woman was often hindered in her effort to spread out, because the two or three large postal bags that arrived daily for the more than ten thousand inhabitants of the campus, often stuffed to bursting with letters and postcards, occupied quite a bit of room on the floor where her numerous piles of newspapers were also lying. There would be much squabbling in shrill voices, and she would stand in a corner, evidently offended, pointedly staring stubbornly out the window. The woman in charge concerned herself with all aspects of running the section, such as necessary administrative work, including handling incoming mail and foreign mail, and sorting of various letters, printed matters, etc., into the numerous numbered slots provided for the purpose. Each section or department had its own compartment, lockable from the outside, like a kitchen hatch. It would have been unthinkable if every recipient of mail had tried to get through the small rooms to pick up mail. On some days there would be crowded chaos as the mail lay about in bags, still unsorted, with various people digging about in the bags until the supervisor put a stop to it one day in an energetic tone. Students and "lowly" people were to kindly wait outside the door if their mail was not ready for them on a table outside.

In the beginning I, too, waited patiently until everything had been neatly sorted into the "foreign bureau pigeonhole." Sooner or later it was almost inevitable that I would lend a hand with the sorting, i.e., I would go through the pile looking only for mail from abroad. Sometimes I would sit there for more than an hour before I managed to empty all the bags, sort the letters into piles, and pick out the ones with addresses in Latin script. After a while the staff here became used to me and my rapid way of working, so much so that on occasions they would express regret if I failed to turn up at the usual hour for some reason. Sometimes the woman in charge of the section would bring me my mail in person. She would telephone me first and enquire as to the cause of my nonappearance. If I merely had been delayed, she would then tell me that there was mail for me, but if I was ill she would stop by in person after work and bring the letters to me.

Today when I think back and reminisce about the mail-room staff I have very fond memories of some of the daily occurrences that took place and the deep bonds I formed with the people there and, in particular, their tremendous sincerity and willingness to help.

I had such an experience with a woman official who worked at the packet counter in the main post office downtown. It was always a major effort having to cycle fourteen kilometers to town and back just to pick up a parcel, not to mention having to stand in line for hours, besides the nerve-wracking fight for a place in line against those trying to push to the front. Incoming and outgoing parcels all underwent a thorough checkup. Especially the outgoing ones were carefully examined as to the contents, and if everything was found in order, the sender would then have to sew up the cloth-wrapped package in front of the offi-cer and if he or she refused there would then be a big quarrel. This usually meant trying to keep calm and wait for one's turn.

And so one day, as I stood before this official, having finally fought my way to the counter, I asked if it might not be possi-ble for me to pick up my parcels at the branch office not far from the university. For some reason this could not be done. How-ever, the woman in charge then offered quite spontaneously to deliver my parcels and packages to me in person. I did not want to accept this offer, knowing just how much effort was involved in waiting for the somewhat irregular bus, not to mention her having to carry the parcels herself. But she insisted. A few of the other postal employees who happened to overhear our discussion encouraged her in her resolve and then enlightened me as to her status within the main post office. She was the exemplary worker in the establishment, and it would mean a great loss of face for her if she should not be able to serve my needs. I succumbed to all this insistence, no longer opposing them. Every time she came to the campus on my account I had some small token of appreciation ready for her, for all her trouble and effort. We both enjoyed our mutual friendliness and our little chats, which inevitably developed in the course of time. All in all she may have come to the campus three or four times. Shortly before I left Y. she appeared one day to bring me not only my Christmas parcels, but also a small farewell gift.

Not all the postal employees were as friendly and helpful as the woman I have just described. One employee at the branch post office was a grouchy-looking young man, whose unfriendly behaviour towards me I attributed to the antiforeigner propaganda to which he would have been subjected during the Cultural Revolution. The man was in his midtwenties. He always had something to criticise about my letters. Sometimes he would complain about the allegedly incomplete address on the envelope, even though he could not read a single letter of Latin script, or he would wail about the fact that the country of destination was not shown on the envelope in Chinese script. The latter complaint could be regarded as justified, and I took care to make sure he had no reason to nag about this in the future. But it was not to be! There was an episode with an important registered letter that is worth telling. I took my letter to the counter, fully and correctly addressed, with "West Germany" clearly shown in Chinese. The aforementioned young man was on duty and the only one behind the counter selling stamps and so forth. When he saw me he just left me standing there and disappeared for some time. When he finally got around to dealing with my letter, he turned it this way and that, weighed it, pasted the required stamps and other stickers on the envelope, and then demanded that I write the name and address of the addressee in Chinese on the envelope and then do the same for the sender. I refused to take part in this nonsense, arguing that the German post office workers could not read Chinese characters and, in any case, I did not know the Chinese name for the German city. At this he assumed a tone of vast superiority and positively bawled me out about my ignorance and lack of education, looking around the spectators for support: "She thinks she can get by with spoken Chinese only, but there are no illiterates in today's China!" With that he handed my letter back to me and informed me curtly that he would not accept it like this and would not issue the necessary receipts. I was furious and demanded to speak to the manager. This was refused on the grounds of that person having "an afternoon off." I then reached for the register of registered letters, which lay in front of him, and showed him my earlier entries in Latin script. I had often sent registered letters to Germany and never had any trouble before. Meanwhile a cluster of interested bystanders had gathered around, and comments in my favour went back and forth. He argued with a number of them, and from these arguments it was evident that I was not the only one whom he treated with such unpleasantness. Many other customers made no secret of their annoyance with him either. It was a huge commotion. Voices rose, and angry words were spoken. The young man, completely unnerved by now, grabbed my letter and started tearing off the stamps on the basis that without stamps the letter could not be sent. But I had already paid. With great difficulty I was able to prevent him from seriously damaging the letter itself, when a number of other postal officials came running from the back room attracted by the noise, among them the deputy manageress. When I was asked the reason for all this commotion the entire crowd present replied in unison that it was his fault, that impolite fellow there, who had refused to accept my letter. I did not have to speak for myself at all. The manageress showed neither disapproval nor surprise but simply instructed the young man to work according to regulations. But in spite of everything he insisted that the missing Chinese characters for the German city had to go on the envelope! The manageress suggested that I might oblige him and get it over with. I looked around and asked one gentleman to help me. When he heard the name "Stuttgart" he looked up and asked the bystanders what the Chinese name might be. I doubt if any of those present had ever heard of German city names, much less had any idea how those names might look in Chinese characters. That made the score one to nil in my favour. I now asked the young man if he himself would oblige me by writing the characters on the envelope, as none of the people present had any knowledge of how to write the name of the German town in Chinese writing, and because there were no illiterates in China! I could help out with a few other foreign languages—might this perhaps help him? Could he also read other languages than Chinese? I was almost speechless with anger at such chicanery. Without another word he tore the letter from my hand, and all of a sudden everything went routinely, as it always had before.

My anger had still not abated when I got back to the campus. As the foreign bureau was there for us to solve problems of whatever origin, I resolved to go there to complain. I had never troubled them about being badly treated or similar experiences I had encountered, but this time it had gone just too far. The new section head, Mr. Y., offered to intervene on my behalf, and I gradually calmed down. We were at dinner later that evening when Mr. Y. came to my table with the manager of the branch post office and the assistant I had met that afternoon. After an exchange of courtesies the manager raised the subject of the afternoon's events. He listened to my side of the story first and then gave me the background of the young man in question. It seemed he was from a poorly educated family, with poor manners from his home background. He did not enjoy his work at all and was in the habit of venting his bad temper on his customers, leading to a number of previous reprimands. However, he, the manager, did not have the authority to transfer this young man elsewhere, although he had made several attempts to bring this about. But certainly his behaviour was in no way connected with any "antiforeigner" sentiment. "We are all extremely grateful if the technologically advanced foreign nations help us with our development into the year 2000. The young man should think of this, too, but he is just too obdurate," the manager said. Finally they took their leave with many apologies and with calming words to the effect that I should not get upset.

When I went to the campus postal station the next morning to fetch my letters I was greeted with much ado and words of support and encouragement. It was high time somebody had complained officially to the management about this youngster. He was insufferably rude to all of them, not selling larger quantities of stamps if he did not happen to feel like it and causing other similar complaints. In any event, the tale of my argument with him in the post office went the rounds like wildfire, and for this day at least there was plenty to talk about.

My next time-wasting adventure, at the same post office, was caused by a package I had declared "diplomatic cargo" and which was to go to Shanghai. It contained a few reels of film, which I had requested from the German consulate in Shanghai to help with my teaching and now wanted to return. It was packed in the same waterproof canvas bag according to postal regulations as they had been when I received them. But no, the official responsible for packages, another such boy, objected to the packing. Packets like this had to go in a wooden box. Soft articles could be sent in a canvas bag, which had to be sewn tight in front of the official after inspection by him; however, rolls of film had to go in a wooden box. And that was that! My companion, who had come along to help me carry the heavy load, was all for just going and thereby avoiding a confrontation.

But I did not want to go all the way back with the heavy bags, having accomplished nothing, only to have a wooden box made and repack. After all, the goods had travelled perfectly well packed in canvas from Shanghai to Y., so why not the other way? Surely there must be uniform postal regulations in China? Of course there were, I was told, but since the first of January 1986, new regulations had come into force. They were pasted on that column over there—why not read them for myself? To his surprise, I did just that—he could hardly have suspected that I could read Chinese characters! I found no mention of a wooden box and pointed out that the regulations dated not from 1986, but the previous year. After consulting his colleagues and with much laughter all round he accepted the bag, and we parted as "the best of friends."

In the Event of Illness

The Chinese have an old and appropriate saying ready for every possible eventuality, which helps to explain and render acceptable much that is otherwise difficult to understand. Whilst such wise sayings rarely help the person concerned, they give much food for thought if one thinks through underlying meanings and then asks oneself why this particular saying was chosen for a given circumstance and not some other; the saying chosen is almost always very apt.

And that was my experience with the saying *shui tu bu fu*, which means "unaccustomed to water and soil." During the first weeks after my arrival in Y., I found that I repeatedly suffered from gastric problems, with varying intervals between attacks, a visit to a doctor being necessary on each occasion. I suffered from diarrhea despite the fact that I was most careful with what I ate and drank. Boiling all drinking water and eating well-cooked food were second nature to me, and I adapted to the Chinese habits and lifestyle to make sure that I did not accidentally and needlessly subject myself to some germs. And yet my digestive system refused to cooperate and would not settle down. Right to the very end of my stay I had to live with this burden, which was sometimes quite severe and at other times bearable.

But in the beginning I was very concerned about it and for this reason repeatedly sought help from a doctor. Surely there must be something I could take for it from the tried and proven herbal pharmacy of China, with all its rich traditions. There were many kinds of grasses, herbs, and blossoms, taken either boiled into a tea, dried, or made into tablets or powders, all of them effective medicines. But none of them really helped in my case. The saying I mentioned above finally made me realise that not every problem is curable, if surroundings and lifestyle are not in harmony with the body. Despite my boiling water, peeling all fruit, and taking all kinds of other precautions, there was always something in the composition of my daily diet to which my system just would not adjust. In my case it was probably the very high lime concentration in the water, or it may have been an unusual pesticide or the unaccustomed fertilizers used. Who is to know? In any event, the many laboratory tests performed clearly showed that it was not a bacterial infection. I was somewhat reassured and just had to live with and adjust to the problem. Once I had rid myself of the idea that there had to be an appropriate remedy and complete cure for each and every ailment, I simply accepted mine as something immutable and that's it. I rejoiced when I happened to be well, and if the problem became too severe I remained at home. Shui tu bu fu. How right were not only the doctors but everybody else, making my health problem and the limitations it caused acceptable to me.

Getting rid of a bad cold was not quite so simple, although the two female doctors who visited my bedside had a similar saying ready: "Unaccustomed microorganisms adversely affect health and well-being."

When my cleaning woman arrived early one morning and found that I had not got up yet and left for work as usual, she was very concerned about me. Without further ado she notified the doctors. And so they came, to my surprise. One of the lady doctors asked the usual questions about fever, appetite, etc., measured my blood pressure and took my pulse, and after auscultation and percussion of my lungs made her diagnosis. The slight bronchial congestion suggested the start of a bout of bronchitis, and I had to expect increasing coughing and a higher fever. Meanwhile the other doctor had looked about the room and put the blood pressure apparatus back in its case, and after they had finished listening to my lungs through my nightshirt they straightened my pyjamas, carefully adjusted my pillow, and wrapped me up to my neck in my blankets. It was all-embracing care, and I felt looked after, with the calm movements, the mild voices, and the reassuring words that they would do everything humanly possible to help me and especially to combat any homesickness, which of course is always particularly strong if one is ill and not at home. Some time later one of them returned, bringing the medicines that had been prescribed. Of the pills, almost as large as plums and black-looking, I was to chew one every three hours and wash it down with boiled warm water. I was to take four flat tablets every four hours and then take this syrup made from licorice with added opium ("don't worry; it only contains very little"), as needed for my cough. Thus taken care of, I just lay there and waited for whatever was to come next. It was not long before the dean and the administration director came by and asked how I was, what they could do for me, and if there was anything special I fancied to eat. For a long time I had had a great yearning for a "real" soup, made from beef or chicken. The soup on our menu consisted only of water and vegetables, with salt and pepper added to give them flavour. My wish was to be granted. The director undertook to speak to the chief cook about it in person. But towards the end of the visit the dean suggested that it might be better if I went into the clinic for a few days, where I would have ongoing care day and night. This suggestion did not appeal to me in the least, particularly as I knew what to expect there. The rooms and corridors were draughty, inadequately heated, and the hygienic conditions not such as to inspire confidence—no, I much preferred to remain within my four walls. I thanked them for their concern and trouble, but I did not want to cause any fuss and would feel much more comfortable in my surroundings. They accepted my suggestion but insisted on providing a female companion to look after me for the next few nights.

One of my colleagues was entrusted with this task. She arrived each evening at around eight o'clock and left my apartment again at six o'clock the next morning. She was given the room to which I had been assigned first. As far as she was concerned, the opportunity to sleep in a comfortable bed designed for two people was most welcome. She happened to have house-guests, her sister and her husband, who were on their honeymoon and staying with my colleague and her husband. Their "apartment" was a single room of some sixteen square metres, with a double bed, a few chairs, and a table and a wardrobe. For four people it was terribly cramped, but the situation improved markedly when my colleague's husband had to go away on a business trip for a few days and she found "temporary shelter" with me.

The cold lasted longer than I thought it would, and I was out of action for almost two weeks. I felt uncomfortable at having to take time off due to illness so soon after the start of my assignment, but I was soon relieved of this concern. On no account was I to worry; worry only slowed down the healing process, and it was no good being impatient, because all that did was further tax the still-weakened body. The most important thing was tasty and nourishing food. And so some of my new acquaintances felt that this was their concern, and they provided me with home-cooked food such as noodle soup saturated with fungi, scrambled eggs, and vegetables. What I had very little of was rest. One afternoon my ten students came in a group to visit me. Like little angels they stood around my bed and waited for entertainment. After an hour I felt so exhausted I had to ask them to leave.

If a foreigner becomes ill in China, he or she can expect the best and most devoted medical care (by Chinese standards). Head physicians are called in and give their time; imported medicines, when available, are reserved for foreign visitors as well as for their own people of high ranks. But this does not mean that Chinese patients are not looked after; the ordinary sick person certainly receives medical care, but that care looks quite different in many cases from the care afforded to important people who happen to become ill.

As a general rule every unit (factory, school, institute, railway, post office, etc.) had its own medical station, a type of polyclinic. Better-placed units could afford a small clinic with operation facilities, dental department, X-ray facilities, and a room for physiotherapy or ECG apparatus. Our clinic had all of these setups, in addition to which there was a well-stocked pharmacy for Western and traditional medicines on the ground floor. A few beds for both slightly and seriously ill patients completed the setup.

How did such a visit to a doctor go? I had a toothache, and a day was arranged to see the dentist. The head dentist himself was to take a look at my teeth. Immediately after the end of my lessons I rushed to the campus hospital, where I was already expected, heartily greeted, and shown to the first-floor treatment room. There I had to sit down in a prehistoric dentist chair. The dentist, a middle-aged man, looked at me with laughing eyes and commented that I was probably trying to imitate my German predecessors, who had experienced constant problems with their teeth. This was probably due to the unaccustomed diet. Be that as it may, he was utterly enthused about my teeth. Using a tiny flashlight, he examined my mouth, going along each row of teeth with a dental mirror. He was full of praise for his German colleague, my dentist in Hamburg, saying, "Outstanding workmanship. I have never seen anything quite like it." He made further comments about my gold crowns and fillings to his two colleagues, whom he called over to "take a look." Meanwhile a number of other people who happened to be present, not only the medical staff, crowded around me also. Everyone wanted to take a look into this foreign mouth cavity, and I felt like the main attraction in a circus. After a thorough examination by means of a mirror and a tooth scaler he diagnosed my problem as "an exposed neck of a molar." From a container he took a pair of long tweezers with which he gripped a bit of cotton wool that had been dipped into a brownish tincture (glycerine-iodine) before applying it on my aching back tooth. It tasted dreadfully sweet. An unhygienic-looking spittoon on the floor made of colourful enamel served as a waste bucket. Cotton wool, blood, extracted teeth, mouth washings, everything went into it. I had to overcome a degree of revulsion before I was able to expel my wad of cotton wool into it, but unless I wanted to swallow it there was little choice. Once more I had to show off my teeth to one and all; the news that the chief dentist was giving a show of foreign dental work must have spread like wildfire. In the end it was too much for me, and as a joke I suggested that every spectator would have to pay me two fen for looking at my teeth. No sooner had I said it than I stood up from the ancient barberlike chair. A prescription was given to me, I was bid farewell with the friendliest, "We hope to see you again very soon." Everyone was most attentive and obviously favourably disposed towards me; once again there was something to gossip about during their otherwise monotonous daily life.

From the clinic's pharmacy I received a small brown bottle and a little package wrapped in yellowed newspaper. When I opened it back in my apartment some brownish cotton wool (caused by sterilisation) and toothpicks appeared. The little bottle contained the same sweet-tasting tincture the dentist had used. These simple means proved their effectiveness after a few days—or would the toothache have gone away in any case?

Who knows? My problem may have been that remnants of the high-fibre diet became caught in my teeth, leading to infection. When I told the dentist about dental floss being used in daily mouth hygiene, he commented that there was nothing better for cleaning the spaces between the teeth.

"Tooth silk" has been known in China for a very long time, because silk sewing thread can be bought everywhere there. I can still remember my old amah (nanny), going through a lengthy ritual with cleaning her teeth every morning. Armed with a cup of warm water, a toothbrush, a tin of pinkish tooth-powder with a menthol taste, and the important "tongue-scraping iron" she would occupy the washbasin for a considerable time. The "scraping iron" was a thin strip of metal, some four to five millimeters wide, bent into a horseshoe shape. Wealthy Chinese had them made from silver. After brushing, thorough rinsing, and gargling the tongue would be scraped and freed from any coating by means of this instrument. To conclude this ritual she would produce a long silk thread from one of her pockets and with it thoroughly clean the spaces between her teeth. Another rinse and gargle, and the daily mouth hygiene was over. As a child I had always watched this procedure with fascination. Even today, early in the morning people perform their oral hygiene this way.

Most houses and apartments in older parts of Chinese cities do not have a bathroom. Personal hygiene, i.e., washing of hands, feet, and faces, is done outside the front door in public, as is cleaning of teeth. An enamel bowl serves as a washbasin. For an all-over bath or wash the public bathhouses are frequented. But back to what happens if one becomes ill.

Shortly before summer vacation my second Chinese German teacher had an accident and was unable to work. I was told that he had injured his leg and was unable to walk properly, and so I decided to go and visit him. He lived in a room with another young man in a hostel for single male teaching staff. He was lying on a plank bed, his injured leg resting on a cushion, and tried to rise as I entered the room. He was unable even to move his leg, which was loosely bandaged with some linen strips, without a lot of pain. When I asked him how the injury happened he told the following story: He had been cycling with his friend quite late one evening, on his way back to the institute from a trip downtown. The evening had been pleasantly warm, with the sickle of the moon far away on the horizon, and both became immersed in a discourse about the beauty of the surroundings in the darkness. A large stone or pothole in the road brought a sudden end to these reveries as my colleague fell from his bicycle. The dark country road lay before them, deserted and pitch-dark. There are no street-lights on the outskirts or in small villages in China, no telephone booth to call for help—nothing. The friend had no alternative but to lift my colleague, who could neither stand nor move his leg, onto his own bicycle and pushed him on foot over the remaining five kilometers. He then walked back to fetch the other bicycle before daybreak.

When my colleague finally managed to see the doctor on duty his ankle was already swollen, as was his foot. The X ray had been entirely normal. His foot and ankle were bandaged with strips of linen, and he was given some homeopathic medicine to take and ordered to take bedrest for the next few days. I took a look at his thickly swollen foot, which was visible through the bandages in all the colours of the rainbow. There was no sign of any open wound, but it seemed to me that his leg was fractured above the foot. It did not lie in the correct position relative to his lower leg. I was able to persuade him to go and see another doctor, on the basis that another X ray might show something new. Next morning he hopped along on one leg, over uneven paths, up and down stairs, until he arrived at the campus clinic. The doctor on duty referred him to the main city hospital for another X ray. The X ray performed the previous evening had shown nothing ("normal") because the equipment had been defective, as it now turned out. How he now got himself to the hospital was, however, his problem. Two of his friends planned to hoist him on the bus and accompany him all the way. The ambulance owned by the university, a rather bulky little bus painted white with a red cross, was busy with transporting things at that time of the day and therefore not available. It turned out that the private trip on which it had been engaged ended earlier than anticipated, and my colleague had the good fortune to be driven to the hospital in this vehicle.

It was indeed a broken leg, a double fracture in fact. Encased in plaster up to his knee, he returned "almost free of pain," according to him. For the next six weeks he had to stay in bed, and in the campus clinic at that. He thought this was quite funny, and he was looking forward to having much time for sleeping. But evidently the stay in the clinic cannot have been all that enjoyable, because after only three weeks I saw him hobbling across the campus. He commented that it had been just too boring sleeping all the time, and time had dragged for him. The doctors were not of the same opinion, but that did not matter to him. He would, however, go back to the clinic to have his cast removed.

For the patient in China there are no medical or hospital expenses; he merely has to contribute a few fen towards medicines, and he has to pay eight fen to be entered onto the list of patients at the start of his treatment. (I, as a foreigner, had to pay one yuan, and the amount I had to contribute towards medication was also considerable higher.) And so it really did not matter whether my colleague remained in the clinic or not.

One day our Japanese colleague did not appear at dinner. This was unusual, because he had always let us know beforehand if for some reason he would not be there. At lunch he had been sitting with us very cheerful, and his appetite, as usual, was excellent. He was delighted when I offered him the indefinable piece on my plate. So what happened? When we went to see him he told us that he had probably overeaten, particularly too much meat. He had become very ill in the afternoon, with vomiting. He had then collapsed during his lesson, and as he had been barely able to walk, his students had virtually carried him to his apartment. But a day of fasting would soon have him right again. Unfortunately, this was not to be. As we heard the next day, he was taken to the clinic late that evening, where he was treated with infusions of glucose for his very severe abdominal pains. However, when his condition continued to deteriorate the next day he was rushed to the city hospital, where only critical cases were normally referred, which could not be diagnosed or treated adequately in the campus clinic. After a thorough examination the head physician diagnosed a perforated appendix, which meant that an emergency operation was unavoidable. But as Mr. S. told me later, this was not immediately possible, and he also insisted on being flown back to Japan immediately. For this, however, there simply was not enough time, as the head doctor told him. He was admitted to the hospital at around midday, and the operation took place six hours later, lasting some four hours. When I went to visit him a few days later he was already feeling much better. His high fever of more than forty degrees had fallen to thirty-eight, and he was being treated with antibiotics by injection. This particular medicine had been specially obtained for him because a foreigner's life was in danger, and everything humanly possible was done to save it.

In a society where the assumption of personal responsibility and decision making is practised rarely, it is understandable why several hours elapsed from the time of admission to the hospital before he was operated on. Even though Mr. S. had already given his consent for an operation, this was not enough to absolve the surgeon in the event that the operation should fail. The head of the work unit, in this case the president of the institute, had to give permission. After he had at last been found after a frantic search, not only had this valuable time been wasted, but the subsequent discussions with the medical team and telephone calls to the city power station to ensure that there would be no disruption to power supply over the next few hours took up a lot more precious time. The team of doctors, the president, and the head of the foreign bureau all agreed that an "immediate" operation was absolutely necessary, but the doctor did not dare attempt a general anaesthetic. A decision was made to use lumbar anaesthetic with acupuncture.

Now a few comments about hospital accommodations for VIP patients, which of course Mr. S. was. Whilst the new hospital had been furnished and supposedly was ready to accept patients, it turned out that it was not quite finished after all. At the time Mr. S. was admitted the wards were just ready, but the operating theatre was still in the old building opposite the wards. As Mr. S. told me later, he was quite shaken up after he had had his operation. While he was being wheeled over an uneven building site to his ward, a big umbrella was held over him to keep off the rain. He was more than happy to be just lying on his straw mat again and able to think about all that had happened.

It was the rainy season and the heat unbearable. Two large electric fans standing on the floor of his suite struggled to provide a little cooling. The suite consisted of a bedroom, a living room with couch, telephone, and television, and a bathroom. His eating utensils of colourful enamel stood on his bedside table. He told me that the food was appalling and that the nursing care he received would have been totally inadequate had it not been for the fact that his colleagues and students (all male) had been taking turns helping to care for him. The care they were giving him was quite touching. They changed shifts every eight hours. All that a Chinese nurse would do was give injections, distribute medicines, and follow the doctors on their rounds. Washing patients and helping them "go to the pot" were not part of their duties, much less in the case of male patients.

Mr. S. got over the operation well, and after four weeks of postoperative care in the hospital he was allowed to return to the campus. There were no complications of any kind, nor did the very large scar cause him any problems.

A duplication of these events seemed to be in the offing a few months later when the new young American teacher complained of abdominal pains one day. Her vomiting and diarrhea, and the manner in which she moved as she painfully rose from her chair holding her right side reminded me of the appendix affair with Mr. S. She was treated initially for an intestinal infection, but when this showed absolutely no improvement she finally succeeded in securing an appointment with a more competent doctor in the city hospital through the foreign bureau. We were accompanied by an interpreter.

We were ushered into one of the many adjoining rooms in a single-story building. A female attendant in a greyish-white smock closed the doors and windows, as it was already quite cold and the room not heated; she then adjusted the whitish sheet on the examination couch and we all waited for the doctor, who eventually came. The examination took place in full view of everybody, and the female attendant commented that the patient's underwear was totally inadequate for this time of year, whilst the doctor undertook a very thorough examination of her abdomen. Diagnosis: appendicitis, and an operation was deemed necessary. The best thing would be if the patient were to remain in the hospital and be prepared for an operation the next day. But the patient would have none of it! She vehemently refused to remain in the hospital, not under any circumstances. The doctor, faced with such "obstinacy," was therefore forced to prescribe an antibiotic. It was all explained to me in detail. Every morning and evening I was to give my coworker an intramuscular injection of so and so many units of the prescribed medicine. If there was any improvement or worsening of her condition I was to adjust the dose accordingly. Due to early training I was a fully trained nurse and completely familiar with the giving of shots. But I did not want to become involved in this case, particularly as I did not even know which antibiotic was being used. There are a great many different antibiotics, some of which are well tolerated by the patients and others with varying side effects. Moreover, the Chinese name of the chemotherapeutic drug involved meant nothing to me. The idea that responsibility would be neatly transferred to me was, from my point of view at least, much too risky. So the campus's own clinic therefore had to assume this responsibility, and each day at the appointed time a senior nurse would appear, accompanied by a woman doctor. For the first two days the doctor in question even established a kind of bivouac in the apartment of the patient, giving her round-the-clock care. It was quite touching but to them a matter of course. But as I had experienced with my cold, C. had very little rest, as everybody came to visit her. After three injections C. awoke one morning with a badly swollen face and with no feeling right up to her eyes. She told the doctor but was not very disturbed herself. But when the numbness by the next day had spread to her mouth, chin, and ears she had me ask the doctor which specific drug was being used. It was always said that it was a kind of "penicillin." Eventually, after much to and fro and thumbing through reference books, there came the answer: streptomycin, of which she had been injected with several grams. Very delicately I suggested to the doctor that this particular drug might be too dangerous, and would she please discontinue it? After all, side effects such as affected sight and deafness were quite well known. But she had never heard of these side effects. In China, streptomycin was prescribed a good deal.

C.'s condition did improve after she was given tablets of a drug that allegedly contained sulfonamide, but all in all, she never really felt well again. During the summer vacation she flew back to the USA for a checkup; her appendicitis turned out to be a form of hepatitis. Although the number of medicines she had been taking made a positive diagnosis impossible, her appendix was completely healthy.

Early in December I noticed that my Chinese colleague was

becoming less and less regular in attending lessons, and so I visited her in her "apartment," the room I described above. She was lying in bed, whilst her husband was sitting at his desk. We started to talk, and from her somewhat embarrassed comments I gathered that she was in the second month of pregnancy. The couple had been married for years and were delighted at the prospect of a family. The woman was about thirty and her husband about to complete his master's thesis. It was time they had a family, and in addition they had prospects of being allocated a two-room apartment towards the end of the year.

There was joy all around, despite the cramped conditions and the indescribable deprivations all occupants of this hostel-like housing for married couples had to endure. The building had a ground floor and three other stories, with twenty-eight rooms of sixteen square metres each on every floor. There were separate toilet and shower rooms for men and women. But not only young couples lived in this building; there was an infant or an even older child peering out of almost every door, and on a few occasions I even saw a grandmother as well. All in all the building housed some 350 people. Cooking was done in the corridor outside one's own room door. Every family had its own "bucket stove" without a chimney standing in the corridor of three meters' width and next to it some basic furnishings that in the main consisted of a few small wooden crates or shelves, which housed the cooking utensils and on which leftovers and other foodstuffs were stored. Often I saw at all times of the day large and small rats scurrying across the floor of this dark corridor, which derived its only light from small windows at each end. The staircases were jammed full of objects that had become useless, such as boxes, cardboard cartons, rusty old implements, and so forth. There was a dreadful filth everywhere, not to mention the unhealthy smoke from all the stoves, which was particularly bad at mealtimes. But the accommodation shortage was serious, and the management of the institute was making every effort to provide better housing for all. Everywhere new apartment buildings were under construction.

Under these circumstances it was understandable that my colleague and her husband did not want a child. But as they could look forward to moving to a larger home quite soon, they were naturally very pleased at the prospect of increasing their family to three people. Any more than that was not permitted.

However, my colleague's condition, after the initial discomfort, worsened from day to day. When I called to see her the second time she complained of severe abdominal pains, but the woman gyneacologist whom she had consulted attributed no importance to it. She assured the patient that everything was normal and that all she had to do was take good care of herself and get a lot of sleep. Well, let it be that.

It was a lucky providence that I went to see her for a third time some days later in order to ask how she was. She was sitting upright in bed, supported by several pillows, gasping for air. Her husband was working at his desk. For days now she had been unable to swallow a single bite without bringing it straight up again. Her colour was a pale grey, with deep shadows under her eyes. When she had showed me her abdomen a week earlier I thought it looked rather rounded for only two months of pregnancy. What a shock I got when I took another look at it this time! She was a small person, weighing no more than one hundred pounds, and yet her belly was swollen as if she were six months pregnant. I implored most earnestly that she consult a doctor again, a real gyneacologist, not just a doctor for "women's affairs," and if necessary she should go to another hospital, i.e., to the city clinic, for this purpose. But this was quite unthinkable. They would not even treat her, because she belonged to a different work unit. As for the main city hospital, she could go there only after referral for examination and on recommendation by her superiors. But such an examination had to take place, I told her, and urgently at that. They were both quite helpless. They, as "little people," could not just go and consult a specialist. They needed somebody to speak on their behalf. I declared myself ready to call on the head of our language department and describe the case to her, but neither of the couple wanted this, quite understandably. The mere fact that I was taking so much trouble over them was already embarrassing to them. And "making so much fuss over one human life" was really not necessary. But even just to live up to the New Year would already be a miracle." Such and similar comments came from her lips. I extracted a firm promise from them both that they would seek another examination.

The next thing I heard about this case was that she was to be admitted to one of the city's maternity and gynaecology hospitals as soon as a bed was available. Her husband told me that she was being treated with "penicillin" in order to reduce as far as possible the risk of infection from the operation that now had become inevitable. The "cure" lasted for almost a week. The day before the operation we all, her class and I, visited her.

One of the external students, who had been able through his connections to one of the many managers of the hospital to arrange permission for me as a foreigner to make such a visit, met us outside the main entrance at the prearranged time. The student introduced me to the manager, obviously proud that he was able to present a foreigner as his teacher. The manager then led us to the upper story. There were no steps in the stairway, but rather a system of inclined ramps leading from floor to floor. Daylight entered this dark place through cross-shaped slits without panes in the outside walls. In the various niches of the landings leading from ramp to ramp I saw groups of men playing cards and women sleeping on padded quilts. All were rigged up in their padded clothing, as there was no heating at all in the concrete building. They were probably relatives who were taking turns caring for ill members of their families, spending their free time in the hospital in this way. Most of them were peasants or rural workers from the countryside, some distance away.

Eventually we arrived at the ward. The manager motioned us to wait outside the wide double doors and went inside. Opposite this door were the large swinging doors leading to the operating theatres. I took a quick glance into this forbidden zone. Apart from the dirty white colour of the walls and the generally dirty and neglected appearance, the corridor with its well-worn lacquered wooden furnishings, washbasins with old taps, the smell, the bags of linen outside some of the doors, and the quietness reminded me of my own time as a trainee nurse in the 1950s.

Our leader came back and motioned us to the ward and handed us over to the care of the nurse in charge, who showed us the room. My colleague lay in a small room of four beds, of which three were occupied. The room was bare, whitewashed (now greyish), and without heating, a neon tube dangling from the ceiling, and the large three-part iron framed window was probably not properly shut, as the plain cotton curtain moved in the draught. Next to each bed was a bedside table with personal eating utensils. One bed next to the window was not occupied, the thin mattress was rolled up, and the bedside table was sitting on the mattress base. There was only one chair in the room, on which I had to sit, with the other visitors standing about the bed. As we entered, the woman's husband was sitting on that particular chair beside his wife's bed with his head resting on the mattress, probably sound asleep. Having been woken by our arrival he hastened to bid us welcome and offered me the chair. He apologised for his tiredness, but he had been spending most of his time at the hospital, supplying his wife with food he cooked at home, which meant that he had to cover the journey by bicycle three times a day. Both of them were immensely pleased at our coming and at the things we had brought. Every one of us had brought something nourishing and tasty to help the sick person restore her health.

My colleague, dressed in her padded "going out jacket," smiled at us from her bed. She was lying under several padded quilts she had brought from home, because bed linen and pillows were not provided. The other two patients lay in their beds similarly bundled up. Our young teacher looked well, although she said that she was not at all well emotionally. A few days earlier, she told us, the doctor had terminated her pregnancy. That intervention by means of a vacuum extractor had been very painful. She had been shown the tiny being in a bowl, but the doctors would not tell her if it was a girl or a boy. Her husband was not allowed to see the foetus. "Sha yi ge ren, jiu yi ge ren" (one human being killed, one saved), was the only sentiment she uttered, with a pained look on her face. And she still had to face the operation the next day. After an appropriate time we took our leave, and her husband accompanied us to the exit gate of the hospital. We were all in a depressed mood, particularly after the husband had told us of the fears held by the doctors. They suspected at least one, if not several, malignant tumors on his wife's ovaries. She was to be operated on at eight o'clock the next morning. He would spend the next few days, and nights as well, by her side. I asked him where he would sleep. "The edge of the bed would do," he replied. As we talked we found ourselves being surrounded more and more by inquisitive passersby. All of them tried their best to catch a little of our conversation, so that they could relate at home their unusual adventure seeing a foreigner talking outside the hospital.

The following evening I happened to meet the secretary from the language department, and I asked her if she had heard anything about how the operation had gone. It turned out that she had been there the whole morning. My colleague had come through the operation well. One of her ovaries had to be removed because the tumor (a cyst) was too large. The other organ had not been affected as much, and it was possible to save it. I asked how she had withstood the anaesthesia, of which she had been very much afraid, and was told that only partial anaesthesia with appropriate acupuncture had been used.

After almost four weeks in the hospital she was discharged with the strict instructions that she was to have at least a further four weeks' bedrest and that she had to make sure she had a good, well-rounded diet. For this reason her old mother was called in by telegram from the town on the Yangtze where she lived. She cooked for her daughter round-the-clock, the results of which I was to see when I went to visit her one day. She had become round as a ball, quite apart from the thick winter clothing. She looked well and was happy that she would be able to experience the coming of the New Year after all and help celebrate the Spring Festival in February. She did not dare to even consider another pregnancy, because she was afraid that this might again result in health problems for her. She commented, resignedly, that her marriage would probably remain childless.

In order to round off my report of what happens in the event of illness I would like to comment on a few minor episodes that occurred more or less by and by. One evening I noticed that one of my course participants had a number of tiny square pieces of paper stuck to his ear. He must have noticed my questioning looks, because he soon explained the reason for them. He had been treated by acupuncture on his left ear at regular intervals, because he suffered from pains below the right side of his lower rib. He did not know whether either his liver or his gallbladder was diseased, causing the pain. When I asked if the acupuncture helped he replied that "it caused neither significant improvement nor worsening." The young man, in his midtwenties, had complete trust in traditional medicine and was of the opinion that one only needed patience. After all, he had had the problem for quite some time, so medical treatment could not be expected to produce quick results either.

And another episode: A man of around thirty suffered

from "tingling in the feet," in traditional medicine called *jiao qi, jiao* being "feet," *qi* referring to noxious factors therein. He had had various courses of acupuncture for this, he told me, but it had done nothing to free him from these annoying symptoms. In particular, he often woke up at night from the unpleasant sensation. Oh, it was all so nerve-wracking! He wanted to go to West Germany to continue his education, but this might have to wait if he could not rid himself of this "tingling." I advised him that his problem might be connected with a lack of vitamin B_1 and suggested he consult a doctor trained in Western medicine who might prescribe the missing vitamin for him. This was no sooner said than done, and some time later he informed me that this treatment had indeed helped him.

Another one of my students excused his temporary non-appearance for classes by explaining that his little two-year-old daughter had become ill and had for some time been lying in the hospital belonging to the petrochemical complex. Why this hospital? His wife worked there, and their pediatricians were much better. Both parents shared the task of caring for their child. Whilst he busied himself with cooking for his daughter, relieving his wife at the bedside for a few hours because she had to work, she stayed at the bedside all night, with mother and daughter sharing the bed. I learnt that the child was suffering from pneumonia. At first tuberculosis had been suspected, but fortunately that was not the case. We discussed this at some length during classes, and it appears that in China the child mortality in connection with TB is quite high. In remote areas preventive inoculations have not yet been introduced.

During the summertime I saw more sick-looking people than in the colder months, because they wore lighter clothing, without any head covering. In general, they all looked rather lean, with thin, apparently weak arms attached to a sunken torso. Bloodshot or inflamed eyes, mutilated or blackish teeth, toothless mouths, severe dandruff, and eczema were all fairly common, and I encountered them all during my frequent excursions into the village.

What other unusual events happened? There was a story going the rounds about a strange death that allegedly had occurred in one of the students' dormitories. Apparently the four young people who shared a room with the young chap in question had been with him until quite late the previous evening, just chatting and having fun. At about six o'clock the next morning, when all had to get up, they found that the young student was dead. His body had already been quite cold and rigid. A doctor was called but had been unable to find anything unusual, no foul play, no external symptoms of injuries, nothing. He just lay there quite peacefully, apparently. His parents came from a far distance to fetch their dead son and take him home. When I asked whether any relevant authority had intervened or whether the family had taken any steps to find out what happened, I was told that on no account did the family want the police or any other public authority notified. Two other children of the same family had died previously in mysterious circumstances. The parents had also been reluctant to look too far into the earlier deaths, because after all, who really understood supernatural forces? Instead of any real effort to find out what had happened there was only speculations about probable heart defects or even previously undiscovered brain tumors. Oh, these rumours!

If one compares the health care available to the Chinese people today with that of some thirty or forty years ago, one sees that despite the inadequacies that exist there has been an enormous improvement in medical care. In earlier years my colleague, being of limited means, would have consulted some quack or even nobody and probably died. Today there are hospitals, medical stations, clinics that offer advice, family planning, and occasionally campaigns about health care in general. The people are informed about diseases, their symptoms and prevention. The country is too large for such campaigns to reach the far corners, and the process of educating the masses that illnesses and their effects have nothing to do with demons or their punishment is a slow and painful process, especially in rural areas where superstition and mythological legend still play a major role even today.

Marginal Episodes

In one of my previous chapters I commented on the heavy physical work even women had to perform in China. Sometime in May, when I was on a train journey, with the lush green landscape passing slowly by my train window, my eyes were suddenly arrested by an unusual spectacle. Not far from the tracks four people were toiling away in a small field, not yet planted. While the man was trying to maintain his plough in a stable position, evidently with much effort, three women with straps diagonally across their chests were laboriously pulling the plough so as to cut furrows into the heavy, rich clay soil. My fellow travellers commented that these particular peasants were probably so poor they could not afford a water buffalo. It was not unusual to find family members, mostly women, having to perform this work. Not all peasants were part of a commune; many farmed for themselves and could sell their produce on the now-allowed free market. Apart from the various wooden farm implements, which had not altered in shape or method of construction for centuries, I did see here and there modern tractors made in China. Generally speaking, however, manual labour predominates in the rural economy. Whether the task is the planting of rice seedlings or thrashing of the ripened grain, it was always people doing the work, people in a stooped attitude, with large straw hats to protect them from the sun, thrashing away at the grain by hand. Almost always I saw women doing this kind of work.

On one occasion a military manoevre took place outside the gates of our institute. It seems that a unit of young soldiers had to perform a practice shooting exercise that day. Lying opposite each other in ditches on either side of the road, they were busily firing away at each other with blank shells. It was quite a spectacular performance, with smoke and noise travelling all the way to my classroom on the fourth floor. Whenever there was a break in the shooting the young lads were busied with marching, saluting, or crawling over the asphalt surface. After taking a meal out in the open, each one sought out a quiet spot in the shade for a well-deserved midday nap.

As I set out at around three o'clock in the afternoon to cycle into the city, I literally had to run the gauntlet of soldiers. A lot of rifles were quite deliberately aimed at me, and a few of them even pursued me to the bend of the road. I felt most uncomfortable, though I knew they were only using blank shells, and was glad to be out of their sight. On my return later the road, which was like a blind alley, was once more peaceful and quiet leading to the northern gate of the campus.

I experienced a somewhat more macabre episode when I was descending the steps from the fourth to the third floor in the company of one of my students one day. On the ledge of a large window in the stairwell, about fifty centimetres wide, a boy of perhaps five years was performing some form of acrobatics. Meanwhile two or three younger children, evidently his brothers and sisters, were playing in the corridor, rolling about, turning somersaults, and very obviously enjoying the chance of so much freedom. They looked somewhat ragged, dirty, and runny-nosed, but well nourished. I asked my companion to point out to the child on the sill outside just how dangerous his actions were and get him to come back inside. Had I spoken to the child myself, I thought, he might have fallen off the sill out of shock at being spoken to by a foreigner, the likes of which he probably had never seen before. My companion, a man over forty and probably a father himself, reacted with total surprise to my request. Why should he concern himself about this child when even the child's own parents did not care? If the parents showed some responsibility, then they would not allow their brood to run about like this, unsupervised. And in any case, what did it matter if this child had an accident, as there were far too many people in China anyway? Surely these were children from a peasant family, who tended not to worry about the prescribed one-child family, in any case. One child more or less did not matter to them. Fortunately, as we got to the ground floor, no child had fallen down.

One day, when we were discussing the topic of vocational training and employment opportunities in class, the following story concerning photography was told. A young couple, the husband a photographer, wanted to take a really nice picture of their little son, not quite a year old, as a souvenir of an excursion to the well-known Yangtze bridge. The mother sat the child on the balustrade, holding the child by only one arm, so that she would not be in the photo. It seemed that the father did not want to have the mother's arm in the photo either; in any case, the mother let go of her child for an instant, the father went "click," and the little boy fell backwards into the waters of the Yangtze stream, never to be seen again.

Such little digressions, certainly not all of them with such sad content, often occurred during lessons, which not only served to liven up the hour and give me insight into the everyday life of the people, but also gave my pupils the opportunity to demonstrate their linguistic prowess and ability to express themselves.

Another story out of my "box of episodes": In October we had moved into the new Experts Residence, a section for foreign teachers in the previously mentioned hotel building for ninety-nine guests. In my new apartment there I was allocated two cosy little rooms, a small balcony, and a tiny bathroom, not more than fifty square metres all in all. The move also meant a change in the way we took our meals. We were to feed ourselves, which meant that we were paid monthly an amount to cover our meals and we could then select our meals ourselves in any one of the various canteens. The food quality did not get any better, and the choice was also very limited. Sometimes the same stew would be offered for days on end. Because it was not very tasty, it was then not on demand, but the dish would not go into the garbage can either. This meant that it was "improved" with tomato puree or by adding a carrot or two or else stretched with potatoes. But it still tasted dreadful. One day *jiaozi* were on offer and I ordered twelve pieces, which was all that was allowed for one person. I had to pay 1.20 yuan, which was a high price for a few boiled ravioli, but at least they were a change from the new "designed" menu plan.

Every day on my way to lessons I had to walk past the canteen kitchen. Through the large, low window I saw one day some of the kitchen staff busily preparing dumplings, and lunch suddenly became something to look forward to. Imagine how disappointed I was when I tried to order some! They were only intended for the kitchen staff to eat themselves. It was too laborious for the staff to make so many *jiaozi* for all of us, the five of us foreigners. By coincidence the chief cook, my countryman, happened to be there, and after I had been refused the *jiaozi* I turned to him. He went to fetch the large rack of woven bamboo that held the uncooked dumplings and motioned to me to help myself, but I would have to boil them myself. I put about fifty of them into a bowl I had brought with me. When it was time to pay, he did not know how much he should charge me. I told him that I had paid ten fen each a little while back, to which he replied that whoever was serving *jiaozi* at that time must have been crazy to charge that much—the few dumplings were only worth a few fen. I gave him two yuan, which he did not want to accept, saying that one yuan was quite enough, but I insisted.

I don't know how all this was squared off with the cash drawer or whether there even was any form of bookkeeping or control over takings, expenditures, and food sold. My impression was that most of them made their own rules, with much of the money finding its way into their private pockets one way or another. Perhaps there was a minimum cash collection that was required, and anything above that was siphoned off into private wallets. Be that as it may, the *jiaozi* were just delicious!

In the new building nothing much functioned initially as it was supposed to do. My neighbours, for example, were able to draw hot water from their taps at any hour of the day as they pleased. But in my case only cold water flowed. The administration had spent a great deal of money on this new building, which towered over all the other buildings of the institute on a small hill overlooking the campus. The fittings were allegedly the very best, direct from Hong Kong, as were the aluminum window frames. There was a new air-conditioning system that was supposed to blow cold air in summer and warm in winter, wine red wall-to-wall carpeting of synthetic fibre, turquoise wallpaper, green velvet drapes, specially made furnishings of varnished wood, and mauve covers for our armchairs; all of these superlatives were bound to delight the foreign heart and appeal to foreign tastes. I soon came to terms with the colour combination, but the draughty windows that suggested sloppy workmanship, the poor functioning of the air-conditioning system, and other defects made living in the new building rather uncomfortable. As my apartment was at the extreme end of the building, and on the third floor at that, it apparently could not be expected that the hot water supply would reach that far. After a number of complaints and the resulting appearance of some workmen it seemed as if the problem was solved. It was true I could obtain warm water and at times even almost boiling water, but it was always a kind of lottery as to whether hot water would happen to flow at the time and on the day I needed it. It was much the same with the highly praised air-conditioning system. By November it was already quite cold, and in the evenings in particular I would have welcomed a little warmth in my apartment. But the "official heating period" of the region around forty degrees latitude started on the twelfth of December. Had I still been in my old apartment I could at least have heated my private room by means of my electric heater.

Punctually on the twelfth of December the tall campus chimney started to belch black and grey smoke into heaven, and the pressure boiler came into operation and supplied every radiator in the entire institute with steam at an appointed hour. If we thought that we in our new building would also get the benefit of some of this heat, then we were to be disappointed. Now that we were the recipients of modern technology, which the simple unqualified worker had trouble coming to terms with in any case, we all had to wait patiently until a repairman had familiarised himself with the system. An additional boiler station was built for our "most modern" heating plant, which would supposedly work accordingly to the newest technology, having been built to entirely different rules. But until mid-December nothing worked at all. At last the system started to operate, but once again my neighbours fared much better than I did. The repairman went in and out of my apartment, but the problem seemed insoluble. My air conditioner blew merely cold air not only from the laminations of the enamelled iron monstrosity in my bedroom, but also from the slits of a wooden grating on one wall under the ceiling in the living room. The only source of warmth left to me was my little spiral cooking plate, which I had somehow managed to smuggle over with me during the move. It was not permitted to have such an item in the new apartment.

There was really no way I could live with these conditions for long. With the best will in the world I could not work properly in a room at only twelve degrees or remain there for any length of time, not to mention the early morning temperature of about seven degrees. One day, as I arrived in class frozen through once again, my pupils told me that they had often spent one or even two days in bed when their heating system failed once again. This prospect held little appeal for me, and I decided to try my own hand at getting my monstrosity of a heating system to work. There were plenty of valves and taps to turn, and taking pot luck, I tried a few of them. But apart from air escaping from the system, nothing happened. The thing growled but continued to emit cold air.

After I had complained variously to the responsible desk, which also served as reception for the adjacent guest house and for the Experts Residence, about my heating I was forced to come to the conclusion eventually that nothing had been done to fix it. I therefore resolved to call on the manager of the building and housing administration in person in order to address the problem. After a long string of excuses and apologies about the stupidity of the heating technicians, I was politely bid farewell with the assurance that he would personally look into this situation which caused so much discomfort. Somehow his intervention must have worked, because a workman who seemed to know what he was about did appear in my apartment and got my system to work. His explanation for the faulty operation was that my apartment was right at the end of the steam line, so the pressure could not reach that far. If he was to increase the pressure, then the heat in the other apartments would be become unbearable. I had to take him at his word, but it was nevertheless still unbearable to live with this situation. We finally agreed that I was to telephone him at the boiler station if the room was too cold, and he would then fire up the boiler for me for a short time. Whilst this was an offer in theory, in practice it looked very different. When I did phone him one day he explained the heating times were from 5:00 to 8:00 A.M., from 10:30 to 12:00 noon, and from 4:30 until 10:30 P.M. But one could not always rely on heat becoming punctually available. It happened that the appointed times were slept through or simply forgotten. My

Japanese colleague and I took turns complaining, as we both spoke Chinese. The Americans would come to me, and I would go to Mr. S. if it was his turn. The heating times did not suit our normal daily schedules very well at all. Most of us were out of the apartment from about 7:00 to 10 A.M. By the time the mid-day break started at around noon any warm air we had received in the morning had already been dissipated through the unin-sulated masonry and the gaps in the windows. Spending one's free time in a cold room was not particularly appealing. On the other hand, one could always take a "face sunbath" on the bal-cony, even during the winter months. The sun shone almost every day, and it almost became a ritual for me to spend my mid-day break there, warmly bundled up, in the sun and out of the wind. I had got used to the cold rooms, but it was rarely what one might call comfortable or cosy.

Sometime or other I just had to go to a hairdresser. My col-league offered to come with me, as she knew a good establish-ment. She did not go there herself, as she considered it too expensive for her, but she thought it might suit my needs. There was a small hairdressing salon on the campus, but it did not inspire me with a great deal of confidence as far as cleanliness was concerned. The floor, which was constantly covered with hair, and the sacks full of the same woolly black contents out-side the "display window" did not tempt me to enter. The two or at times three barbers in their grubby smocks were usually more concerned about their sleep needs in the reclined barbers' chairs than they were with caring for their customers' hair. I was advised not to try their skills. The salon in the city did not appear to be very different at first sight, except that it was much busier and really large, with two separate sections for ladies and gentlemen. The cash register was next to the entrance door, where I had to pay eighty fen for a wash, dry, and cut in advance. A blue ticket was given to me, and I was automatically propelled forward by the woman behind me. Feeling somewhat lost, I looked about me to determine whom I should see next. My colleague did not really know either. As we entered, every pair of eyes turned to us, or rather to me. Even all the heads inside the old-fashioned drying hoods tried hard to turn in our direction. Those ladies who were attached to the electrically heated permanent wave clamps were disadvantaged. They simply could not disentangle themselves from the clamps quickly enough without taking the risk that they would pull the whole apparatus from the ceiling. The place was a hive of activity, with only male Figaros in sight. All chairs as well as all the waiting benches were occupied. Every head seemed to be undergoing attention. Women who had not been able to gain an empty chair were walking up and down or stood about in the general tumult busily chatting; gossip was probably the main topic.

Once I had felt my way somewhat I simply walked up to a man in a whitish smock and asked him to cut my hair. He referred me to an older barber, who turned out to be the head barber. In no time a chair was freed for me in front of one of the large basins affixed to the wall in a row. A cold and dampish cloth was stuffed into my collar, and then I had to bend forward. The woman attendant responsible for washing held the red rubber hose that was connected to a tap over my head, but what a shock I got when a cold stream of water poured over my head, positively making me cringe! I decided to forgo a thorough wash with such cold water, but warm water was not available. I was dripping like a drowning poodle, and my blouse also felt damp already. I asked for a dry towel and promptly had another damp, cold cloth wrapped about my head by the attendant. My hair was dried after a fashion with this cloth, which was wrung out from time to time. This procedure was repeated a few times, and finally she handed me over to the head "coiffeur" as "well dried." Without asking me how I wanted my hair cut or how long or short I wanted it, he brushed my comments aside very energetically, indicating that he knew quite well how a foreigner's head should be treated. I abandoned myself to my fate and hoped that I might finish up with an acceptable hairstyle at the end of it all. The hairdresser was busily putting on a show, keeping up a running commentary to all the onlookers, who kept inundating him with questions about his hairdressing art. They also wanted a haircut like he was doing with my hair, despite many of them being themselves covered in soap suds or in curlers. What was so very special about the end result was something I, at least, could not determine. In fact, I was a little annoyed, because I thought I was now looking quite bedraggled. The Figaro assured me that the untidy ends of hair would soon be put in beautiful order by artistic drying. I let him go about his business, not wanting to get into an argument or become upset. He had hardly started brushing, rolling, and drying when suddenly there was an electricity failure. There we were, all of us sitting in the gloom and waiting for the electricity to work again. It seemed as if the blackout might take a while, and I wanted to get back in time for lunch, as otherwise the canteen would be closed. I was about to rush out into the cool May air with my hair still damp, coat on, and almost at the door when suddenly there was much shouting and I was called back. The power was on again, so now quickly to the drier before it failed again. I no longer cared about the looks of the hairstyle; all I wanted was to get back to the institute with a dry head, and indeed I would achieve this. After this adventure I always cut my hair myself, and I don't think I looked any the worse for it either.

One concluding episode: It was in Beidaihe, the well-known seaside resort, which was not reserved only for diplomats and businesspeople. High functionaries, particularly those from the military, also knew how to appreciate this very special, lovely spot with beautiful pine forests, golden beaches, and green hills, not to mention the many bungalows built in the style of country residences by foreigners before 1945, with their attendant grounds. These villas were used by their former owners as summer resorts. Almost all of them had by now been allocated to the military, with the especially exclusive ones being used by the central government. It was therefore not surprising if one saw limousines or other vehicles with military or government markings in the streets. Outside the many gateways leading to the individual villas armed soldiers stood posted in little guardhouses.

One afternoon I was sitting in the garden cafe Kiessling. Cafe Kiessling was a well-known name in the Far East before and during the war years, and the name guaranteed first-class cakes, confectioneries, bread, and ice cream made from original German recipes, as the founder was a master confectioner from Saxony. The main business, which was founded in Tianjin around the turn of the century, with a branch in Beidaihe for the summer season, continued to exist and operate under foreign management until after 1949. On my first visit to Tianjin in 1980 I was told that the name Kiessling in Latin script outside the cafe was the only remnant of the time of European domination in China. Today Chinese characters and the transcription "qi shi lin" appear under the original lettering, which is so familiar from my childhood, complementing it.

And so I was sitting in Cafe Kiessling, although of course there was nothing left of the former atmosphere, and looking about. A big, black, highly polished car stopped outside the cafe. Whilst the chauffeur was still sitting behind the wheel, a young man jumped out enthusiastically and opened the door for a young lady sitting in the backseat. The young man was dressed in the Chinese version of the "dandy look," grey suit in Western style, pink tie with an even more colourful shirt, white gloves, dark sunglasses, a cigarette dangling casually from the corner of his mouth. Thus attired he was busily escorting his female companion in a pink chiffon dress, pleated and three-quarter length, with long puffed sleeves plus white gloves, into the cafe.

A picture of ladylike virtue, the young woman looked out from under her black "wagon wheel" hat, drawing occasionally on her cigarette in a long holder. Oh, how up-to-date and elegant they must have felt themselves to be! I felt certain that these young people must have had parents who were part of the upper level of the political hierarchy and therefore lived accordingly. People from this high social milieu evidently met in Beidaihe for the summer season. The much lauded equality for all never applies to the happy few, regardless of which particular government happens to be in power at the time.

A Stroll through the Old City

It was already December, and in another month and a half my year in China would draw to a close. A lot still had to be done. For example, I had to make arrangements to obtain my exit visa. For this purpose somebody from the foreign bureau had to accompany me to the security bureau, which was located in the old inner city. It was a cold, windy day with a light frost. Clouds of dust were whirling about the streets, blowing scraps of paper and plastic in our direction. Imagine how pleased I was when I was finally seated in the somewhat warmer security office, with a cup of hot water in my hands. The smoky air in the room was something to which I had already become accustomed, so it did not worry me much. It was a relaxed atmosphere, without any official air or the usual grudgingly expressed official questions. Quite the contrary, the woman official was most interested in my personal background, asking me about my family and general conditions in Germany. Whilst she was talking and asking questions she rummaged about in a drawer for the appropriate stamp and red ink pad. As she stamped the visa into my passport, she looked at me mischievously and said, "If I had not issued you with a visa you would have to remain here and continue to teach us. You must be feeling relieved, but your students and the institute will regret your leaving very much." And indeed I confess that I did feel relieved. She must have noted my slight uneasiness. After all, who knows what takes place in the minds of these officials? The woman accompanied me to the door, wishing me well and also a happy return home. The entire process had taken no more than half an hour.

I had no desire to return directly to the campus, nor did my companion. My impression was that he was glad to have escaped from his office for a little while. And so we cycled about the streets hither and thither without any particular goal, and in the end we found ourselves in one of the numerous small alleys in the old part of the city, which had not yet been demolished. According to information I had been given, there were plans to pull down the many-centuries-old single-story buildings in the traditional manner and replace them with large concrete blocks. Should this really occur it would mean that the city Y. would become one of the thousands of identical-looking cities that had been "modernised" as part of a thrust for progress and then became overpopulated by the masses migrating from the country.

But on this day there was still plenty of activity in the narrow streets and lanes, no more than six metres wide, and behind the large doors of the houses, some of them opened. The old quarter was crisscrossed by rather bumpy clay thoroughfares, stamped hard by years of pedestrian traffic, with shallow ditches on either side intended to serve as sewage drains. Most of the narrow lanes were taken up by cyclists, thumbs constantly at the bell, and running and walking between them were children and other pedestrians, including itinerant merchants carrying their wares in two large baskets hanging from the ends of long shoulder poles. Flip-flop, flip-flop, they went as they made their way in a kind of bouncy walk through the mass of humanity. On one corner there was a display case with a glass front resting on two large wooden wheels, behind it a merchant with a whitish smock over his padded clothing, a white cap on his head. On the top of the case lay an assortment of bones and bits of skeleton; on closer inspection it turned out to be the skull of a dog, with two bones stuck into the eye sockets. The anatomy looked somehow familiar, and I had the feeling I had seen it on my plate at some stage. This was a dog meat seller, who had quite an impressive array of cuts on offer. Seeing this brought back to me the comment made sadly by one of my students earlier, about city dog catchers taking their young dog one day while nobody was at home and throwing it into a cart. Those of their neighbours who saw it could do nothing about it except report the sad event later.

We pushed our bicycles farther through the tumult. There was quite a stink in the air, as if there was a public convenience nearby. The solution to that riddle was, in fact, rattling and shaking its way along the road before us, the more we made our way into the lanes. It was a large, crudely made open wooden box of perhaps 150 by 80 centimetres on two wooden wheels, which was filled with the contents of the latrines belonging to all the many houses and was being pulled along by an old man in a stooped posture. [Translator's note: These conveyances were known to old China hands as "honey carts."] Dripping merrily from cracks in the woodwork, the cart slowly clattered down the alley, with everyone doing their best to get past it as quickly as possible, without running the risk of being pushed up against its side. Eventually we worked our way out of the stink zone.

At the corner of the next alley stood a heavily bundled up man, a fur cap with earflaps down on his head and both hands stuck in sleeves as if they were a muff. Smiling with his toothless mouth he invited me to buy some of the goods he was offering. He was roasting sweet potatoes in the clay-clad old oil barrel before him, full of hot ashes and glowing embers. It was a sheer joy to bite into one of these hot, delicious fruits and brought back childhood memories. As in the past, still today they were wrapped in newspaper and offered to clients in that way. And they were still cheap, too. From another merchant I bought a kind of flat cake, a specialty of the region, freshly baked for me on a grubby-looking sheet of steel brushed with oil. I could not resist these delicacies, rediscovered memories from my childhood, knowing full well that with my touchy digestive system I was likely to regret it. But happily all agreed with me very well indeed.

And so, on we went. Behind the shop windows the most varied range of different goods was piled, not only foodstuffs but also small items of furniture made of bamboo, wool and knitting needles of polished bamboo, cloth, including silks, crockery, household utensils, and ironware. One shop sold vinegar, oil, and soy sauce, poured into the buyer's own bottles, and in another the shop assistants were weighing out various types of rice and flour. There seemed to be no shortage. The only exception seemed to be fresh vegetables, which were scarce. And prices in general were significantly lower than in Beijing.

During my pilgrimage through this old quarter I came across much that I remembered from the past and which I had believed was now long dead and gone. For example, I saw one middle-aged woman standing and gossiping with a few neighbour women whilst working on a shoe sole of cloth. This was made out of several layers of scrap cloth, coated with flour glue and then dried. Three or four layers would be cut to the shape and size of a foot, and the various layers would be sewn together with a large needle and hempen thread and then pulled tight. My old amah, when doing this task, would occasionally stroke the needle through her hair in order that the oil from her hair would make the needle glide through the layers of cloth more easily, and this custom also survived.

Yet another merchant tried to solicit customers with a monotonous rattling sound. He was a seller of rat poison, who drew attention to himself by means of this instrument.

In the past the night watchman doing his rounds used the same sticks of bamboo, about the length of a pencil and some five centimetres wide, tied together at one end and used like Spanish castanets. By rattling them at defined intervals he not only announced his presence and therefore a peaceful night's sleep, but also gave an indication of the time.

I halted opposite the poison seller and out of pure sentimentality tried to acquire the rattle. He could sense the deal of his life here; evidently the neat row of stuffed dead rats lying before him, grey and black and adorned with red ribbons, did not convince potential buyers of the efficacy of his poison and business was slow. He asked the proud sum of ten yuan for his nicotine-stained rattle. This gave rise to a great deal of whispering and discussion among bystanders. Would the foreigner be crazy enough to pay this much money? She was not! She just laughed at him and made as if to leave. He called her back and asked what she was willing to pay. This would be a lot of fun. After much haggling and bargaining, in which all onlookers present eagerly participated, we finally agreed on two yuan, even though I knew I was still paying several times too high a price, and he knew that I knew. For those few strips of bamboo fifty fen would have been too much. But what won't one do for the sake of mere sentimentality?

Shortly before we cycled out of the tangle of alleyways we came past a large, wide open gateway. There were long white wooden boards hanging on the grey brick walls on either side, on which was inscribed in black characters: "Competent Court of such and such a district of the city of Y." I dismounted from my bicycle and went into the courtyard, in order to find someone who could supply me with information about what went on here. The gatekeeper hurried over and answered my questions most politely. I asked whether it might be possible for me to attend court one day and to whom I should turn to obtain the necessary permission. I learnt that this particular courthouse only served the purpose of registering and recording a particular misdeed; the actual trial and pronouncement of sentence took place in the district court. After I had told him by which work unit I was employed he suggested I apply to the foreign bureau there. He could foresee no difficulties with my plan as long as everything was arranged through the proper channels.

My companion, as an employee of the foreign bureau, was quite
thrilled at the prospect of being permitted to observe a legal
proceeding also. He immediately offered to start making all the
necessary arrangements and make contact with the officials in
charge. My companion thought that my idea was just great and
kept on repeating over and over what a wonderful idea I had
had. I, on the other hand, was somewhat skeptical and chose to
wait and see.

A Day in a Court of Law

Less than two weeks had passed since our excursion to the security bureau when my companion on that outing telephoned me and told me that a visit to the court had been arranged for a given day for all the foreign teachers. In order to prepare us for this event we had to attend a one-hour briefing session at our foreign bureau first, which would serve not only to inform us about the process of Chinese law, but also to give us instructions as to how we had to behave whilst in court and during the trial.

The hour commenced with the head of the bureau, Mr. Y., explaining to us with an air of importance and reverence how quickly the foreign bureau had reacted to my request, making my wish a reality, and what an honour it was for us to be permitted to attend a process of law. During the long history of the city, stretching back over thousands of years, never before had a foreigner been granted such permission. We would be the "very, very first" such guests. Via the city foreign bureau the court had requested our foreign bureau to brief us thoroughly first and to read out the rules of the court for us. With that the head got out his notebook and started going through each point in turn. The trial would not be taking place at the high court of the city, but in a middle district court. Two hours, from 8:30 to 10:30, had been set aside for the trial. We were to leave the institute together by the campus minibus punctually at 8:00, so that we would arrive at the court by 8:15. For this particular case the judges, associate judges, and lawyers for both prosecution and defence would appear in full regalia. There would be ninety onlookers, and a row of seats would be reserved for us. After all the others had taken their seats we, as guests of honour, would be permitted to enter the courtroom last. It was made very clear to us that something extremely special was about to take place here, and the head repeated this several times. We then had to listen to the basic ground rules of conduct: We had to be quiet, which meant that we must not speak or converse with each other, and there would be no photographs, no taking notes, and no questions. Should there be questions we wanted to ask, these should be put afterwards and would be conveyed to the court via the foreign bureau. In addition, we must not move about, i.e., we were not to stand up or leave the courtroom, nor might we smoke. Any instructions from the judge had to be followed strictly. The reason for arriving a quarter of an hour early was to allow us to meet the judge in the reception room.

It would be a very ordinary case, a public session. Trials for capital crimes and political trials always took place in camera. Very serious cases were tried at the main city court, not the district court. An explanation from the head of the form the trial would take was also necessary so that attention could be given to due ceremony.

Once we were all seated the secretary would read out the rules of conduct, after which the judges, lawyers, and so forth would be called up one by one to take their chairs. Last, the accused would be led in and asked by the judge about his personal particulars and informed of his rights. Following this the prosecuting attorney would read out the charges, witnesses would be heard, and the case for the prosecution would be presented. After this the defence attorney would have his say, and last, the accused would make his statement. After all this had taken place, the judge, associate judges, and prosecuting attorney would retire for half an hour in order to confer, after which they would return and pronounce sentence. A sentence once pronounced was final and immediately valid, with no right of appeal.

Armed with all this knowledge we proceeded to the court the next morning. We were advised to dress very warmly, because as in every other building in the city, there would be no heating. On this particular morning my thermometer registered minus three degrees Celsius!

Half of our foreign bureau staff rode with us in the pre-ordered minibus. On arrival at the court we were met by several uniformed court attendants, who led us to the upper floor in order to get to know us and acquaint us with details of the case. Four men were charged with theft and had been in detention for six months during the investigation. Three hours had been set aside for today's trial and for the subsequent pronouncement of sentence. As soon as we had warmed ourselves with a cup of hot tea it was time to enter the courtroom.

The medium-sized room was already well filled, and only the second row of seats had been kept free for us. Apart from the odd nose being blown or throat being cleared, it was utterly quiet in the room. I took a look about me and saw many eager pairs of eyes looking in our direction. Most of the spectators were elderly people of both sexes. The courtroom itself with its simple chairs, bare concrete floor, bare walls, neon lights, and the armed court attendants, who looked very smart in their blue uniforms with red and gold epaulettes, plus the stern and motionless expressions on the faces of all the official attendants, all combined to have a rather intimidating effect on me. I could detect nothing in any way human, be it the usual hum of voices, any muddle or untidiness, or makeshift arrangements, nothing! The chairs stood dead straight in a row, the floor clean, the windows polished clean and properly shut. The aisle and the only entrance were strongly guarded.

In the space not much before us, which reminded me of an altar apse, the judge's bench stood raised in front of a wide pleated curtain. The state emblem hung above it. On either side of the judge's bench was another bench, with two chairs behind it. The vacant area in front of the judge's bench was intended for the accused. The unbelievable correctness of every detail of the room, with all officials in their place at attention with side arms in holsters, and the utter silence gave me the impression of a very strict ceremony, particularly as I had never seen the inside of a courtroom except in the movies. There seemed to be no chance at all to depart from the established form ever so slightly, and somehow the overall effect was somewhat oppressive.

Punctually at 8:30 an official sitting in the row before us rose, strode with measured step to the judge's bench, and took a seat to the extreme left of the judge's chair. The official adjusted the microphone and started to read from a sheet of paper a lecture about appropriate conduct in this court of law. It was forbidden to leave the room during the trial, to talk, to take photographs, to spit, to disrupt proceedings by interjection, or to speak to the accused. The instructions, read out in a monotone, were brief, precise, and delivered with a stony countenance. He then asked the spectators to rise. The official then nodded to a few gentlemen in a row in front of us, calling them by their titles, "Mr. Judge" and "Mr. State Attorney," and asked them to take their seats. Two gentlemen dressed in thickly padded blue coats, flat peaked caps with the emblem of justice, a decorative column with two scales, on their heads, stood behind their chairs with rigid facial expressions. One by one the other gentlemen and one lady took their places next to those called previously at the side benches adjoining the judge's bench. After this ceremony there was silence for a few seconds, after which all were permitted to be seated. The trial had started.

First the four people at the side benches were introduced. Sitting to the left of the judge were a man and a woman, introduced as defence lawyers, both in civilian dress. Opposite them two police officers in thick green uniforms were making themselves comfortable in their chairs. They had recorded the incident and were thus present as witnesses.

Before going into details, I want to record, in order to not repeat myself, that all the people seated on the dais and the two court officers standing before the bench not once during the entire proceedings altered their stern and apparently cold expressions and attitudes. They stared down on the delinquents with unchanging expressions, and questions were put, or instructions were given, in a severe, sharp voice at all times.

The prosecuting attorney read the charges. The crime was theft of state property. A copper machine part valued at 3,000 yuan had been stolen from a factory and offered to a fence for 600 yuan. During this transaction the thieves had been observed by one of the policemen sitting on the side bench, and thus the arrest.

After the charge had been read, iron gratings were brought in and assembled in three cages with a floor area of barely one square metre each. The judge then nodded to one of the officials, who led in the accused one by one. A small man in prison grey shuffled in and let himself be locked in one of the cages. Meekly, with his shaved head drawn back into his shoulders, he stood before the judge in a bowed attitude and answered the latter's loud questions in a very soft voice. First the accused had to state whether he was a Han Chinese or a member of a minority group. The first part of the interrogation also concerned his name, age, address, place of birth, background, marital and family status, work unit, and education, and each of the four accused had to answer the same series of questions one by one. By occupation two of them were rag collectors, one a factory gatekeeper, and one a labourer. As there were only three cages for the four accused, two of them were locked inside the same cage, because theirs had been assessed as being a less severe case than the others. Behind the cages, pistols at the ready, stood two court officers.

Once the personal particulars had been determined, and it had been established that none of the four belonged to an ethnic minority (for whom there were different laws), the main process of the trial could commence. The accused were between twenty and forty years old, two were married, and they all came from different areas.

The small man described the break-in into the factory where he worked. The particular machine part was just lying there unused, apparently belonging to no one, and he thought there was no reason he shouldn't take it. Due to its weight alone he could not have taken it away by himself. An interested helper, one of the two rag collectors, declared himself ready to help with the theft in return for an appropriate share of the proceeds. The gatekeeper, who knew the man working at the factory, was content with a bribe in the form of six fresh fish and was willing to let the worker and his "friend" pass through the factory gate without checking the wrapped parcel on the luggage rack of his bicycle. Answers to questions concerning the fish varied considerably.

Whilst the thief indicated a length of some forty centimetres between his horizontally held hands, the gatekeeper indicated that they were about half that length. "They were about this big," he said, indicating a somewhat shorter length vertically.

"There were six fish," said one.

"No, there were only three," said the other, "and they were not at all that fresh either."

Finally the judge put an end to all the argument back and forth with a loud command to maintain order. Both were instructed to speak only in answer to a question, and only with "yes" or "no"; otherwise they would face additional penalties for contempt of court. The main accused man, the thief, tried to adhere to these instructions, as did the gatekeeper. But one of the rag collectors was somewhat "refractory." It seemed to me that he wanted to explain himself better, rather than give clear-cut answers to what were often quite leading questions. A veritable thunderstorm rained down upon his head, and in the end he had no option but to meekly do as he was told. The other rag collector, who had helped steal the machine part, had intended to sell it to his coaccused and take his cut of 100 yuan as middleman. "No, it was 200 yuan," "No, 150 yuan," and here, too, it was impossible to get a clear statement. Each of the accused tried to shift the blame on the others; only the gatekeeper appeared to know little of all these negotiations. He was also the first to admit his misdeed and concede the right of the court to sit in judgment over him. He could see how he had done great harm to the state. It seemed that one of the less serious cases was resolved; after a time the evidence and the statement of one of the policeman witnesses were regarded as concluded.

It was now the defence attorney's turn. He reviewed the essential parts of the case and evidence and on behalf of the gatekeeper asked for a fair and sympathetic judgment. His client was a good husband and family man who had never before been guilty of any crime, and he was a good, industrious worker. His failing had been that he weakened when tempted with the fresh fish, with which he wanted to give his family a treat. The other accused had acted despicably with regard to state property; the main blame lay with the thief who had shown no patriotism or national conscience and drawn others into his web. Despite this the defence attorney asked for a fair sentence, because the thief had also fallen victim to a human weakness, albeit one that was inexcusable. The two rag collectors had been entangled in conflicting statements, let themselves be led astray by the main accused man, and had been unable to resist the temptation of a quick profit. These and similar short arguments were those used by the defending attorney, who represented all four accused.

After this the accused themselves had the opportunity to

make a statement. One by one they asked for a mild sentence, and the main accused threw himself on the floor with repeated kowtows, literally begging the highly placed gentlemen for mercy and not to punish him too severely. He promised that he would change his ways and appeared to be extremely repentant.

The faces of the three representatives of law and order maintained the same stoic expressions, without the slightest change. Together they rose from their seats, the judge announced that there would be a recess for about half an hour during which the judges would confer and determine the sentences, and after that all three left the room. We were allowed to use this break in order to stretch our legs.

After the half hour had elapsed we all filed back into the room. Reading the sentences did not take long. The main accused was sentenced to eight years' banishment and the two rag collectors from five to seven years'. The gatekeeper had to serve three years in an open institution, where he had to perform agricultural work.

The accused had listened to their sentences with bowed heads, and at the end each of them thanked the judge for his just sentence and then was led away, and the trial was over. While the sentences were being read the main accused was shaking and shivering uncontrollably over his entire body.

Our little group of foreigners felt somewhat awkward as we assembled in the antechamber afterwards. The judge came over in order to personally bid us farewell. I was introduced as the initiator of the project, with appropriate comments about my origins and knowledge of language, and was immediately asked whether I had noticed any difference from trials "before liberation" (prior to 1949). I felt, as I had on other occasions when I was asked for comment on similar matters by others, that they were really not interested in hearing an opinion. What they wanted to hear was, again and again, how good, how positive, and how progressive the Communist government was compared to past governments.

On my own behalf, and on behalf of my colleagues, I thanked the principal judge for the most interesting trial, the friendly reception, and the permission given to us to witness the trial. We were conscious of the honour bestowed upon us and wished the gentlemen of the high court well for the future, with continued success. Our leader of our foreign bureau was quite delighted about my appropriately put words and good manners, as he repeatedly assured me. After a while we took our leave and made our way back to the campus.

Whilst the principal judge had not once altered his stony expression or stern voice during the entire trial, I was quite taken aback at being faced in the antechamber by such a relaxed and very approachable man in casual conversation. He was happy, he laughed, and no hint of official worries clouded his cheerful face. This change in him was quite astounding.

During the recess I had a chat with one of the female court employees and learnt, among other things, that sexual crimes were on the increase. Rapes and attempted rapes and sexual molestation, especially by school janitors against young female pupils and the like, were the main reasons women turned to the courts. In general, men found guilty of such crimes were punished by long sentences of imprisonment or banishment. I read between the lines that women nowadays were less ashamed than in former times in accusing the man involved. As far as I recall, women in the past had no way of protecting themselves against sexual molesters, much less any legal redress.

Other crimes that came to trial were simple or aggravated breaking and entering, theft, and purse snatching. Capital crimes were very rare. Depending on each individual case the court decided whether or not the trial was open to the public.

In the case of the trial we had witnessed, the public was admitted because the case seemed suitable as a lesson to the people that they must not steal state property, and also to show what would be the result of such a crime—namely, banishment. When questioned about where sentences of banishment were served the court official said that criminals were generally sent to the most remote regions, i.e., the desert in Xinjiang, Uygur. There they did not live in prisons built for them, as such things were rare in China. They had to live in camps where they were free to move about and had to perform specific labour for the good of the people. If they had no skills, they had to take part in schooling and vocational training. Reeducation was of course a major part of the schooling process. I wanted to know if anyone had ever escaped from banishment. No, almost nobody managed to escape. From the place where banished criminals were sent there were no trains and no other transport to facilitate an escape. Prisoners were taken there in trucks and at the end of their sentence were brought back the same way if they still wanted to return. Many married there, started a family, and became worthy members of society once more. Was it difficult to resume one's place in society after completing one's sentence? Could one go back to one's home and workforce? I was told that those released from serving their sentences had to be taken back into society and given work; no work unit could refuse to take them. But if an individual should commit another crime leading to a second or subsequent sentence, then there was probably no way back into society for that person.

In the camp itself alcohol and smoking were forbidden, and for many this was in itself a not inconsiderable punishment. Those banished could be recognised from their grey prison garb, shaved heads for men, close-cropped hair for women. It was very rare for family members to visit those serving banishment—after all, who would travel thousands of kilometres and sacrifice time and money just to stay a few weeks? From time to time there was probably mail, but in general, camp inmates led lives of their own.

Where sentences of more than six years were handed down they were generally served as banishment. Shorter sentences were normally served in open penal camps that, in the overall public interest, were located in regions not quite so far away. Did they receive payment for the work they did? As a rule they were only paid a minimal sum for their own needs.

Now when I think back to that December afternoon I can only reflect that the day at court, which was an aftermath to my little excursion through the many lanes and streets, was an interesting addition to my other experiences in China, as was the rediscovery of familiar old scenes of daily life in the streets and of everyday life in China generally.

The Year Draws to a Close

There is not much more to report about my teaching activities or everyday occurrences. Once I had obtained my exit visa, the next step was to arrange for the transport of my possessions back to Germany. This turned out to be not as easy as I first thought. The post office in Y. only arranged for the shipping of books and printed matter to countries abroad. I could have arranged for my many crates and trunks to be conveyed to friends in Beijing (which was my point of departure) and asked them to take care of my things until my arrival there. I would then take care of customs and other formalities myself later. But that would have been too much of an imposition for my friends, who would have had to pick up all the items from the post office in Beijing.

On the assumption that the foreign bureau of our institute would have some experience with the means of transportation of personal effects, I turned to one of the employees there for advice. It all appeared to be no problem, *mei wenti*, but to begin with at least, they did not know how to go about it either.

Meanwhile I made my own enquiries from the Beijing office of a German forwarding agency. The reply was that arranging transport from Beijing to Germany was also *mei wenti*, no problem at all; I should just send my things there, and the firm would take care of everything else. However, I had to make sure that the boxes and trunks were left unlocked, i.e., customs officials had to have unhindered access for the purpose of inspection. My problem was the distance of some 850 kilometres from Y. to Beijing, and that's where the problems arose. Transportation from Y. to Beijing was something the German firm could not arrange either. I continued to make enquiries. The foreign bureau's attitude was that there was still plenty of time before mid-January. *Mei wenti*; in four weeks surely a solution would be found.

I asked my students if perhaps they had an idea as to how one might arrange to send personal effects back and forth through their vast country. It appeared that, in case transmission by post was too inconvenient, the following was the method used: One started by borrowing the rail ticket of an acquaintance who happened to be making a business trip by rail, and one then declared the trunk or crate concerned as accompanying baggage the day before by using this ticket. The baggage slip was then either handed to the holder of the ticket, who then gave it to previously notified friends at the destination, or sent by registered mail. Armed with this information, I went back to the foreign bureau and asked for the matter to be handled this way. They took up this suggestion and advised me to have all my cases and trunks packed and ready to go by the date of my departure, January 23, so that everything could take place with minimal trouble. The bureau would make enquiries re locating a business traveller to Beijing on that particular day. I was somewhat reluctant to rely on this promise entirely and made my plan public to my students as well. As already mentioned, I still had four weeks left.

Meanwhile Christmas was upon us. The foreign bureau wanted to arrange a cheerful Christmas for its foreign teachers, and we were all invited to participate. On an appointed day we met with the head of the bureau to talk over the plans; a few students from Tanzania were there also. Although it was my impression that the whole thing already had been planned by the foreign bureau, we were to be consulted just the same in order to give the whole undertaking a "democratic" appearance. After all, it was a Western holiday, and we were to celebrate it in the manner to which we were accustomed. I thought that this was a really nice and friendly gesture. Somebody was to decorate the tree, another arrange for musical entertainment, and a Father Christmas had to appear as well. Naturally, the important long-hooded "Santa Claus" gown, red with white borders, not to mention the white long beard and main attribute of a Santa Claus, the large sack for all the presents, were required. The Americans and the Tanzanians were responsible for the Christmas carols, which immediately brought the first interference from the foreign bureau: "Cheerful songs without any Christian content." This was really easily arranged by choosing songs such as "Jingle Bells" and "White Christmas." The gardener was instructed to provide a palmlike green tree as a substitute for a coniferous tree. Later, during the actual celebration, this turned out to be a kind of a green potted plant about a metre high, which stood somewhere in the corner undecorated and largely unnoticed. My task was to turn the Japanese teacher into a Santa Claus. The "how" was left up to me. Since I could not make a costume without material, I asked, who would bear the cost? They had not thought about costs. *Mei wenti*; I would come by the red cloth somehow. The problem of the presents was to prove much more difficult. During the last Christmas party all presents for the foreign teachers had somehow mysteriously disappeared, and having become the wiser for this experience, the foreign bureau had decided that presents this time should be handed out by numbers. Everyone who wanted to take part had to bring a gift with the value of at least two yuan to the bureau, in return for which he or she would be allocated a number entitling the holder to take part in the distribution of the presents.

Since everything had already been organised by the bureau, we did not concern ourselves with these details, democracy or not. Only my task caused me some headaches. There were only a few days left before the twenty-fourth of December, and still nothing seemed to be happening. I started to press the foreign bureau for action, and in a short time one of their female employees came with two giant flags of red silk, as well as masses of white cotton wool apparently from the pharmacy for the beard and the borders on the costume. I obtained needles and thread myself, and within a day I had sewn or rather basted complete Santa garb for Mr. S. with all necessary frills. I still had some double-sided adhesive tape, which I used to make thick white eyebrows, and the white beard turned out quite well also. Mr. S. looked rather adventurous.

So, as far as we were concerned, Christmas could start; we were ready. As we learned from the foreign bureau, members of the foreign bureau of the city Y. as well as other "important" people had been invited. Before the actual festivities were to start, all the foreigners working at the institute had been invited to a festive banquet consisting of a Western dinner. The meal was then a compromise between Western and Oriental cuisine. It was quite touching to see how much trouble the management had gone to in order to make the occasion as festive for us as they possibly could. After spending two hours together over dinner in one of the canteens, we were invited to go into the large dining hall in the new hotel, where the crowd of local guests was already waiting for us. When we had all assembled, the head of the foreign bureau gave a short speech, after which he announced the arrival of Santa Claus, who had come with his helper (me) to see all the children. The Chinese name for Father Christmas, probably taken from the Russian translation, is Old Man Frost (Grandpa Frost). My Japanese colleague, who had by now fully assumed the worthy role of Old Man Frost, and I were waiting to make our entrance. Fortunately, I was spared the need to dress up as an angel.

Our appearance was greeted by huge applause, and Santa Claus was asked to the microphone in order to wish everyone a Merry Christmas. Mr. S. acted his role superbly. He told all the children present about the long journey he had undertaken to get here; after all, the long trip from Japan and then by rail to Y. had not been without difficulty. But he was pleased at having arrived at last and at being able to greet so many guests. He received a huge ovation and was invited to do a round of honour, shaking the hand of every child present. Whilst he was busy doing that I had to walk alongside him carrying the large sack, which was filled with crumpled paper. Parents with their children crowded around us and begged for a souvenir photo with Santa Claus. I heaved one child on his left, another child on his right knee for a lengthy time, whilst poor Old Man Frost tried to be merry, although he must have felt as if he were in a sweatbox in his thick padded clothing. (He had put on another padded jacket under his gown in order to look a bit "fuller.") From the moment of our first appearance until our eventual exit we were followed by searchlights, and even the local television station showed the celebration live as part of the evening programme. After we had completed our round, the young Americans and the Tanzanians sang two or three current American Christmas songs for the attentive audience, following which some of the other Tanzanians presented an absolutely beautiful song about their native land in the form of antiphony to an African rhythm. With that the foreigners' contribution to the Christmas festivity was concluded, and the Chinese part began. A three-man band appeared. A type of Hammond organ was rolled in and somehow connected to a cable, as were two microphones. A young woman of about twenty together with a young man about the same age combined in some utterly deafening singing, so much so that the organist had to struggle to be heard above their voices. If the organist had a solo number he was not to be outdone in the decibels department. The louder the sound, the more it was supposed to be Western disco! The amateurish gestures and the almost painfully uncoordinated movements of the two singers were probably intended to demonstrate the spirit of progress and the modern attitude of the today's youth in

China. Be that as it may, all of them tried their utmost to make it a really wonderful Christmas for us, and it is much to their credit that they gave us the day off also.

After helping with the distribution of presents I left the turbulent scene. Numbers were exchanged for presents, with everyone wanting to be the first out of fear that they might miss out.

The Chinese idea as to how Westerners liked to celebrate Christmas, i.e., loudly, colourfully, and with presents, dancing, and Santa Claus, was probably derived from Anglo-American films. In any event, I was glad that I had something to do on Christmas Eve.

For New Year's Eve (not Chinese New Year) nothing had been planned. During the last few days of the old year my students had shown little interest in serious work. The evening lessons ceased because some department was arranging a New Year celebration. Somehow I was also invited, even though I had nothing to do with either computer or mathematics courses. But some of my students came from these faculties, and so I was to have the experience of taking part in a truly Chinese pre–New Year's Eve party. Something was happening in almost every classroom. Music of every kind, from popular hits, waltzes, and tangos to Chinese operatic arias, filled the entire campus through the open windows. It was a real cacophony. The rooms were decorated with colourful garlands and the tables pushed together to form a single rectangular surface, with the chairs arranged all around. We all sat there very politely looking expectantly to the head of the table, where the organisers sat and regulated the party.

First of all, guests of honour, which included myself, were introduced by name. Each of us had to rise and make a bow of thanks in all directions. Individuals were then called upon to make a contribution to the merriment, which again included me. I think I struck the right note with a short song and two Chinese nursery rhymes I still remembered from my childhood.

A member of the festival committee served all guests beer or soft drinks, and there were sunflower seeds and other snack food on the tables, to which we helped ourselves. In no time the floor was covered with shells and lolly wrappers. The gathering consisted, as I experienced (the second fete took a similar course), of everyone contributing short sketches, songs, or anecdotes, encouraging everyone to participate and promote a happy gathering—a custom practised some thousands of years. After some three hours I took my leave, not before having taken a turn on the dance floor. New Year's Eve itself was spent by us teachers by ourselves in one of our apartments.

The year was drawing to a close, and my next task was to make some more intensive efforts to organise my return journey. My farewell party with my students and my coworkers also required a lot of planning and organising, although my students suggested it was all no *wenti*, no problem. They would look after the necessary drinks, and I could leave the lugging of bottles to them, but not the paying for it. They were really most helpful and eager. The sale attendants would not have delivered the drinks for me.

During the remaining interval before my departure for Beijing I hardly had time to catch my breath. Not a week passed without two or three invitations. I was generously showered with beautiful gifts and served delicious dinners. Again and again I was assured how much they all regretted the fact that I could not stay with them longer. Saying good-bye was really made difficult by all the sincerity and trust shown towards me. During my farewell party several of my students gave short speeches of thanks in almost fluent simple German and promised to keep in touch by letter, which they would do.

All the official functions were behind me: the festive banquet arranged by the president and the foreign bureau complete with presentation of a formal gift—a coffee service for six persons with the name of the institute in silver characters—and speeches, ordering of the rail ticket with sleeper, reservation of a room in Beijing for five days, and handing over of several special books on the German language to the library of the language department. I had obtained these books and much information material as generous donations from various German organisations.

The matter of transportation of my effects was not to be resolved until the last moment. Trunks and crates had been standing ready for days. Just a few days before my departure on the twenty-third of January an employee of the foreign bureau came rushing to me in order to inform me that the matter of transportation of my things could be arranged that afternoon. He had been able to obtain the rail ticket of a business traveller that evening. As occurred so often, it all happened at the last minute and had to be rushed.

I could have despatched my belongings on my own ticket, but as I had heard luggage seldom went on the same train, it would have been too risky. Transportation of luggage usually took a couple of days, and it was safer to send my baggage in advance. It would be held for me free of charge for up to four days at the main station in Beijing.

We arrived at the baggage counter of the main railway station in Y. that afternoon and waited patiently in the long line. It was bitterly cold that day, and the long waiting in the open air gave the cold the opportunity to really penetrate.

At last it was our turn. Baggage stickers and slips had to be filled out in triplicate and assurance given that nothing flammable was contained in the freight goods. Now I understood why we had been waiting for so long. The Spring Festival was drawing close, and it had happened once too often that fireworks were shipped that were not properly packed and subsequently exploded. So every item was subjected to a very thorough inspection before acceptance. We must have been trustworthy, because when we offered to open all the trunks and cases again the official just shrugged tiredly and allowed our things to pass.

After I had paid the transportation fees, we returned to the institute. I was glad that everything had taken place so smoothly. In my apartment, which was now rather bare, I felt somewhat out of place. The empty desk and wardrobe, no pictures on the walls, no more flowerpots, there was nothing that made a home cosy and habitable. I no longer belonged here, but the feeling I was safely home again had not struck me either. I was somehow suspended in an emptiness. Despite the joyous expectation of soon seeing family, friends, and acquaintances again, mixed in with these feelings were doubts as to how easily I would be able to readjust to the affluent society.

The last few days were, unfortunately, marred by a few unpleasant exchanges with the woman leader, Mrs. Z., of the foreign bureau, about my salary among other things. Verbal arrangements that had been made in the summer suddenly now were considered no longer valid. At the time I had asked for a written confirmation of these arrangements, which had been dismissed with the assurance that everything had been noted. I was very disappointed, with a feeling of having been exploited, and was overcome with anger at so much brazenness. My main anger was over the reduction of my salary. Since I had planned to depart on January 23, the semester having ended on the seventeenth, the woman leader saw no need to pay me a full month's salary, on the basis that as I was no longer at the institute I was not entitled to payment. Had I remained up to the end of January twiddling my thumbs I would have been paid. I was not so much concerned over the few yuan, but I was determined to resist such deliberate alteration of the rules and arrangements, and in the end I won my point. I happened to find out that according to the law, a worker who completed his/her employment after the fifteenth of a month was entitled to a full month's pay, and this applied in my case.

The day of departure came, and all the farewells started.

My Japanese colleague left first, his journey being to the south. The three Americans and I were on our way north to Beijing. We were accompanied to the railway by a huge following of students, friends, and colleagues and were given a wonderful, sincere farewell with many good wishes. We departed at about 10:00 P.M. and arrived in Beijing the next morning at around 11:00. An employee from the bureau travelled with us, and he was to assist me with arranging transportation of my baggage.

In Beijing I bade farewell to my three American colleagues, who intended to stay a little longer in China, two of them looking for a new job. I was then driven to my hotel and made the arrangements to meet them the next morning in order to pick up my trunks from the railway station. We sat out punctually the next day, and after just one hour of standing in line and visiting various counters to make sure we had all the necessary stamps, we finally took possession of my unharmed baggage. From there we proceeded as quickly as possible to a Chinese despatch and expedition company just outside Beijing, because by now it was almost midday. Even though the midday break had been abolished in Beijing, we wanted to be sure we got there in time, because one never knew what really took place in one of these firms. Imagine our disappointment when we finally got there! Not that the responsible officers were asleep, oh no! The customs officer was seldom there after noon, and it would be much better to telephone him first in order to arrange a time. But as it was the weekend, nothing could be done before Monday, and we were to come back as early as possible. We agreed to be there at 10:00 A.M. My baggage, which we had already unloaded, had to be stowed back in our van, because nobody wanted the responsibility for safe custody over the weekend. And so back we went, baggage and all, to my dark little hotel room.

I spent the weekend with friends. The crowning highlights not only of my last days in Beijing but my year in China were a visit to a beautifully preserved old monastery still in use by Buddhist monks and an invitation to dinner.

Full of concern, I set out on Monday morning back to the firm handling my belongings. We were early and the customs officer late, so that we were forced to waste valuable time in fierce cold of minus ten degrees. After he had finally arrived he carefully inspected each item from the outside first and then asked about the contents. Were there valuable antiques, paintings, calligraphy, or old books in the crates? From my lists, copies of which had to be packed inside the baggage, I was able to translate for him the exact contents. He was quite delighted about the detailed listings and saw no need to inspect the inside of even a single box. He gave me red stickers with the characters "cleared by customs" for all my belongings and collected twenty-five yuan for his trouble. It seemed as if it was all resolved; however, we had to take the baggage personally to the point of despatch. An employee advised our driver of the address and how to get there. After much searching we finally found the place. A large container was found for my baggage, comprising less than one cubic metre in all, and once my goods had been stowed in the still-empty space it was all closed and locked three times. I could just relax. The container was to travel by the trans-Siberian freight train, and the items should arrive in Hamburg in about forty-five days. Indeed I did receive them after just two months in undamaged condition.

I spent the last evening before my departure with an acquaintance who had invited me to dinner. A last journey in a cold subway and a last trip in an extremely crowded bus, which I doubted I would ever get out of alive, completed my sojourn in China.

Flight: Beijing–Frankfort

It was true! There I was, at Beijing Airport, and through the large windows I could see the Lufthansa aircraft from the waiting section. What a feeling of "home" that meant!

By the time we were all seated in the plane and had fastened our seat belts some time had elapsed. I was very comfortable and relaxed in the soft seat and was looking forward to the flight.

As for the flight itself, I will only quote the following extracts from my diary:

First stage Beijing–Karachi (eight hours; we have just flown over Wuhan). 2025 take off Beijing by LH 663. I am enjoying everything on board, the cleanliness, the trained and friendly manner on the part of the cabin crew, the service, the music in stereo with excellent sound quality, the Schweppes, clean toilets, the small snack and the opulent dinner consisting of a small piece of fillet steak, salad, wine, cheese, black bread, butter, dessert. Though everything was very tasty and attractively presented, I discovered that I was no longer used to eating so much. I left the meat after taking one or two bites, ate only vegetables and a little salad, and did not touch the dessert either. Instead I ate black bread, with thick butter on it, and with it enjoyed a dry red wine, delectable. Not for a long time had I felt so alert and up-to-date as I do right now. Goodness, it is only now that I realise what a year of deprivation I have behind me.

Karachi (which was a fueling stop)–Frankfurt. I think we are somewhere above the Mediterranean, with two and a half hours to go to Frankfurt.

When I think back to the twenty-eighth of January (the day before yesterday) I just cannot believe that I am about to land in Frankfurt. Two days ago I had a heavy cold and was invited to the home of a friend. The trip on the hard seat of a rattly, draughty bus was uncomfortable, then across into the overcrowded underground. Dust, garlic breath, cigarette smoke, the garrison smell, and noise, noise, and more rattling, tinny, constant noise.

The trip by bus back to the hotel had almost been dangerous to the point of being life-threatening. I am surprised that I got out of it without injury. With brute force I was shoved in the back. My outstretched arms against the windowsill gave me a little breathing space; otherwise I think I would have been squashed flat against it. My arms were aching, and at times I was afraid that a sudden push or a strong jerk as the bus stopped would break them. Getting out again was a pure boxing match, where I had to literally fight my way through in all directions.

From my description of these experiences it will be understandable why I enjoyed the flight so much. We landed earlier than scheduled. It was a strange feeling to be surrounded by only white-skinned people once again; in the plane I had not noticed this so much; I had been too occupied enjoying myself. Eighteen hours earlier I still had to express myself in the Chinese language; now I had to switch back to German. The few words I had exchanged with some passengers, or with the stewardess, did not seem to count. Once, instead of saying, "Danke," for some information I found myself inadvertently uttering, "Xiexie."

The last stage, Frankfurt–Hamburg, "flew" in the most literal sense. What was sixty minutes with eighteen hours already behind me?

The weather was clear, the snow-covered landscape visible below me. Reminiscences of my very first flight some thirty years ago were awakened as we approached Hamburg and prepared to land. How would I find it this time, settling back again? That first time I was arriving in what was for me a strange country, whereas today I was coming home to my family and my friends. And yet now, like the first time, I was curious and somewhat reserved in the face of the many questions I was about to face, to many of which I knew I would have no answers.

A Brief Postscript

Many months have passed since my return home. Settling back into the affluent society was something that did not come easily, because I could not help making constant comparisons with the frugal life in China.

Even the brief transit stop at Frankfurt made me realise how one can come to take friendly customer attention for granted, how it was only a matter of course that everything functioned without a hitch, and that I could accept information given to me as being factual without question. I became aware how spoilt I had been before my stay in China, and how unspoilt I had come back.

After a year of fumes, smoke, and smells, I was struck by the clean air on the airfield at Hamburg-Fuhlsbüttel. And yet I am sure that by our standards it was not at all clean. I was surprised at how few people there were on the streets. I enjoyed the smooth and noiseless ride in the taxi and even little things such as the regularity of traffic lights, which I used to take for granted but now I noticed suddenly.

I had hot running water at any time, day or night, and a comfortably warm home. In the shops I barely knew what to buy, so rich was the choice of goods on offer. I succumbed to a shopping orgy, which, fortunately, did not last long. It took a little while before I came to realise that hamsterlike purchasing was no longer necessary and that I could, for example, spread the jam a little thicker on my slice of bread without worry. There was plenty of everything, and I felt gratitude that in this regard I was so well off.

And yet something was missing from this feeling of well-being. I miss the human touches and the natural way in which human foibles and weaknesses were accepted as part of life in China. Society here will not tolerate any weakness, making no concessions to human shortcomings or inadequacies. One has to function as a cog in the larger machine and be a part of it. Conversations remain superficial, and people are no longer to detect the nuances in dialogue or "read between the lines," much less take any notice. Everyone tries to get further than they are already, and still they are unsatisfied. I have always had difficulty with the definition of the term *poverty*, and this difficulty was in no way diminished by my stay in China. When is someone "poor" here in Germany? When someone cannot afford a car, TV, house, vacation, or perhaps kiwifruit? Everything seems to be relative.

Travellers to China, most of whom have only the basic or at best scarce knowledge of the country, will find what is by our standards a socially and economically poor but culturally rich country. One is fascinated by the idea of "China." Words such as *mysterious* and *exotic* are still part of what those travelling to China expect to find when they get there, part of the vocabulary when it comes to China.

Although much is still inadequate in China, as I have covered in my book, and there is much progress and improvement still to be made, there can be no denying that generally speaking, the people of China are very much better off now than they were during my childhood days. If one wishes to judge whether progress has been made, then one has to draw comparisons between their own country's and Chinese history. There is certainly a need to remove the stuffiness from the strictly regulated offices of the Chinese bureaucracy so as to make for more efficient and effective thinking. But it will be a long and difficult process before the way people think is changed in China. Society there is still governed, as it has been for centuries, by clan thinking, hierarchical behaviour, and the ability of the authorities to control every aspect of life. Here in the West we try to draw speculative conclusions from the smallest attempt at reform by the Chinese government and predict from it a new concept for the Chinese future. According to the Chinese way of thinking, there is nothing that does not change. Everything is subject to continual change, and adaptation to that which is new ensures ongoing life and survival.

The opening of the "bamboo curtain" took place too quickly and grew too large, so that much that was new came into China from the outside world, some of it good and some bad; the result of this is a rigorous attempt now to control the flood. Anything undigested causes stomach complaints, and in order to prevent this from happening the curtain is being closed a little again and efforts are being made to uncover the cause of illness or, at least, find a way of making the new and strange food a little more digestible.

The policy of the sixties and seventies, when China was hermetically sealed off from the rest of the world, was a terrible mistake. This is what these Chinese themselves see today, but progress is not happening as quickly as most of them, especially the younger ones, would like. What is missing is a steady, phased development, a solid building on what was already founded. Often I had the impression that whole phases of development were skipped entirely and that this still occurs now, all in the interest of catching up as fast as possible. This is, of course, understandable, but in the end ambitious and costly plans and projects are often not fully thought through and are just predestined to failure. Those achievements that have been made seem to be superficial and not integrated.

It may well be that it is the very history of China, with its many ups and downs over the centuries, together with the strongly developed feeling of nationalism and tradition and the ability of the Chinese people to endure suffering, that has given

China her real underlying strength. Perhaps this strength, from its cradle thousands of years ago, has gradually attained the enduring power that enabled China to survive into the twentieth century as the only one of the ancient cultures of our world.

Despite the many inadequacies, the numerous bureaucratic hurdles and difficulties, the year I spent in China gave me a great deal that was positive and worthwhile. I am grateful to my husband and my two sons for giving me the freedom to go and for being happy to have me back. I also want to thank my many friends and acquaintances, who helped me to maintain my contacts with home by their many letters and little parcels.

Very special thanks are due to my many Chinese friends and acquaintances; they permitted me to share their lives and their many joys and sorrows, thereby allowing me to gain a very real understanding of their lives and everyday existence.